THE SEDUCTIONS
OF BIOGRAPHY

CULTURE WORK

**A Book Series from the
Center for Literary and Cultural Studies
at Harvard**
Edited by Marjorie Garber

Media Spectacles
Marjorie Garber, Jann Matlock, and Rebecca L. Walkowitz, Editors

Secret Agents:
The Rosenberg Case, McCarthyism, and Fifties America
Marjorie Garber and Rebecca L. Walkowitz, Editors

THE SEDUCTIONS
OF BIOGRAPHY

Edited by

Mary Rhiel and David Suchoff

ROUTLEDGE ○ NEW YORK AND LONDON

Published in 1996 by

Routledge
29 West 35th Street
New York, NY 10001

Published in Great Britain in 1996 by

Routledge
11 New Fetter Lane
London EC4P 4EE

"Outing History" from *Out* Magazine, February–March 1994, by Blanche Wiesen Cook. Copyright © OUT Publishing. Reprinted with permission. "Inventing and Interpreting Malcolm X" from *The New York Times Book Review*, 29 November 1992, by Michael Eric Dyson. Copyright © 1992 The New York Times Company. Reprinted with permission. "Bisexuality and Celebrity" from *Vice Versa*, by Marjorie Garber. Copyright © 1995 Simon and Schuster. Reprinted with permission. "Taking a Life" from *Signs* 20, by Doris Sommer. Copyright © 1995 The University of Chicago Press. Reprinted with permission.

Library of Congress Cataloging-in-Publication Data

The seductions of biography / edited by Mary Rhiel and David Suchoff.
    p.   cm. — (Culture work)
    Includes bibliographical references and index.
    ISBN 0-415-91089-7.   —   ISBN 0-415-91090-0.
    1. Biography as a literary form. I. Rhiel, Mary. II. Suchoff, David Bruce.
III. Series.
CT21.S42   1996   95-25777
814.009'492—dc20   CIP

◯ Contents

Acknowledgments

THE LIFE STORY of this volume begins with the group of Andrew F. Mellon Faculty Fellows at Harvard University who gathered for one year of discussion and research on Biography: Jeffrey Decker, Maurice Isserman, Dennis Trout, and the editors of this volume contributed to that year of colloquy and fellowship and to the conference "Life-Likenesses: The Seductions of Biography" that gave life to this volume. The pre-history of this biographical venture was made possible by the scholars who both seduced us into this project and supported us in it. The directors of the Mellon Faculty Fellows in 1992–1993—Richard Hunt, William S. McFeely, Marjorie Garber, and Henry Louis Gates, Jr.—co-planned that conference and made the selection of speakers and topics as cogent and pleasurable as we hope the resulting volume has turned out to be. We thank all the participants of that conference and those whose hard work and planning made it possible, especially the Andrew F. Mellon Foundation, Harvard University's W. E. B. DuBois Institute, and the Center for Literary and Cultural Studies at Harvard. Thanks are due as well to Jay Maclean, Andre Craddock-Willis, and Herrick Wales. Invaluable editorial life-support was provided in outstanding, timely, and professional fashion by Grace Von Tobel, Sarah Richmond, Judy Daviau, and Zarin Mistry of Colby College. We are also grateful to Paula Krog, for disk-doctoring beyond the call of duty, and to Eric Zinner, Stephen Magro, Christine Cipriani, and Bill Germano at Routledge for their invaluable assistance.

○ Preface

WHY BIOGRAPHY?

William S. McFeely

WHY BIOGRAPHY? This is a question that invites conjecture rather than strict definition. To begin with, biography is seductive. I like the treachery of that descriptive term, that wonderful word, and I invite you to follow its scent into the essays on biography which follow. In them there is room to explore the subject in intimate, uneasy ways without wasting time trying to achieve the unattainable: a definitive statement of what biography, or its cousin, autobiography, is.

But it is something. When we write a biography or read one, when we tell our own story or see ourselves in someone else's, we are embarked on what can be an exciting journey. Books and other biographical texts draw us into our culture. The silliest public-relations account of a rock singer's life may expose more than had been bargained for. And, to be honest, the most serious of scholarly tomes can obscure quite as readily as the best of them can illuminate. This volume seeks to explore some of the ways in which biographies shed light.

There are, of course, those who see no light in the genre at all. Martin Amis, reviewing a biography of Philip Larkin, wrote: "Biography, besides being a lowly trade, may also be attritional...." Andrew Motion, the author of the Larkin book, had said in his rationale for the work, "'All good biographers insist on separation, as well as connection.'" Amis disagreed, "No, what they do, or end up doing, is insist on connection. And Motion connects *ad nauseam*: 'obviously on the spur,' 'the message for Ruth in these poems,'…and so on. Biographers may claim separation, but what they helplessly insist on is connection. What the hell are they doing day after day, year after year (gossiping? ringing changes on the Zeitgeist?), if the life doesn't somehow account for the art?"[1]

Closing her study of an artist, Ruth Butler, author of *Rodin: The Shape of Genius*, writes, "After seven years of steeping myself in the long and vivid life of Auguste Rodin, I searched for one word that might encapsulate it for me. The word that fits best is 'lonely.'"[2] I doubt Butler could claim that Rodin's loneliness would account for his art in a way that would satisfy Amis or anyone else. But she does suggest that Rodin's loneliness gave the artist space in which to create one of the great biographical statements of our culture, his "Balzac."

If not *Zeitgeist*, there is sound social history in Butler's work to ground us in Rodin's France; if there is gossip, it certifies Rodin's humanity. And Mr. Amis might note that the most serious of historians recognize how skillful a tool of social maneuverability gossip can be. Similarly, it can help an author and a reader of a biography move into perspective on a subject. Skillfully and tactfully used, gossip can even give a certain meaning to the space around great poetry.

I am not sure that there is a neat line between literary biography and studies of people involved in other pursuits. For example, both the soldier Ulysses S. Grant and the agitator Frederick Douglass, about whom I have written, wrote with daunting skill.[3] Neither American would normally be thought to be the subject of a standard literary biography, and yet with both I had to contend with fine writing in their autobiographies—in Grant's case, his *Personal Memoirs*, in Douglass', his three works, *Narrative of the Life of Frederick Douglass*, *My Bondage and My Freedom*, and *Life and Times of Frederick Douglass*.[4] Whether writing about a poet, a painter, a general, or a radical agitator, the biographer is confronting the work of the person contemplated.

Let me indulge in a bit of autobiography. I can remember the surprise—and dismay—the first time I heard myself referred to as a biographer. I had thought I was a history teacher doing what history teachers are supposed to do: writing about one's period in one's field. I had looked at President Grant as a Reconstruction politician because my field was the history of American race relations; I had tracked General Grant back into the Civil War because my students were anguishing over their relationship to another war, the Vietnam War. In those contexts, I had told the story of that politician and that soldier; suddenly, I was a biographer.

About all I knew about that label was that it marked the doom of one's reputation in the historical profession. I had never stopped to think of biography as a literary genre. And I have to admit to being innocent still of any theoretical grasp on biography as distinct from other ways of trying to make sense, with words, of the world I am struggling to understand and explain. But when I had completed my look at Grant in his world, I could see no reason not to own up to the question of the worth of a biography. The very first words of the book are "Why Grant?" Why should I have bothered myself with him for so many years? Why should I inflict him on anyone else?

Apparently, I needn't have worried about asking "Why Grant?" (and then attempting an answer). It was fascinating to me how many reviewers picked up on those two words. It was as if their disingenuousness was tonic. I had not written "Why was Grant a man of great importance?", which would have aroused the expectation that I would give the reader a definitive answer by the book's end. It was, more simply, the matter of being curious—of wanting, in the case of the general, to figure out what brought an ordinary, likable man into one of the ugliest businesses we have, the making of war, and what made him so damn good at it.

I hope I did not hammer home my personal connections to the matters that Grant confronted—war and racial strife—in the manner that so irritates Martin Amis. But it would be disingenuous of me to say that I stood separate from such concerns. I hoped my readers would make similar connections of their own, and was pleased when some did. I am proud not so much of the reviews of that book as of the letters from people like the man who had fought in the Korean War and wrote, "Do you mean on page 78 that that's what happens in a war?" He then, without pausing, likened what I had said to what he remembered experiencing in his war. That reader had made my text his, and I was deeply moved that he had done so.

The reader of this volume may wonder at the absence of Augustine and Rousseau, of James Boswell and Dr. Johnson, or, for that matter, of Plutarch. I do regret a bit that there wasn't room in these essays for a look back beyond our soiled twentieth century, but as this book took shape, celebration or analysis of great monuments of the genre did not seem to be the task. The questions that seemed the most compelling were more contemporary ones. Notable in the book's contents, too, is the absence of the century's big boys. There is no Truman here, no Churchill. They were excused from class on the grounds that problems in the handling of historical evidence involving global political matters would deserve their own volume.

In short, we knew we could not attempt everything that came to mind. Instead, we wanted to plunge straight into what haunts many of those of us who write: how do we know when we've got it right? And, if we have done so, how will the reader's concerns connect to our own and those of our subject?

As either the writer or the reader engages a biography or autobiography, there is a conjunction of the private and the public. I suspect that few of us any longer believe that a strict separation between the public and the private makes sense in imagining any life. I could not have been true to Frederick Douglass if I had not told of his troubled but long relationship with his wife, or the problems his children faced in the shadow of a sometimes-distant public man, or his compelling friendships with women. But there is room for caution.

In the summer of 1993, I met not a biographer but, rather, the object of a biography. She was a quite grand old lady and her story, involving one of the nation's leading newspapers, was surely a matter of public concern. Janet Malcolm's indictment of biography was in *The New Yorker* that week, and as I walked into the room, my host greeted me as a second-story man. Turning to the guest of honor, he explained not only that I was a biographer, but also that Malcolm had, scathingly, called any such writer "a professional burglar."[5] The lady looked straight at him and said, very quietly, "she has a point."

Her son, whose death was crucial to the newspaper story, had been killed in a freak automobile accident. Calmly, his mother reported that the biographer, doing his research, had asked the son's wife, "what did it sound like when Tom's neck broke?" Is there, for biographers, no shame? My own view is that there should be.

I once was asked who in other disciplines was doing work that came closest to my efforts as a historical biographer. I think the inquirer expected me to pick a political scientist or a psychologist. My answer was quick: I named a portrait painter. Like Marion Miller's work on canvas, my words have to achieve just the right hue, have to travel from note cards to the contours of the narrative just as Miller's brush moves from palette to canvas and shapes a face.

I am not alone in recognizing the pull of the pictorial in the writing of history and biography. Edmund Morgan, a distinguished scholar of seventeenth-century New England, once said how hard it was to write about a person of whom there is no portrait, how lucky he felt that there was one of John Winthrop, how regretful he was that there was not one of Margaret Winthrop. (I might add that he did a good job of imagining one.) His fine biography, *The Puritan Dilemma*, is not only a sensitive rendering of a marriage, but also does a remarkably clear and concise job of explaining early-seventeenth-century New England theology as well as the establishment of unique government processes. A good deal of work can be accomplished in a biography.

I, too, was guided by a portrait, or rather by a photograph taken in the field. It was an 1864 image of Ulysses Grant, standing in front of an ordinary soldier's tent. I was looking at a youthful, relaxed, confident man. I knew from research that confidence had not been his hallmark during the years before the war in which he was engaged. And I knew too that the man leaning unpretentiously on a post outside that tent was the commanding officer of perhaps the greatest army to take the field up to that point in history, the culminating year of the American Civil War. Here was my challenge. What made this man tick?

The essayists in the volume that follows have sought to get past the obvious *People*-Magazine sorts of remarks toward the challenging, important theoretical questions raised by autobiography and biography. There are issues raised by our inescapable confrontations with psychology—with matters of race, gender, sexuality, of class and violence—that cause us to doubt any story of a life, however heavily documented, that is one-dimensional. What is there that we as writers, as readers, can trust in the re-creation of a life?

It seems to me, finally, that at least a hint of an answer lies in the riddle, "Why biography?" Impeccable research, although absolutely essential, does not alone insure that trust. There is another ingredient, one that I think is hinted at by our question, "Why biography?" To the subject must come the basic human curiosity about our fellow humans. We are a curious race and as much as we seek the self, the ego—as determined as some of us still are to conceive of a just society rather than a celebrated individual—we do conceive of human activities in personal terms.

Rhys Isaac is a historian who knows that history, however collective its consequences, hurts individually. When contemplating slavery in Virginia in the eighteenth century, where individual voices are hard to hear in the dim chorus of records of importations and purchases, Isaac does not let his eye go past a newspaper account captioned, if I recall correctly, "A Distressing Happening." The newspaper told of a slave just dragged off a boat from Africa and bought by a man whose language he cannot understand to a strange and terrifying farm, who looked around at this new world, walked over to farm implements lying on a bench, grabbed a knife, and cut his own throat.[6]

Life does happen to each of us singly. The biographer is looking at just such a singular individual. Not all of our stories are this tragic, but, whether as writers or readers, we seek in them some way of seeing ourselves in better relation to a troubling world. That is why biography.

NOTES

1. Martin Amis, "Don Juan in Hull," *New Yorker* 69 (12 July 1993), 81.
2. Ruth Butler, *Rodin: The Shape of Genius* (New Haven: Yale University Press, 1993), 514.
3. William S. McFeely, *Grant: A Biography* (New York, 1981); idem, *Frederick Douglass* (New York: Norton, 1991).
4. Ulysses S. Grant, *Personal Memoirs of U. S. Grant*, 2 vols. (New York, 1885–86); Frederick Douglass, *Narrative of the Life of Frederick Douglass, An American Slave* (1845; reprint, Garden City, N. Y., 1963); idem, *My Bondage and My Freedom* (1855; reprint, New York, 1969); idem, *Life and Times of Frederick Douglass* (1892; reprint, New York, 1962).
5. Janet Malcolm, "The Silent Woman," *New Yorker* 69 (23, 30 August 1993), 86.
6. Rhys Isaac in an informal discussion of his work at a conference, "Large Questions in Small Places," Charles Joyner, convener, Myrtle Beach, S.C., September 28–October 1, 1989.

○ Introduction

THE SEDUCTIONS
OF BIOGRAPHY

Mary Rhiel and David Suchoff

WRITING OR READING A LIFE STORY, as we've implied by the title of this volume, *The Seductions of Biography*, has an appeal that challenges the rhetorical victory of postmodernism over the tradition of the self-sufficient individual. Or does it? Reading the title carefully, we see that the attraction to biography is plural, not singular, allowing for multiple pleasures in the postmodern mode that mixes genres and strikes ironic poses. Yet in the past few decades biography as a genre has suffered from a lack of legitimacy in the worlds of contemporary critical theory, social historiography, and even highbrow journalism. While traditionalists vilify attempts to revise the stories of "great men" in curriculum debates, the truth-content of biography is being openly questioned. Simultaneously, biography has become a multi-faceted genre for minorities telling life-stories that have been previously unheard by the larger culture. These battles over biography ask us to reexamine the selves that constitute culture.

Biography plays an important, even seductive part in these contemporary culture wars. Both conservatives and their opponents turn to the life-story to lay claim to a cultural inheritance which now seems up for grabs. One critic, for example, belittles contemporary Afro-American culture and its focus on biography as "ethnic role models' fantasies of a glorious past."[1] While this critic worries that excessive biographical attention to black writers might cause the "decomposition of America" as a homogenous entity, writers who represent African-American and "other" lives previously lost to mainstream American culture make use of a quite traditional, even confessional, mode of autobiographic self-telling. This historical moment is a productive one, and it provides the cultural context for the essays that follow. "The New Biographers," as some of the volume's contributors have been called, make use of seductively traditional modes of self-telling, even as they challenge the status quo.[2] This challenge often involves the new biographers' questioning of the lures of traditional forms. One of the central issues driving many essays in this book is thus a properly postmodern one: how should the individual life-story—biography—be treated as an increasingly "popular" genre at the very historical moment when new identities, and life stories, are making themselves heard?

The essays in this volume suggest no easy answer to this question: representing new subjects is not always the same thing as giving voice to powerful criticisms of a culture. Feminist perspectives on the writing of women's lives offer a crucial case in point. While many feminist auto/biographers challenge the ease with which eliminating the belief in referentiality might "ignore the crucial referentiality of class, race, and sexual orientation,"[3] other feminist biographers rush to reassure their readers that they have not written biographies in any normative sense of that word. "Changing the Subject," as one chapter of this book puts it, does not necessarily mean that culture has been changed, if "new" identities have been fetishized for mass consumption. Several recent biographies have been written as reminders that biography is not a search for a true self, but rather a way of calling established cultural history into question. As these biographies point out, much established historiography excludes the multiple discourses on gender which constitute culture at any given moment. Such feminist approaches to biography rest upon the belief that the cultural memory represented by biography is always shaped in a contested, critical cultural field.[4]

Thus while it is no great surprise that Biography returned to cultural prominence as racially and ethnically different individuals articulate their life-stories, writers in this volume question whether traditional forms of self-telling neutralize or vocalize the claims of cultural difference. The stable individuality presumed by Ralph Waldo Emerson's "Representative Men" or Thomas Carlyle's *Heroes and Hero-Worship* made biography, to be sure, the domain of the unique and exemplary citizen: such selfhood, however, was racially and ethnically exclusive. To attain one's "best self," as Matthew Arnold argued in the nineteenth century, the particularities of one's class history, or stubbornly persistent ethnic background—coded as the "Hebraic" tendency of culture—were to be left behind. Yet while structuralism's "death of man" motif can be understood as registering the decline in the centrality of the biographies of Western, white males, the postmodern plurality of biographical subjects exercises a constraining as well as liberating cultural force. Feminist and postcolonial critiques represented in the essays that follow question whether a liberated plurality is always a liberating one, when the new subjects who speak lose resistant cultural particularity in the cliches of the confessional form. Writers in this book rightly view the opening up of the private lives of public figures as a critical advance for culture and scholarship, while questioning the dominant ideologies of private life (reproduced, for example, in the Hollywoodization of culture) which biographical entrance into this domain may serve.

What we have to learn from feminist and multicultural contributions is fundamental to the rethinking of biography this volume represents. Both approaches demonstrate that the production of meaning in biographical form is a powerful force in shaping and reshaping cultural memory. We no longer view the present as the end point of an agreed-upon narrative of progress, a view of history that fueled traditional biography's emphasis on great men and great deeds. With multiculturalism comes an insistence that biography has limited the fullness of our culture's memory, but biography can also be a means of challenging and recasting that memory. The life text is, like history, open-ended.

Perhaps for this very reason general readers have remained interested in biography even as the genre became a kind of critical taboo in academic studies. The "new criticism," with its "intentional fallacy," told college-trained readers to ignore the author of a work of literature, and to avoid using his—and it was usually a male—life to explain the letters a "great" writer produced. The structuralist and poststructuralist writing of figures such as Michel Foucault and Roland Barthes speculated on the "death of the author," or even the "disappearance of man." The autonomous, acting individual who provided the subject for traditional biography was decentered by social structures and social codes; the individual came to be seen as spoken by language, rather than as language's speaker. In Weimar Germany, the German cultural critic Siegfried Kracauer had attacked biography in just these terms: stories of self-sufficient individuals, he claimed, were becoming fictive compensation for a society in which the acting individual was controlled by the mass.[5] Kracauer had pointed out the shift biography as a genre was making from its high literary form—for him, in the hagiographical accounts of Goethe's life—to its function as a form of false autonomy offered by mass culture.[6] Today, as different essayists in this volume suggest, biography opens up the cultural marketplace by portraying different kinds of lives. But the critical perspective raised by Kracauer remains crucial for different writers in this volume as well: when does the seductive move toward biographical inclusion become the mass-marketing of difference? How does the urge to destablize traditional culture, by telling the stories of different lives, mesh with the stabilizing generic conventions of the traditional, unified self on the road to self-consciousness?

These differing perspectives on the cultural politics of biography illuminate the current rejuvenation of biography this volume represents. They also fueled the lively and well-attended 1993 conference at Harvard University, "Life-Likenesses: The Seductions of Biography," which provided the inspiration for this book. The sections that follow indicate different moments in the process of the critical reconstruction of our cultural memory at work in the stories of the self. "Mass Media, Biography, and Cultural Memory," introduced by Anthony Appiah, appraises the intersection between popular life stories and modern media, looking frankly and critically at the way market forces proffer biographical images for consumption, images that become part of our national mythology. "Private Lives, Public Figures," introduced by William S. McFeely, examines biography's role in transforming our notion of public figures, now that private lives and sexual identity play such central roles in our cultural-political debates. "Changing the Subject," introduced by Betty Sasaki, considers biographers and biographies of figures whose racial, ethnic, or gender differences had been excluded from "standard" biography, but also examines biographies of individuals—such as Madame C. J. Walker—which ask us to rethink what we now call identity politics. "Whose Life is it Anyway?", introduced by Barbara Johnson, examines the pitfalls and promises of biography's confessional lures: this section explores the ethical questions faced by biographers in a new era of sexual exposure, and examines the ways biography's promise of intimate self-exposure can be contested by the nonheroic, yet resistant postcolonial subject. The concluding section, "Postmodernism and the Possibility of Biography," introduced by Marjorie Garber, offers three different reflections on the redefinition of Biography in the postmodern age.

The proliferation of theories and practices of biography represented in this volume tells us that the seductions of biography cannot by reduced to a generic formula. As William McFeely points out in his preface, this volume does not aim to subject biography to a new set of limiting definitions, now that it is no longer compelled to tell the stories of great men alone. Instead, this volume records moments in our contemporary culture wars when definitions of the individual are being contested. In this sense, the vital currents of biography as it is currently practiced merge with the most crucial questions of contemporary cultural criticism. Biography marks the transitional point at which critical theory, which sought to deconstruct the subject, and multiculturalism, which seeks new forms of subjectivity, meet and carry on a debate with each other as well as with the biographical tradition. What follows is a group of essays by cultural critics, historians, and art historians whose theories and practices affirm the relevance of biography to our basic yet seductive need to tell the story of our selves, and thereby to construct the multiple cultures in which we live.

NOTES

1. See Arthur Schlesinger, Jr., *The Disuniting of America* (New York: Norton, 1992), esp. Chapter 4, "The Decomposition of America," 101–121.

2. Karen J. Winkler described many of the contributors to this volume this way in "The New Biographers," *The Chronicle of Higher Education*, October 27, 1993, vol. XL, No. 10, cover article, p. A6.

3. Brodzki, Bella, and Celeste Schenck, eds. *Life/Lines: Theorizing Women's Autobiography* (Ithaca and London: Cornell University Press, 1988).

4. See, for example, Biddy Martin, *Woman and Modernity: The Life-Styles of Lou Andreas-Salomé* (Ithaca: Cornell University Press, 1991).

5. Biography in its modern form, as Michael McKeon has argued, did not emerge until the notion of an independent individual developed in the eighteenth century. The independence of the subject of biography was figured from the start as an outpost of individuality implicitly set against the forces of commodity culture. Michael McKeon, "Writer as Hero: Novelistic Prefigurations and the Emergence of Literary Biography," in William Epstein, ed., *Contesting the Subject: Essays in the Postmodern Theory and Practice of Biography and Biographical Criticism* (West Lafayette, Indiana: Indiana University Press, 1991), 17–42.

6. See Siegfried Kracauer, "Die Biographie als neubürgerliche Kunstform," in Siegfried Kracauer, *Das Ornament der Masse: Essays*, mit Nachwort. von Karsten Witte (Frankfurt am Main: Suhrkamp, 1977).

①

MASS MEDIA, BIOGRAPHY, AND CULTURAL MEMORY

○ Introduction

K. Anthony Appiah

IT IS A FAMILIAR IDEA that modernity allows the ordinary citizen to make a national identity central to an individual identity: being-American has been central to the self-definitions of many Americans of all races and classes, as being-English (and, later, British) was to so many Englishmen and -women. For these patriots, the story of the nation was a crucial element in their sense of themselves.

It is a slightly less familiar thought that the identity of this nation is tied up with the stories of individuals—*Representative Men* and women, in Emerson's formula—whose stories, in helping to fashion a national narrative, serve also, indirectly, to shape the individual narratives of other patriotic—nationally identified—citizens. Horatio Alger famously contributed to the development of a narrative of success, constructing an American pattern that many—from Booker T. Washington to Henry Ford—read into their own life-stories; fitting this pattern was, for them, as for those who celebrated them, a crucial element of their American-ness, a necessary part of what made them suitable objects of the identifications of their fellow citizens.

Another commonplace insists that postmodernity obliges us to live "after the subject": and, while it is extremely difficult to say what this means in the context of French philosophy in the late twentieth century, it is not hard to explain some of what it has meant for American literary studies. The critique of the subject had at least two significant consequences for the approach of literary studies to biography: first, it led to a skepticisim about the author as an explanatory concept; and second, it led to a rejection of the notion that each individual is a unitary subject. This second consequence encouraged doubts about those accounts of the self that narrate a life with a coherent system of causality in which the early life prefigures, and determines, the later pattern. Postmodernity is, therefore, as it ought to be, skeptical of the modern biography, the Horatio Alger story; and it is, of course, even more doubtful of the imaginary unity of the autobiography, where the now-deconstructed subject-author purports to narrate the now-deconstructed wholeness of his or her own subject-life.

Since the wholeness and coherence of the national story is the product of narrative conventions that seem to draw on the conventions of the life-story—America is a young nation, whose civil war is the identity travail of her adolescence—skepticism about the latter should go with skepticism about the former. And so it does, with the constant invocation of the topos of the imaginary or constructed character of national identities—*Imagined Communities*—as, indeed, of collective identities quite generally.

And yet, as the three essays that follow show, the deconstructed nation continues to be read into and through its representative women and men. This is so even if the tales we tell of the nation are as fragmented, mixed up, and incoherent as the cultural narratives of the sexual ambiguity of stars and the disrupted lives of assassinated political hero-villains, or the horrifying visual recycling of the intersection of personal and national histories in the moments of the Kennedy assassination, the Challenger disaster, or the Rodney King incident.

These essays can all be seen as reflections on the intersection of collective identities—bisexual, African-American, American—each of which is, as the essays in their juxtaposition unintentionally reveal, entangled with the others. These essays also insist on the instability of each collective identity and its affiliation with the instability of the biographies—of a Malcolm X, a Greta Garbo, a Christa McAuliffe—that we know we cannot grasp as coherent, whole things, because we doubt the wholeness and coherence of their subjects.

Here, we are exploring the conventions that give the biographical moment its continuing power (even in a time when the subject matter of the biography seems to have disappeared) and we learn to see how these conventions allow us to explore our connections to each other through the narratively-constructed national, sexual, and racial identities that both unite and divide us. Reading biography as genre can provide each of us another patch in the quilt of our postmodern lives.

But biography can also lead us to examine the sense in which we really do live after the subject. The old subject was constructed through a narrative of internal homogeneity and cross-temporal consistency, and with a Cartesian self-transparency; all this fails to fit the experiences of many of us. All this we must indeed live after. But the selves with which we now live, in the challenging circumstances of our postmodernity, are not the less real for being fragmented, internally conflicted, multiple, and conscious as much of their temporal mutations as of their continuities. The old subject did not understand itself as the social construct that it was, and thus took itself and its solid essence more seriously than it was entitled to; but it was also, perhaps, at least in its manifestation in the novel and the late nineteenth- and early twentieth-century biography, a fiction well-suited to the solid circumstances of bourgeois life. What we see in such less comfortable stories as the tales of "bisexuality" and the multiple readings of Malcolm X are, of course, reflections as much of changing social realities as of changing understandings of the self. There were lives and selves before the subject—Augustine's, for example—and there are selves and lives after the subject; the changing forms of biography (among them the new televisual codes that narrate the fifteen minutes of fame of the contemporary representative woman and man) are both causes and reflections of the new circumstances of that self.

BISEXUALITY AND CELEBRITY

Marjorie Garber

I awoke one morning and found myself famous.
                                    —George Gordon, Lord Byron[1]

"EVERYBODY IS BISEXUAL," bisexual poster-boy Gore Vidal is famous for saying. "Not that everyone practices it."[2]

When we are told that legendary screen lover Errol Flynn was bisexual and that he spent "an enjoyable night" with the eighteen-year-old Truman Capote, we tend to shrug it off as Hollywood excess. Capote himself is said to have remarked to Marilyn Monroe, when asked whether he had a good time, "If it hadn't been Errol Flynn, I wouldn't even have remembered it."[3] Flynn, Dietrich, Garland, Tyrone Power, Cary Grant, James Dean; the bisexuals of the Golden Age of Hollywood were as numerous and as omnivorous as the rock-and-pop bisexuals of Glitter and the Sexual Revolution—Bowie, Jagger, Joplin, Joan Baez, Elton John—or the postmodern bisexuals of MTV and David Letterman—Madonna and Sandra Bernhard.

Is bisexuality just another publicity device for calling attention to the larger-than-life transgressions that make a star a star? Is bisexuality, like Greek or Shakespearean tragedy, something that happens to the great or near-great, who live on a scale with higher highs and more melodramatic lows, an occupational hazard or a professional perk? Something celebrities do because they have the opportunity, the stress, or the need for novelty in private as well as in public life? Do people become stars because they are bisexuals or do they become bisexuals because they are stars?

"I am bisexual, in some circles famously so." This declaration—one could hardly call it a confession—is that of formerly-famous glitter-rock spouse Angela Bowie, the ex-wife of David Bowie, in her 1993 autobiography, *Backstage Passes.* "David and I may in fact have been the best-known bisexual couple ever. We were certainly the most famous couple ever to admit and celebrate our bisexuality so publicly. So if you didn't know before, now you do."[4]

For Angela Bowie, bisexuality is her claim to fame. But why should someone be famous for being bisexual?

A scene in Wendy Wasserstein's hit comedy, *The Sisters Rosensweig,* opens with Geoffrey Duncan, wryly described as an "internationally renowned director and bisexual," entertaining his female lover, her sisters, and their dinner guests with a story. It is apparently a hilariously funny story, since the guests all enter "laughing hysterically," and to indicate that the story is already in progress the scene begins, *in medias res,* with "So":

"So Danny Kaye supposedly dresses up like a customs inspector at the New York airport, and when Sir Larry comes through, he calls him aside into a special room, strips him buck naked, and inspects every single bloody part of him!"

"Why?" asks Sara, one of the sisters, who has been cast for this exchange in the role of the straight man. "Was he smuggling?"

"Sara," explains Geoffrey, "they were, as we say, 'very close personal friends'."

"Danny Kaye!" exclaims Sara in disbelief. "As in Hans Christian Andersen!"

"And then apparently they went off and spent a very warm and funsy night at the Saint Regis."

"Has this beem documented?" Sara demands.

"Who gives a damn?" says Geoffrey.[5]

Celebrity—bisexuality—biography.

The source from which Geoffrey is gleefully quoting—and which does *not,* as it happens, specifically document this by-now-so-well-known story—is Donald Spoto's biography of Laurence Olivier.[6]

> During the stopover at New York's Idlewild Airport, he was stopped by a customs officer who inspected his passport and tickets, inquired in a nearly incomprehensible accent about Olivier's travels and promptly informed him that a body search would be required.... After submitting to the indignities of an inspection of every inch and crevice of his body, Olivier was astonished to see the customs officer step back and slowly remove a complex disguise (a dark wig and a heavily powdered latex mask) and there before the naked Olivier stood Danny Kaye.

(At the risk of sounding like Sara, I can't help wondering whether at this point Kaye burst into a chorus of "the king is in the altogether, the altogether, the altogether...".)

The story itself was featured in virtually every review, together with other details of Olivier's sex life—and the sex lives of his wives. His first wife, Jill Esmond, was a lesbian: "the trauma of the wedding night, as she turned away from her husband with a resolute revulsion for sex, must have caused him to feel not only unattractive and ashamed but also inadequate and incompetent."[7] His second wife, Vivien Leigh, "began to suspect Olivier's sexual ambivalence," both in the triangular relationship he and she developed with actor Peter Finch and "especially in the increasingly frequent visits and almost obsessive attention of Danny Kaye."[8] His third wife prevailed upon him to remove from his autobiography accounts of "the numerous homosexual escapades of his adult life."[9]

Rumor linked Olivier sexually with lifelong friend Noel Coward (Spoto says, in a sentence that is a masterpiece of double negation, that "whether Olivier was disingenuous in his insistence that he never wavered and whether the relationship with Coward was briefly carnal is impossible to ascertain"[10]) as well as with reviewer and "Ultimate Fan" Kenneth Tynan. "Sexual intimacy with Tynan might well have been consistent with their mutual admiration," writes Spoto, in the could-have, might-have mode so dear to (some) contemporary biographers—a mode we might call the prurient wishful subjunctive. "Whatever may have transpired privately—and an overtly homosexual affair cannot definitely be established—Tynan's threat a few years later to publish a book about their relationship caused Olivier to become violently upset."[11]

Olivier has been celebrated for years for his cross-gender magnetism, an aspect of his performing self that is in fact characteristic of all the greatest stars of this century. Film director Elia Kazan noted, with approval, his "girlish" quality, by which he meant his ability to "tease and play the coquette"[12]; Tynan himself wrote memorably that "Olivier's relationship with his audience is that of a skilled but dominating lover."[13]

Now it turns out that there is a referent to this figure, a ground to this metaphor. Laurence Olivier "was bisexual." He had affairs with men, with women, with the audience and with the camera. What does this say about stardom? About living up to one's own legend? About how legends get produced and disseminated? And what do the revelations of the Spoto biography, so gleefully retailed by the buoyant Geoffrey of Wasserstein's play, tell us about the interrelationship of bisexuality and biography in today's mass market readership?

In a literary era dominated by postmodernism, it is interesting to look at celebrity biographies, for in a way no literary form could be *less* postmodern. These are books that aspire to the condition of the well-made novel, full of "explanations" for why characters act as they do. Many employ the mind-reading techniques so notoriously deployed in Joe McGinniss's book on Ted

Kennedy, techniques which are a staple of the genre: he thought to himself, she wondered, their hearts leapt up. What is sought, what is seductive in celebrity biography is a narrative, a coherent, consistent "story"—a true life story—what we might think of as the antithesis of the post-modern.

The postmodern celebrity biography, we might suppose, would be something closer to the Alek Keshishian film *Madonna: Truth or Dare*, with its bold graphics, discontinuous narrative, intrusive camera, alternation of black and white documentary and color concert-footage, and post-credits interchange between director and star. Truth—or Dare. While postmodernism might be characterized as opting for the Dare, the celebrity biographies I will be considering, and which constitute a multi-million-dollar business in the US today, opt for the "truth"—the truth that sells. And what is that truth today? Bisexuality.

The publishing industry seems indeed to have gone in for "bisexual advertising" in a big way, as trumpeted by jacket copy from recent biographies of James Dean, Angela Bowie, Judy Garland ("Many of her lovers were gay men, and she frequently turned to other women for romantic solace"[14]), Marianne Faithfull, Elton John, and others. The jacket flap of *Jagger Unauthorized* by Christopher Andersen promises "the full story of his bizarre relationships with David Bowie, Rudolf Nureyev, Andy Warhol, and one of today's biggest male rock superstars"—who turns out to be Eric Clapton.[15] "Eric and Mick were caught in bed together, it's true," claims an acquaintance. "It was a very narcissistic scene, very ambivalent sexually."[16] The inside flap copy for *Malcolm Forbes, The Man Who Had Everything*, by Christopher Winans asserts that "the man who squired Elizabeth Taylor to society functions one evening was not the same man who the next night was racing his motorcycle through the steamy, seedy underworld of New York's downtown streets, a handsome young man clinging tightly to his back."[17] (How can there be *a* biography of a man who is "not the same man"?)

The back cover of *Howard Hughes: The Secret Life* by Charles Higham quotes an excerpt from an advance review: "An outing of the billionaire closet bisexual…. Strongly documented…a hypnotic portrait of a great American monster,"[18] while the flap promises an account of "Hughes' seduction in his teens by his uncle Rupert, a famed novelist and playwright" after which "Hughes became bisexual, and was later to have affairs with several male stars, including Cary Grant and Tyrone Power." Thus does the copywriter neatly dispose of the question of bisexuality's cause and effect, which has occupied psychotherapists, geneticists, social science researchers and doomsday prophets for countless hours over time. "Marlon would openly acknowledge the tie between his bisexuality and his search for meaning in life," flatly declares the author of *Brando: The Biography*. "Rumors linked him with novelist James Baldwin; actors Wally Cox, Christian Marquand, and others; and even Leonard Bernstein and Gore Vidal."[19]

Clearly, bisexuality sells books, or is thought to do so. Is it the bisexuality of the protagonist that attracts researchers' (and media) attention? Or is it that bisexuals tend also to be especially newsworthy and celebrated in their fields? Either bisexuality makes you a celebrity, or a remarkable number of celebrities are bisexual. Is "bisexuality" here in the position of the subject or of the object?

As the form of my question will suggest, I believe that the answer is "both"—or rather, that it is impossible to distinguish, when it comes to the lives of people who live in the limelight, between object and subject, between desirability and desire.

Many "ordinary" bisexuals—that is to say, un-famous people who have been interviewed by clinicians or talk show hosts, "explain" their bisexuality by some version of the following rhetorical question: why should I overlook the erotic possibilities of half the human race? As Woody Allen has more memorably phrased it, according to formerly self-declared "bisexual"—now "gay"—mega-producer David Geffen, "Say what you will about bisexuality, you have a 50 percent better chance of finding a date on Saturday night."[20] Or, as James Dean is said to have remarked to one of his male lovers, "I'm certainly not going to go through life with one hand tied behind my back."[21]

For performers and artists, and arguably for anyone in the media-inflected public sphere, this question of universal attraction cuts both ways. "Good actors," writes one critic, "exist inside a monosexual world. Great performers—an Olivier, a Garbo, a Dietrich, a Chaplin—are often flecked by sexual ambiguity."[22] And in the case of celebrities like these, "sexual ambiguity" and "bisexuality" are not—or rather, not only—pathologized. Childhood adjustment problems, over- or under-attentive mothers, over- or under-dominant fathers—all of this is grist for the performative mill. "Bisexuality was a Hollywood tradition, one upheld with some style by such stars as Tallulah Bankhead and Marlene Dietrich,"[23] reports Judy Garland's biographer. Singer k. d. lang speaks of "making your sexuality available, through your art, to everyone. Like Elvis, like Mick Jagger, like Annie Lennox or Marlene Dietrich—using the power of both male and female."[24] "Monty's bisexuality was practically legendary," says Bill Gunn, a screenwriter and playwright, about his friend Montgomery Clift. "I think that's what made him so exciting to people in the theater—just about everybody felt they had a chance with him."[25]

Marlene Dietrich's cross-dressing, one of her biographers suggests, "not only capitalizes on an aspect of the actress's bisexual nature; it also enables women in the audience to love her and simultaneously establishes…an identification with men."[26] Among the extraordinary roster of Dietrich's lovers over a long and gallant career were a number of women, including the Berlin music-hall performer Claire Waldoff, playwright and screenwriter Mercedes de Acosta (who also had an affair with Dietrich's rival Greta Garbo) and Edith Piaf.

"She always admitted to me that she preferred women to men," said Dietrich's secretary Bernard Hall after her death. "She said, 'When you go to bed with a woman, it is less important. Men are a hassle.'" Needless to say, however, the list of her male lovers is a roll-call of the famous and the powerful: among them Douglas Fairbanks, Jr., Erich Maria Remarque, Maurice Chevalier, Jean Gabin, John Gilbert (for whom she also competed with Garbo), Michael Wilding, Yul Brynner, Frank Sinatra, Eddie Fisher, Generals Patton and Gavin—and even, her daughter claims, Adlai Stevenson and Edward R. Murrow.

All great stars are bisexual in the performative mode. Dietrich herself once remarked, "Each man or woman should be able to find in the actress the thing he or she most desires and still be left with the promise that they will find something new and exciting every time they see her again." Her great skill lay in the personification of bisexuality as the performative sign of stardom.

A clever director will deploy these energies on the stage or the screen, in effect quadrangulating triangular desire, as Josef von Sternberg does with the kiss in *Morocco* (Gary Cooper watching Dietrich in top hat and tails) or as Nicholas Ray does with James Dean and Sal Mineo in *Rebel Without a Cause*: "Nick Ray was not averse to using Jimmy's bisexuality to good purpose. The director knew that Sal was homosexual, and encouraged him to explore that part of him that would love Jimmy. At the same time, according to Ray, Jimmy fell in love with Sal."[27]

Whether it is actualized in sexual relationships or remains on the level of elusive attraction, this heightened performative state, this state of being simultaneously all-desiring and all-desired, incarnates in the celebrity the two, sometimes apparently conflicting, definitions of bisexuality: having two genders in one body, and being sexually attracted to members of "both" sexes. I put the word "both" in quotation marks, for the number two seems to me a starting point rather than an end-point for the enumeration of "the" sexes, or "the" genders.

"He can be masculine and feminine but never neuter," wrote one of Olivier's reviewers, and Kenneth Tynan is famous for remarking that Dietrich had "sex but no particular gender." Photographer Cecil Beaton said of Mick Jagger, a favorite model, that he was "feminine and masculine: a rare phenomenon." "He is sexy, yet completely sexless. He could nearly be a eunuch."[28] Clifton Fadiman wrote of Judy Garland that "she seemed to be neither male nor female."[29] Columnist Joe Hyams asserts that James Dean was "one of the rare stars, like Rock Hudson and Montgomery Clift, who both men and women find sexy."[30] Despite Beaton and Hyams, though, this quality is not "rare"; it is the indefinable extra something that makes a star.

"Bisexuality" for stars often means gender-envy, gender crossover, cross-gender identification. "Mick wanted to *be* Tina Turner," one of Jagger's friends reports. "He told me that when he's performing that's the image he has of himself. He *sees* himself as Tina Turner."[31] Elton John claimed that David Bowie "has always wanted to be Judy Garland."[32] Michael Jackson models his looks on Diana Ross or Elizabeth Taylor.[33] Singer Annie Lennox "did" Elvis on "Saturday Night Live." Director Josef von Sternberg, in a famous pronouncement, remarked that "I am Miss Dietrich, and Miss Dietrich is me."

But equally often the crossover is in "object" as well as "subject," for performatively bisexuality functions as a "shifter" in grammatical terms, taking love songs addressed from an "I" to a "you" and giving erotic permission to cross gender boundaries. Janis Joplin has been compared to Edith Piaf and Billie Holiday—both, like her, bisexual singers—as a powerful "diseuse," or performer of monologues. "To hear Janis sing 'Ball and Chain' just once is to have been laid, lovingly and well," wrote one music critic.[34]

It is no accident that both Marlene Dietrich and Judy Garland developed fanatically loyal followings among gay men. I remember with heart-stopping clarity attending a Garland concert at Forest Hills stadium late in her career, when the audience called out to the faltering star, "You're a real trouper, Judy." "Talk it, Judy—we don't care." As Garland's biographer notes, "the combination of her turbulent private life, her repertoire of songs about men who got away, and indeed her whole melodramatic persona had made her into something of a camp icon."[35] As for Dietrich, she herself acknowledged the power of the bisexual shifter:

> You could say that my act is divided between the woman's part and the man's part. The woman's part is for men and the man's part is for women. It gives tremendous variety to the act and changes the tempo. I have to give them the Marlene they expect in the first part, but I prefer the white tie and tails myself.... There are just certain songs that a woman can't sing as a woman, so by dressing in tails I can sing songs written for men.[36]

Songs such as "I've Grown Accustomed to Her Face," sung without a gender-switch in the pronoun.

In a famous formulation about the "homosexual wishful phantasy of *loving a man*," Freud described how the unconscious proposition "*I* (a man) *love him* (a man)" could be translated into more apparently tolerable conscious forms: "I do not *love* him—I *hate* him," or "I do not love *him*—I love *her*," or "it is not *I* who love the man—*she* loves him" (for women, "it is not *I* who love the women—*he* loves them"), or "*I do not love at all—I do not love anyone.*"[37] Freud took a rather dismal view of these options; to him they were signs, respectively, of paranoia, erotomania, delusions of jealousy or megalomania—but then, we might say, that's show business. These sentiments are the stock-in-trade of pop, rock, blues and torch songs, where the singer becomes the conduit for the doubly identificatory emotions of her, or his, audience. Doubly identificatory because, once again, the object of identification is both the entertainer and the ventriloquized protagonist of the song.

In another essay, this one on "Hysterical Phantasies and Their Relation to Bisexuality" (1908), Freud theorized that "hysterical symptoms are the expression on the one hand of a masculine unconscious sexual phantasy, and on the other hand of a feminine one,"[38] and followed up this on-the-one-hand-and-on-the-other-hand formulation with a concrete example of such handiwork: "when a person who is masturbating tries in his conscious fantasies to have the feelings both of the man and of the woman in the situation which he is picturing." We might also want to recall here James Dean's remark about his own bisexuality, "I'm certainly not going to go through life with one hand tied behind my back."

However uncomfortable—or comfortable—the analogy with the masturbating fantasist (or the bondage slave) may make us, this is a good description of the complicit relationship of audience to performing star. In fact Freud unwittingly sets up such a comparison by framing his essay on fantasy and bisexuality with a reference to the "strange performances with which certain perverts stage their sexual satisfaction, whether in idea or in reality." One particularly memorable case involved a patient who "pressed her dress up against her body with one hand (as the woman), while she tried to tear it off with the other (as the man)."[39]

It is neither a joke nor a mere witticism to suggest that such staged "performances," with their manifestations of bisexual desire and satisfaction, are an important part of the mechanism of stardom for Mick Jagger, David Bowie, or Janis Joplin—as indeed for James Dean and Montgomery Clift. It is not only the "performer," but also the "performance," which can be bisexual, and can derive from the complex deployment of fantasy effects of enormous power and pleasure. Not for the first time we can see that what is perverse in the private individual may be culturally valued in the celebrity. What is pathologized in the clinic is celebrated on the stage and at the box office. In fact "bisexuality," which is so difficult to pinpoint "in life," is perfectly recognizable as a performative mode.

Marlene Dietrich's daughter Maria Riva explains that in the Dietrich household the phrase "in life" was used to distinguish real life from things that were "movie star" related and therefore unreal.[40] Yet the paradox of Marlene Dietrich was, of course, that the "movie star" *was* the real. "I don't ask you whom you were applauding—the legend, the performer, or me," she confided to the audience for a Marlene Dietrich retrospective at the Museum of Modern Art in 1953. "I, personally, like the legend."

"Life" is what is sought in biography. But it is precisely in eroticism that the real life/stage life distinction breaks down, as Truman Capote's remark about going to bed with Errol Flynn makes clear. Celebrity loves celebrity itself—loves the simulacrum with real love.

We tend to use the phrase "sex life" either as a shorthand term for the sexual experiences and sexual tastes of an individual over time, as in "his sex life was largely confined to occasional encounters with willing strangers," or else as an euphemism for the considerably less socially acceptable "gettin' any?" "How's your sex life?" means "how are you doing in bed these days, and who are you doing it with?" Broadly speaking, one sense is diachronic and the other is synchronic—one characterizes, the other particularizes, one looks at sex as a history, the other looks at sex as a story. But can a "sex life" be, or tell, a life story?

In the preface to his one-volume life of Henry James, published in 1985, Leon Edel notes some important changes in the practice of biographical writing over the years that bear upon this question of a "sex life." His original study had been written between 1950 and 1971; the redacted single volume benefited from—or at least responded to—subsequent changes in social attitudes towards privacy and sexuality, what Edel characterized as "the candor which prevails, the freedom we now possess in writing lives to deal with the physical as well as cerebral side of men and women":

> I am not trying to suggest that I have, in my revisions, gone in quest of a "sex life" or even a "love life" for Henry James.... What I have been able to do is to discard certain former reticences, to take less advantage of certain "proprieties" I practiced out of respect for surviving members of the James family.... Selection, taste, tact, and certain decencies still remain: and biographers will have to be judged by the skill with which they adhere to what we humanly want to know rather than load us with gossip and the modern bedroom. We are able to offer a more forthright record of personal relations, of deeper emotions and sexual fantasies, and need no longer wrap indiscretions and adulteries in Victorian gauze.... I have accordingly inserted some new passages and an inevitable amount of speculation—the stock-in-trade of all biographers.[41]

Now, this is a fascinating account of a scrupulous scholar's scruples. Edel first observes that biographers now feel freer to talk frankly about items formerly regarded as backstairs gossip. The same, we might say, is true for the media, who used to protect philandering politicians and what were then called "AC-DC" actors and film stars from prying public eyes. His figure is that of unwrapping, removing the layers of gauze, the reticences and proprieties, that have in the past cloaked indiscretions and adulteries; there's more truth, apparently, as well as more enterprise, in walking naked. But, he tells us, biographers will still select, still abide by "certain decencies," giving us "what we humanly want to know" rather than tediously loading us with "gossip and the modern bedroom."

Leaving aside whether this latter is not in fact exactly what we, humanly or inhumanly, want to know, let us consider the method Edel employed for achieving this new and desirable level of candor: not only the insertion of "some new passages," but also "an inevitable amount of speculation, the stock-in-trade of all biographers." Rather than merely subtracting obfuscations, then, or even selecting from among available facts, the contemporary biographer will add something: speculation. Instead of revealing the "truth" beneath the gauze, the newly liberated biography, freed from the convention of reticence, replaces concealment with augmentation—good guesses, connecting the dots, speculative fictions. Even if there were a tape recorder or a videocamera set up in the "modern bedroom" (or the "postmodern bedroom," which is to say, any room in the house) it could only suggest, and not define, the elusive and shifting contours of desire. To locate the deeper emotions and sexual fantasies of their subjects, biographers, it seems, have to have a few fantasies of their own.

Some celebrity biographies have taken for granted a certain public awareness of the protagonist's interesting sexuality—indeed that is one presumptive reason why the book is being purchased, reviewed, read, or in fact written. Malcolm Forbes's biographer chronicles his own research as if he were an investigative reporter. He tells the story of a hapless predecessor who was also working on a biography of Forbes, and "asked him about the rumors that he was bisexual." "Christ!" Malcolm replied. "What sort of book is this?"[42] "The rumors about [Forbes's] sexuality swirled for decades," he reports. "Virtually everybody interviewed for this book raised the question without being prompted." And again, "The question was inevitable. Usually it would surface without coaching within the first five minutes of an interview. Was this book going to mention Malcolm's alleged appetite for young men?" Like Angela Bowie's even less subtle hints about future disclosures ("Maybe Mick is still a little pissed about my appearance on Joan Rivers's show, where I recounted my finding him and my husband in bed together. Well, more on *that* anon"[43]) this is a come-on that predicts the hot stuff that lies ahead. "It didn't take a lot of digging to uncover evidence to back the rumors."[44] At the same time such a device takes the biographer off the hook; it is not he but those he interviews who bring up the subject.

Historian Daniel Boorstin lamented in the sixties the concomitant rise of "the celebrity"—"a person who is well known for his well-knownness"— and the "pseudo-event"—a staged or incited event, often timed to coincide with the evening news. The typical pseudo-event was, he said, "not a train wreck or an earthquake, but an interview."[45] Since the purpose of the interview is to produce and disseminate celebrity, and since celebrity is found to be bound up in some peculiar fashion with bisexuality, we should not be surprised to find that it is in the pages of magazines like *Interview*, and *Rolling Stone*, and *The Advocate*, as well as on television interview programs like *20/20*, that the attempt is constantly being made to establish bisexuality as a "fact" (a "fact of life"). Yet language can function *as* a sexual act, not just as a way of naming one. That is why explicit sexual vocabularies are so often censored. When sex is discussed, the discussion is itself sexy. Sexual language is never merely descriptive or constative; it is performative. To ask a celebrity for the correct name of his or her sexuality is to attempt to pin it down—as if it were possible to do so—in the constative, and not the performative, mode.

As for bisexuality as the "truth" of a "life," we find that the very stars whose biographers are marketing bisexuality as truth are themselves in a more complex and *narrative* relation to it. Bisexuality, like celebrity, appears as an infinite regress. Bisexuality seems always to be being ascribed, claimed, denied, and disavowed. Thus Boy George, returning to the celebrity spotlight after recording the title song for *The Crying Game*, told *Newsweek*, "I used to say I was bisexual, which is a lie, and I felt really bad about it."

Producer David Geffen, in an article proclaiming him the gay and lesbian *Advocate*'s 1991 Man of the Year, was asked why he previously claimed to be bisexual in an interview with *Vanity Fair*—an interview that described him as having gone from being "in love with Cher to being in love with Marlo Thomas to being in love with a guy at Studio 54."[46] "It was a big step for me when I said in *Vanity Fair* that I was a bisexual man," he explains. "That was as much as I could do then. This is what I can do now. I'm OK with where I was then and where I am now."[47]

Flamboyant rock star Elton John told *Rolling Stone* in a much-publicized interview in 1976 that he was bisexual. In fact, he confided to interviewer Cliff Jahr, "I think everybody's bisexual."[48] In 1984, on Valentine's Day, he married Renate Blauel, a sound studio recording engineer, after an engagement of four days. "Bisexuality's not a solo proposition," he told the press. "Everyone does some experimenting. I'm not denying anything I've said. But I have a right to make a choice."[49] *People* magazine speculated about whether the new Mrs. John was "a lover or a cover," and at the wedding— attended by numerous celebrities, including drag star Dame Edna Everage— a five-tiered fruitcake was served to the guests.

By 1992, long divorced, Elton had changed his tune. "No longer calling himself bisexual, Elton says he's quite comfortable being gay," *Rolling Stone* now reported.[50]

When David Bowie made *his* famous claim, in an interview with the British journal *Melody Maker* in 1972—"I'm gay and I always have been, even when I was David Jones," he did so from the (relatively) safe ground of bisexuality. After all, he was married to the equally publicly bisexual Angela, he was the father of one year old Zowie (who later changed his name to Joey) and his escapades with women were well-known. His word "gay" was *read* by the media as meaning "bisexual," just as Elton John's word "bisexual" was, inevitably, read as meaning "gay." A decade later, in the conservative baby-booomer eighties, Bowie confided to the ever-interested *Rolling Stone* that saying "I was bisexual" was "the biggest mistake I ever made."[51]

Where Elton and David Geffen and Boy George repudiated bisexuality in favor of coming out as gay, Bowie at this point sought to erase or revise it in the "other" direction, toward the straight and narrow, and Jagger followed suit. "In interview after interview he claimed that he had never really taken drugs...and that rumors concerning his bisexuality were just that— rumors."[52] The question of which is "worse" in the public mind, to be bisexual or to be gay, is complicated in the case of certain celebrities by the need to be on the cutting edge, where "worse" is "better" and *Bad* is good. How to be on the cutting edge without cutting yourself off?

Folksinger Joan Baez writes in her autobiography, "In 1972 I was talking with a young reporter from a Berkeley paper. He asked me if I was heterosexual. I said simply that if the affair I'd had ten years ago counted, then I was bisexual. I didn't realize what a catch he had when he left my house and tore back up the coast to print his story."

The next day reporters thronging her doorstep were met by a woman friend who was helping Baez with child care after her split-up with her husband. "Just my luck to have a woman greet them at the door in her nightgown," she notes wryly. She also reports the friend's offhand question to her: "Did you tell someone you were a lesbian?"[53] Notice "lesbian," not "bisexual." In 1972 lesbian was the riskier, the more scandalous, thus the more newsworthy category. Even when the term "bisexual" is acknowledged it tends to disappear. Baez writes that she hasn't since had another affair with a woman "or a conscious desire to."[54] *Is* she bisexual? *Was* she? Was she if she said she was? Is the term constative (descriptive) or performative?

Tennis star Martina Navratilova, described by *Time* magazine as Aspen's "most famous bisexual"[55] told Barbara Walters on the television show *20/20* when asked whether she considered herself "bisexual, a lesbian, what?" that she liked both "men and women, but I prefer to be with women." Sports columnist Robert Lipsyte hailed her "description of her bisexuality to Barbara Walters" as "one of the most provocatively intelligent I've heard."[56] But Martina herself, once the target of a palimony suit and now a celebrity lesbian on the fundraising circuit, had earlier disdained the label, announcing in her autobiography, "I'm not a one-sex person, and yet I hate the term *bisexual*. It sounds creepy to me."

Her former lover, ex–Texas Maid of Cotton Judy Nelson, who had left a doctor husband and two sons to live with Martina, is even more resistant. "Judy believes that the labels of 'heterosexual,' 'homosexual' and 'bisexual' need to be deemphasized and that the word sexual can stand alone," Nelson's biographer explains, adding, perhaps unsurprisingly, "Judy feels that the label 'lesbian' has a very negative connotation."[57] Judy's new lover is Martina's ex, best-selling lesbian novelist Rita Mae Brown.

Meanwhile, elsewhere on the tennis circuit Billie Jean King, who had an affair with hairdresser Marilyn Barnett while still married, as she was until 1985, to Larry King, first told a press conference that she didn't "feel homosexual," and then explained that she hadn't meant to deny the facts of her former attachment. "I meant only that I had never lived as a homosexual, in that full life-style, and that when I had the relationship with Marilyn I felt no differently than I ever have. Obviously I must be bisexual. I suspect many people are, only they're not aware of it. I couldn't have sustained the affair with Marilyn and not be bisexual." But for Billie Jean, since she "felt no differently with Marilyn than I did when I made love to a man," the point she sought to get across was, "please, no labels."[58]

For both King and Navratilova "bisexual" was the right term and the wrong one at once. This is partly the kind of resistance to labels that leads people to say, for example, that they believe in equal rights for women but that they're not feminists, as if feminism meant something other, something scarier (something more lesbian?) than that. But in the particular case of bisexuality it is not only phobia but also something about the term's odd relationship to temporality and to performance that is at stake.

"Everybody is bisexual," Gore Vidal says. "Not that everyone practices it." The more we look at celebrities and bisexuality, the more it seems as though perhaps *no one* is bisexual, although almost everybody practices it.

"Jimmy was neither homosexual nor bisexual," one of James Dean's lovers declared, "I think he was multisexual. He once said that he didn't think there was any such thing as being bisexual."[59]

Gore Vidal once teased an interviewer with the idea that he might in fact be "trisexual." "Why, when young," he asserts, "even an unescorted can-teloupe wouldn't have been safe in my company."[60] Here Vidal joins (he would probably rather say, leads) the creative erotic company of bisexual "sexpert" Susie Bright, who told Phil Donahue it didn't matter whether one's partner was "man, woman, or grapefruit," and bisexual painter Larry Rivers, who feelingly describes in his autobiography his teenage sexual relationship with a blue velvet armchair in his mother's living room.

But what would it mean to say that someone "is" bisexual?

Leonard Bernstein declared in 1984 that "although he had been homosex-ual and heterosexual, he had never been both during the same period."[61] Does that mean that he is never bisexual? Or always bisexual? Clinicians these days tend to characterize bisexuality as either "sequential" or "con-current," depending upon whether the same-sex/opposite-sex relationships are going on at the same time. But although this will at first seem useful in making gross distinctions, it is finally less clear than it appears. For one thing, what, precisely, is "the same time"? Alternate nights? The same night? The same bed?

Many of James Dean's friends believed that his "homosexual activities ceased" when he came to Hollywood to film *East of Eden*; "the Jimmy we all knew in Hollywood was very much a swinging heterosexual."[62] Yet his biographer acknowledges that his ambiguous sexuality is central to his fame and fascination. Is it helpful to see James Dean as a "sequential" or "serial" bisexual?

Cary Grant lived with fellow actor Randolph Scott in a gay relationship well known in Hollywood circles. He was also erotically involved with Howard Hughes. All three men married—Grant five times—but gossip columnists and the movie community were well aware of their bisexuality. In the *Hollywood Reporter*, Edith Gwynn described an imaginary party game, of a kind quite common in those days, in which the guests arrived dressed as movie titles: In this fantasy Dietrich was said to have come as *Male and Female*, Garbo as *The Son-Daughter*, and Grant as *One-Way Passage*. As for Howard Hughes, in his prereclusive days, his lovers included, in addition to Grant, Scott, and Tyrone Power, Katharine Hepburn, Ginger Rogers, Gene Tierney, and Olivia de Havilland.

"Lavender marriages" were common in Hollywood—the star-studded liaison of Robert Taylor and Barbara Stanwyck, for example, or, in a slightly different way, the marriage of Judy Garland and Vincente Minelli. Should we consider such marriages, because of their heterosexually "legitimating" aspects, somehow not "real" marriages? This judgment is occasionally proffered both from the left and from the right—that is, from the direction of gay-affirmative politics (and the controversial"outing" of celebrities) as well as from the direction of family values. The celebrity in question is "really" gay or lesbian; the marriage is a cover or a sham. "Bisexuality" is regarded as an artifact of the closet, of Hollywood public mores, or of patriarchy. But how does this kind of marrying for social position differ from other kinds? From, for example, the quest of older, wealthier men for younger, ever more beautiful wives? So-called "trophy wives"? Or, for that matter, the collection of "trophy husbands," ever younger and more muscular, by the likes of Judy Garland and Elizabeth Taylor. Is it possible that the artifact here is not "bisexuality" but marriage?

A biography of Rock Hudson co-authored by the star and published after his death describes his three-year marriage to Phyllis Gates: "the story that was told and retold until it became canon was that the marriage had been arranged to kill rumors that Rock was homosexual. The question of whether the marriage was real or phony is the central conundrum of Rock Hudson's life. It is still unresolved, and perhaps never can be, for one of the principals is dead and the other is not sure what happened."[63]

Phyllis came to believe that publicist Henry Willson and Universal Studios *did* arrange the marriage to forestall a devastating exposé in *Confidential* magazine, although she claimed she knew nothing of it at the time. "Now I don't believe it was genuine," she says. (To complicate things further Rock, now dead, is said to have told friends that Phyllis was bisexual, something she denied.[64])

Phony or real, "not sure what happened," still unresolved—the difficulty of narrating the truth of a "sex life" is compounded internally by the conventions of institutions (like marriage and "Hollywood") and externally by the conventions of biography itself. Manipulated by studios, publicists, fan magazines, gossip columnists, rumor, and conscious self-fictionalizing, it seems as if celebrity biography is "Dare" rather than "Truth. "I had heard the rumors about Jimmy," writes James Dean's friend and biographer in the preface to his book. "But I knew the difference between rumor and fact, and I really didn't care what Jimmy did or who he did it with. Even had the rumors been true it wouldn't have mattered."[65]

Even had the rumors been true. "Don't believe those rumors," Madonna winks to her audience as she performs with Sandra Bernhard, and Sandra comes back grinning, a half-beat later, with a reply: "*Believe* those rumors." The exchange is captured on videotape, and featured in *Truth or Dare*.

When the Kinsey Report on *Sexual Behavior in the Human Male* was published in 1948, Rock Hudson bought a copy and found it "reassuring."[66] The idea of a sexual continuum, from exclusively heterosexual to exclusively homosexual, appealed to him. He was looking for himself in the Kinsey

Report, just as Radclyffe Hall's lesbian protagonist Stephen Gordon discovered herself in the pages of her father's copy of Krafft-Ebing. But even in that 804-page repository of facts about sex lives, bisexuality existed, so to speak, between the lines. It was a question not posed as such, an answer that happened by accident. "Bisexuals" in the Kinsey Report were the product of a statistical overlap.

Hudson told his co-biographer that he "was attracted to women," but he "preferred to be with men." "He preferred it if they had also slept with women, if they 'had a story.'"[67] The "story," the conquest *over* heterosexuality, the transgressive seduction, is part of what is erotic. Stories are seductive; it is with stories that we fall in love.

"Bisexuality" is not a fixed point on a scale but an aspect of lived experience, seen in the context of particular relations. What is peculiarly postmodern about these celebrity biographies is the way in which bisexuality, though it appears at first to be everywhere—on the jacket blurb, in the headlines, in the index—is ultimately, not nowhere, but elsewhere. Like postmodernism itself, it resists a stable referentiality. It performs.

Truth or Dare—that is to say, constative or performative, the mode of "fact" or the mode of enactment. (A far cry from Truth or Consequences, the quiz-show hit of the 40s and 50s, in which, by a logic of reward and punishment, you "get" what you "deserve.") The public adoption or disavowal of one sexual label or another by a celebrity does not constitute a *description* of a sex life but rather an *event* within it. Just ask anyone in the military who pronounces the sentence, "I am a homosexual." To narrate a sex life is itself a sexual performance; if you could simply and objectively state the truth of a sex life it would cease to be truly sexy. To see an equivalence between celebrity and bisexuality is to attempt to *fix* two terms which are similar only in their naming of a process of self-reinvention, self-transgression. The terms "celebrity" and "bisexuality" can't settle into a happily married couple because if they did both partners would immediately cease to be what they are. It would be in effect another lavender marriage.

Celebrities do constantly re-invent themselves. Look at David Bowie. Look at Madonna. Look at Michael Jackson. One of the ways in which they have done this—as these examples will suggest—is by renegotiating and reconfiguring not only their clothes, their bodies, and their hair but also their sexualities. But the cognate relationship between postmodernism and bisexuality merely underscores the fact that *all* lives are discontinuous—a fact well known to biographers.

To shock and to give pleasure: these are the arts of the erotic icon as consummate star. At a "come-as-the-person-you-most-admire" costume party in Hollywood in 1935 Marlene Dietrich went dressed as Leda *and* the Swan. Her escort was "Marlene Dietrich," the young English actress Elizabeth Allen dressed in Dietrich's *Morocco* top hat and tails. One of Dietrich's biographers notes that this was "perhaps the ultimate bisexual statement for those who got it."[68] For the sheer diversion of inventive role-playing—and an object lesson in the theatrical joys of self-love—this is an image more arresting than any in Madonna's *Sex*.

NOTES

1. George Gordon, Lord Byron, after the publication of the first two cantos of *Childe Harold's Pilgrimage*. Thomas More, *Life of Byron* (1930) chapter 14.

2. Richard Grenier, "Gore Vidal: What It's Like to be Talented, Rich, and Bisexual." *Cosmopolitan*, November, 1975, 167. Hector Arce, *The Secret Life of Tyrone Power* (New York: William Morrow, 1979), 187.

3. Charles Higham, *Errol Flynn: The Untold Story* (New York: Doubleday, 1980), 227.

4. Angela Bowie with Patrick Carr, *Backstage Passes: Life on the Wild Side with David Bowie* (New York: G. P. Putnam's Sons, 1993), 18.

5. Wendy Wasserstein, *The Sisters Rosensweig* (New York: Harcourt Brace, 1993), Act 1 scene 4, 49–50.

6. Donald Spoto, *Laurence Olivier: A Biography* (New York: HarperCollins, 1992). The account of the customs officer ruse can be found on page 246.

7. Spoto, *Olivier*, 60.

8. Spoto, *Olivier*, 223.

9. Spoto, *Olivier*, 230.

10. Spoto, *Olivier*, 61.

11. Spoto *Olivier*, 323.

12. Kenneth Tynan, *The Sound of Two Hands Clapping* (New York: Holt, Reinhart and Winston, 1975), 130.

13. Kenneth Tynan, *Othello: The National Theatre Production* (New York: Stein & Day), reprinted in Tynan, *Profiles* (London: Nick Hern/Walker, 1989), 205.

14. David Shipman, *Judy Garland: The Secret Life of an American Legend* (New York: Hyperion, 1993).

15. Christopher Andersen, *Jagger Unauthorized* (New York: Delacorte Press, 1993).

16 John Dunbar, in Andersen, 167.

17. Christopher Winans, *Malcolm Forbes: The Man Who Had Everything* (New York: St. Martin's Press, 1990).

18. Charles Higham, *Howard Hughes: The Secret Life* (New York: G. P. Putnam's Sons, 1993).

19. Peter Manso, *Brando: The Biography* (New York: Hyperion, 1994), 91, 164.

20. Paul Rosenfield, "David is Goliath." *Vanity Fair*, March 1992, 162.

21. Jonathan Gilmore, in Hyams, *James Dean*, 80.

22. Mihael Billington, "Lasciviously Pleasing." In *Olivier in Celebration*, ed. Garry O'Connor (New York: Dodd, Mead, 1987), 72.

23. Shipman, *Judy Garland*, 137.

24. Leslie Bennetts, "k. d. lang Cuts It Close." *Vanity Fair*, August 1993, 144.

25. Robert laGuardia, *Monty: A Biography of Montgomery Clift* (New York: Primus; Donald I. Fine, 1988), 181.

26. Spoto, *Blue Angel*.

27. Hyams, 209.
28. Andersen, 139.
29. Clifton Fadiman, *Holiday* magazine, (in the first weeks of 1952); Shipman, 399.
30 Hyams, 209.
31. Andersen, 127–28.
32. Susan Crimp and Patricia Burstein, *The Many Lives of Elton John* (New York: Birch Lane Press, 1992), 96.
33. Randy Tarraborelli.
34. Richard Goldstein, quoted in Amburn, 129.
35. Shipman, 399–400.
36. Art Buchwald, "La Dietrich Great Anywhere She Goes," *International Herald Tribune*, December 13, 1959; Spoto, *Blue Angel*, 268–69.
37. Sigmund Freud, "Psycho-Analytic Notes on An Autobiographical Account of a Case of Paranoia" (1911) *SE* 12: 63–65.
38. Sigmund Freud, "Hysterical Phantasies and Their Relation to Bisexuality" (1908). *SE* 9: 165.
39. Freud, "Hysterical Fantasies," *SE* 9: 166.
40. Maria Riva, *Marlene Dietrich* (New York: Knopf, 1993),
41. Leon Edel, *Henry James: A Life* (New York: Harper & Row, 1985), xi–xii.
42. Winans, 19.
43. From the author's statement on the first page of the book, signed in longhand "Angela Bowie"—thus by implication an especially "personal" and "direct" communication.
44. Winans, 18; 19; 141.
45. Daniel Boorstin, *The Image* (1962)
46. Paul Rosenfield, "David is Goliath." *Vanity Fair*, March 1991, 162.
47. Brendan Lemon, "David Geffen." *The Advocate*, December 19, 1992, 38.
48. Cliff Jahr, "Elton's Frank Talk...The Lonely Love Life of a Superstar," *Rolling Stone*, October 7, 1976.
49. Crimp and Burstein, *The Many Lives of Elton John*, 223.
50. *Boston Globe*, March 4, 1992, quoting a *Rolling Stone* inteview with Philip Norman, author of *Elton John: The Biography* (Harmony Books, 1992).
51. Kurt Loder, "Straight Time," *Rolling Stone*, May 12, 1983; Edwards and Zanetta, *Stardust*, 393.
52. Andersen, 376.
53. Joan Baez, *And a Voice to Sing with* (New York: New American Library, 1987), 81–82.
54. Ibid, 82.
55. *Time*, December 14, 1992, 55.
56. Robert Lipsyte, "Connors the Killer Is Really Just a Child," *The New York Times*, September 6, 1991, B12.
57. Sandra Faulkner with Judy Nelson, *Love Match: Nelson vs. Navratilova*, introduction by Rita Mae Brown (New York: Birch Lane Press, 1993), 75.
58. Billie Jean King with Frank Deford, *Billie Jean* (New York: Viking Press, 1982, 27.

59. Hyams, *James Dean*, 79.
60. Grenier, 184.
61. Peyser, 301.
62. Hyams, 209.
63. Charles Higham, *Cary Grant: The Lonely Heart*, 81.
64. Hyams, 2.
65. Hudson and Davidson, 57.
66. Hudson and Davidson, 57.
67. Steven Bach, *Marlene Dietrich: Life and Legend* (New York: William Morrow, 1992).

2

PERSONAL STORIES AND NATIONAL MEANINGS
Memory, Reenactment, and the Image

Marita Sturken

THE REMEMBRANCE OF EVENTS AND BIOGRAPHIES of national importance moves between the realms of cultural memory and history. History is composed of narratives that have been sanctioned in some way, that often tell a self-conscious story of the nation. Cultural memory represents the stories that are told outside official historical discourse, where individual memories are shared, often with political intent, to act as counter-memories to history. This tension between cultural memory and history, between different levels of public discourse, converges in particular ways around those biographies that are important to national image. Within national discourse the stakes of biography are high; the meaning of certain life stories helps to shape the ways in which the nation and its history are defined. Yet, there is a way in which biography as a form can be seen to exist in the porous boundary between cultural memory and history, emerging in the tension between the history and counter-memory. Biographies and autobiographies mark the moment when personal stories are imbued with cultural meaning.

The fragments of memory that cohere in biographies come to us not only through the written text, but through camera images, as stories evoked through photographs or told through cinematic narratives and television movies. Increasingly, the biographic form includes the stories told through the media, through tabloid television and courtroom TV. Reenactment emerges as the primary mimetic form, the cathartic means by which the nation relives its traumas and difficulties.

In the 1990s—the era of Amy Fisher, O. J. Simpson, and Waco, Texas— the realms of documentary, reenactment, biography, and history have merged in complex and troubling ways. Cultural images of historical events, both documentary and docudrama, biographical and fictional, have the capacity to usurp and replace the personal memories of those who participated in those events and lives. In fact, it is questionable whether one can ever speak of a personal memory of historical and biographical events that is distinguishable from the cultural narrativization of those events, or that one ever could. This is testimony to the way that memory works both individually and culturally. While the status of biography (as camera image and reenactment, in postmodernity) would seem then to be one that undermines any notion of biographical truth, I would argue that memory, the fabric of biography, has always been about forgetting and inventing.

In the same sense, the shared memories of a nation are also always in flux, and camera images play a central role in this process. Historical events and biographies often acquire their national meaning through shared images, and it is primarily through images—photographic, cinematic, televisual, documentary, and docudrama—that a shared sense of the nation is constructed.

The construction of national identity in the United States takes place in part through nationally "experienced" events—the events for which we remember "where we were" when it happened. The Kennedy assassination, the first moon walk, the assassinations of Martin Luther King, Jr., and Robert Kennedy, and the Challenger explosion, for example, stand out as some of these moments of shock, not the continual flow of history or biography but its rupture. This remembering "where we were" is a kind of witnessing, and increasingly, American spectators participate in this witnessing through camera images: "where we were" was in front of the television screen. This particular kind of embodiment, whereby we imagine our bodies in the spatial location where we were, is a means by which we situate our bodies in the nation. This remembering, through the memory of the body in space, is a kind of reenactment.

Within this complex arena of public and private in the creation of national myth, there are personal stories that acquire national meaning. In the case of public figures, such as presidents, or national figures such as Martin Luther King, Jr., this confluence of personal and national biography is to be expected. However, there are also so-called "ordinary" citizens who by chance become figures in the stories that nations tell about themselves, whose biographies are no longer their own: to name just a few, Emmett Till, Rosa Parks, Patricia Hearst, Willie Horton, Christa McAuliffe, Anita Hill, Rodney King, Baby Jessica.

I would like to examine the intersections of the camera image, the docudrama, the public figure, and the ordinary citizen, in particular the moment at which personal biography becomes national biography. At what point does a biography become a national story, symbolizing an aspect of the nation's self-image, its longing, and its fantasy? How does the camera image, in particular the docudrama, allow for participation in national stories? I will look briefly at three famous images of recent American history—the Zapruder film of President Kennedy's assassination in 1963, the television images of the Challenger explosion in 1986, and the video image of the Rodney King beating by Los Angeles police in 1992. The trajectories of these images in postmodern culture reveal the ways in which national biographies are, like memories, always changing, mutating, and accommodating, in their mix of fact, desire, fantasy, and invention.

THE ZAPRUDER FILM: THE STILL, THE MOVING IMAGE, THE REENACTMENT

The Zapruder film of President Kennedy's assassination in 1963 is perhaps the most famous piece of documentary film in American history. It is both a still and moving image icon: for 12 years it was seen in public only as a series of still images. The representation of the Zapruder film as history is thus individual frames sliding forward in slow motion, offering only fragments of clues to what happened. Never before had a piece of film been so dissected (as a surrogate for Kennedy's absent corpse), with the belief that it contains the truth—a truth that exists somewhere between the frames.

In the Zapruder film, the limousine carrying President Kennedy, Jacqueline Kennedy, and Texas Governor John Connolly and his wife Nellie drives toward and then past the camera in a matter of seconds. Briefly obstructed by a stand of trees, the camera captures Kennedy the moment after he is shot for the first time, witnesses the impact of a second shot, and then follows the car swiftly to the right as it speeds away. Jacqueline Kennedy, clad in a pink suit with a pillbox hat, first cradles her husband's head, and then crawls backward on the trunk of the car, presumably to aid a secret service agent running towards it. It is a grainy color image, its detail blurred and obscure, an image that hides as much as it reveals.

The status of the Zapruder film changed several times. It was initially an amateur film, shot on a home-movie camera by Abraham Zapruder as he watched Kennedy ride by. It was immediately purchased by Time-Life for $150,000, which published it the following week as still images in *Life* magazine, without mention of Zapruder. This allowed the amateur status of the film to be erased, and for *Life* to present "exclusive" photos as if one of its photographers had been present. The film was then locked away by Time-Life, which allowed only select viewers an opportunity to see it. (Dan Rather—whose journalism career was largely made by his proximity to this event—was among them.) Some assassination historians have contended that frames were reversed when they were printed in the Warren Report, and that the captions and order for the frames published in *Life* were misleading.[1] The film thus has a different meaning as still images than as a moving image. It is also rescripted in retrospect; for instance, for subsequent generations, this film has become so synonymous with the assassination that many people think it was seen live on television.

The Zapruder film thus changed from an amateur film to a copyrighted commercial image to legal evidence to "evidence" of a conspiracy. This image, so central to American historical consciousness, so inseparable from the event itself, has played a particular role in symbolizing Kennedy's life and what is scripted in retrospect as a crucial moment in American history and a loss of national innocence. It is not possible to imagine the effect and affect of this event in the absence of that image. Any scientific analysis of the Zapruder film cannot fix its meaning because the story of national and emotional loss outweighs it. Science cannot satisfy this loss. We cannot have—and perhaps ultimately we do not want to have—a definitive answer to why the assassination happened.

The Zapruder film is also an image that has changed status through reenactment. In 1975, at the time the film was first shown on television, Ant Farm and T. R. Uthco, two media art collectives in San Francisco, went to Dallas to reenact the film on video in a performance called *The Eternal Frame* (1976). In what they saw as an exercise in bad taste, they drove repeatedly through Dealey Plaza, with various members of the group (one in drag as Jackie) replaying the famous scene. Yet, these artists, in striving for macabre humor, did not adequately anticipate the power of mimetic interpretation, and rather than stand in horror, the tourists at Dealey Plaza wept and reminisced, apparently under the impression that this was an officially sanctioned event.

The reenactment of *The Eternal Frame*, replayed in constant repetition, had a small audience, but it has now been usurped by the Zapruder film's incorporation into Oliver Stone's controversial film *JFK* (1991). This docudrama contends, among other things, that the Zapruder film is a crucial piece of evidence that the conspirators who killed Kennedy had not counted on, thus accounting for its suppression.

The opening sequence of *JFK* ends with Kennedy arriving in Dallas, and the motorcade moving through the streets. Intercutting historical footage with reenacted scenes of the crowd, the film builds to the moment of the shot, yet defers its image. As the shot rings out, the screen goes black, and viewers see its aftermath—a flock of birds flying to the sky and fleeting glimpses of the limousine speeding away. It is not until much later, during the courtroom scene of Louisiana District Attorney Jim Garrison's attempt to convict Clay Shaw as a conspirator of the assassination, that the Zapruder film is shown—in a new, improved, close-up version. Thus, *JFK* reenacts both the absence of the Zapruder film and its charged presence as an historical image; the audience waits for the image—the moment of impact—again.

Much of the controversy surrounding *JFK* concerned Oliver Stone's audacity at playing the historian. Yet, what the media critics overlooked in their criticism of Stone is the power of his role as docudrama-maker. The meanings of the Zapruder film continue to shift each time it is reenacted, and mimesis becomes history, from the original mimetic image to the most recent reenactment. The Zapruder film replaces personal memories of the Kennedy assassination, becoming those memories, and *JFK* has the capacity to replace the Zapruder film. All subsequent depictions of the Zapruder film are irrevocably altered by its inscription in *JFK*.

In its transformation from still image to moving image to reenactment, the Zapruder film raises issues about the phenomenological relationship of the image to history, and the role of the docudrama as the site of postmodern history-making. It is the reenacted image that carries the weight of historical narrative, that allows for a sense of participation in history. The docudrama allows us to experience history as reenactment, and part of what makes that mimesis cathartic is our anticipation of the event we know is coming. Our bodies wait for the moment of the shot.

THE CHALLENGER EXPLOSION: VOYEURISTIC HISTORY

The Zapruder film was a secret image, restricted from the public eye in its original form. In contrast, the television image of the Challenger disaster of 1986 was an instant image, unanticipated, unedited, live. With the Challenger, the television images were unyielding and distant at the same time they were relentless and voyeuristic. The blurry image of the cloud of smoke from the exploded space shuttle was emphatically a video image, an image of surveillance as viewers watched, live, Christa McAuliffe's parents and students at the moment that they realized that she had just been blown up in space.

The capacity of television technology to transmit images live via satellite implicates spectators in new ways. With the Challenger explosion, Americans were witness to a technological space-exploration spectacle gone awry that had its roots in the Cold War space race. The image of the explosion and McAuliffe's parents was endlessly repeated, the repetition itself forming a kind of reenactment. Voyeuristically watching via television surveillance, the American public was prescribed to share their pride at the public relations event of an "ordinary" teacher experiencing outer space via American technology, an event that was timed to allow President Reagan to interview McAuliffe in space during his State of the Union address. As a nationalistic project intended to promote American technology and give the average American a personal stake in the space program, the Challenger failed spectacularly.

How do we feel when we are witnesses to the McAuliffes' realization? At this moment, they are primary actors in the construction of American myth, the family's sacrifice for the nation, all American parents mourning the loss of their children. In an essay on remembering Christa McAuliffe, Constance Penley notes that McAuliffe was chosen for the role not because of her talents (there were many other more qualified candidates) but, in essence, for her ordinariness, and she knew it.[2] She was to be emphatically normal in space. Ironically, her story has almost completely obliterated the lives and deaths of the other astronauts. Her role dominates the 1989 television movie, *Challenger*, which begins, eerily, with Karen Allen as Christa McAuliffe rehearsing what was to be McAuliffe's message from space. Christa McAuliffe's journey, designed to make American viewers identify with her ordinariness through their own non-astronaut experience, backfired in inviting viewers to imagine their own ordinary deaths in space. Yet, the image of McAuliffe's naivete and patriotic earnestness, chronicled in her biography *I Touch the Future...* and the *Challenger* movie, has functioned ironically to recuperate an image of NASA as the Kennedy-inspired, optimistic promise of a future in space.

Both the Zapruder film and the television image of the Challenger disaster are images that allow us to witness, yet they are central in the American historical imagination in part because they defer what they witnessed. The Zapruder film does not tell us who fired the fatal shots and why, and the Challenger image does not reveal what happened to the astronauts. NASA has since acknowledged, for instance, that it knows that the capsule of the astronauts of the Challenger continued to climb for another 25 seconds after the explosion and then descended for three minutes to the water—that the astronauts did not die instantly in the explosion but at the moment of impact with the water. NASA has also acknowledged the existence of audiotapes of the final moments after the explosion, which it has, despite several lawsuits by media organizations, managed to keep secret. According to *Time*, the tapes reveal that pilot Michael Smith can be heard saying "uh-oh," and that among the last words heard is one astronaut saying to another, "Give me your hand."[3]

In 1993, what purported to be a transcript of the tape, supposedly from McAuliffe's personal recorder, appeared on a private computer bulletin board. This transcript supposedly documents someone yelling, "What happened? What happened? Oh God, no-no." Other voices say, "Turn on your airpack! Turn on your air," and yell in desperation, and the transcript ends with a voice saying the Lord's Prayer. While very unlikely to be true and completely unverifiable, this transcript nevertheless speaks of a desire to know what the image defers and of fantasies of bearing witness. The haunting question, how did they react to imminent death? becomes how would I react in the face of death? This desire, and the fantasies it produces, are components of cultural memory. In the world of computer bulletin boards, where information moves from one system to another, from private space to public space, cultural memory is shared, pushing at the official history, the memorialization of the Challenger as a Florida Memorial license plate, and the ongoing guise of the military program of the space shuttle as a civilian and scientific mission.

Does the American public have the right to this information? Penley makes the argument that empirical evidence facilitates mourning. However difficult, we need to know those stories, those details, for mourning and closure. She notes that people continue to bring in artifacts from Florida beaches that they claim are refuse from the Challenger, although NASA says that it has recovered all possible parts. These are rituals of mourning, the collection of objects, the construction of a fantasy of death.

For those of us who remember where we were when Kennedy was assassinated, the Challenger disaster may seem less significant. But, for the contemporary generation that was in school at the time, many of them watching the launch live as part of the promotion for the teacher-in-space program, it was a defining event. Studies have examined the trauma felt by children who all remember years later where they were when they saw or heard about it, and who identified McAuliffe with their own teachers—sometimes fantasizing about themselves exploding, sometimes fantasizing about the obliteration of their teachers.[4] Christa McAuliffe's biography is not only a public story but her death the subject of nightmares, sick jokes, and fantasies.

The memory of "where we were" when the Challenger exploded is, like all memories, a fluid memory of rescripting, reenactment, and fantasy. Psychologists Ulric Neisser and Nicole Harsch interviewed a group of students the day after the explosion about their "flashbulb" memories of where they were when they heard of the accident and what their reaction had been; they then reinterviewed them several years later. Many of the students not only misremembered where they had been in part or whole, but when shown their initial recollections, were still unable to remember them. Significantly, the study seemed to demonstrate not only that the "original" memories had disappeared, but that students who had heard of the explosion in a variety of contexts remembered that they first heard of it while watching television.[5] The insistent television image is thus highly instrumental in rewriting the memory script. As Neisser and Harsch state, "The hours of later television watching may have been more strongly rehearsed, more unique, more compatible with a social script than the actual occasions of first contact."[6]

By remembering themselves watching the Challenger explosion on television, these students are situating themselves within a "national" experience of the event, sharing the shock of its spectacular and tragic failure with a national audience. The Challenger disaster situated the American spectator before the television set, and the viewing public participated in the nation by placing themselves in the event through the image. Just as the Zapruder film is often "remembered" as having been seen live on television, many people remember themselves experiencing the Challenger disaster while watching television with the rest of the American public, sharing in the disbelief and shock.

Ironically, the original image that allows the American public to feel like it is participating in the event does not aid us in mourning. Rather, we invest it with a truth it cannot reveal. It is the reenactment, the replaying, the fantasizing of the story that allows the mourning process to proceed and the event to acquire meaning. In the retelling of this story, Christa McAuliffe becomes the figure through whom the national trauma of the Challenger explosion can be smoothed over and recuperated into a narrative of patriotic sacrifice.

RODNEY KING: THE PROBLEM OF REENACTMENT

While the Kennedy assassination and the explosion of the Challenger are inarguably events of national consequence, the confluences of biography, image, and national meaning can also be seen in certain "ordinary" events and biographies through their chance intersection with the desires of public discourse. This trajectory takes us from the public person to the aspiring public person to the reluctant public figure, from the still film image to the television image to the home video camera, yet in each, the question of reenactment and memory emerges. In the 1990s, the boundary between domestic and public is increasingly blurred as amateur videotapes move effortlessly into the public realm of popular entertainment, news, and history, and as a home video camera turned toward an incident on the street, the brutal beating of a black man by white police officers, became one of the most famous images in American history.

In some ways, George Holliday's videotape of the Rodney King beating is the Zapruder film of the 1990s, although its meaning is still urgent: While the Zapruder film symbolizes a moment of national loss that prompted a nostalgic mourning, the King video signifies the relentless violence of the present. Although Abraham Zapruder's film was an exception as an amateur film that changed cultural status, Holliday's videotape was made at a time when video images are everywhere; in the uprising/riots that ensued in Los Angeles after the Rodney King verdict, home video cameras proliferated as much as news cameras. Like the Zapruder film, the King video changed meaning when it became a series of still images—its repeated dissection and slow-motion viewing lessened the violence of the blows, watched frame-by-frame by the jury.

We are all familiar now with the story of Rodney King's reluctant role as a public figure, his every move under public scrutiny. At what moment did Rodney King's story become part of national biography? Not at the moment when the police beat him up—that incident was appalling ordinary. Nor was it at the moment when George Holliday's camera was focused upon the incident—community organizations in Los Angeles had been distributing cameras and gathering footage of the Los Angeles police's excessive violence for years, but the media had never before been interested. Rodney King's story became the nation's story at the moment when a local news organization deemed it newsworthy—perhaps at the moment when the mystique about video vigilantes coincided with concern over urban violence. The awkwardness with which King has become a public person is precisely because of the clash of this image's narrative with nationalistic themes. This is an image of rupture and Rodney King can't be an American hero; here, national image and biography collide.

The Rodney King video has, of course, shifted status, primarily at the moment during the Los Angeles riots when a helicopter news crew video-taped the brutal beating of a white truck driver by four black men. From that point on, the King video became the symmetrical half of two images that defined the event: America at war over race. The amateur, low-to-the-ground image taken by George Holliday was replaced by the slick, omniscient view from the helicopter, one that does not show the heroic actions taken by four strangers to save Reginald Denny's life. The participation of television is crucial here; it was only after they saw him being beaten on TV that these people came to help Denny. Another reluctant public figure, Denny awoke in the hospital without memory of the incident and confused to find Jesse Jackson and Arsenio Hall waiting to see him.

There will probably be no TV movie of the L.A. riots. *LA Law* reenacted the uprising by having one of the lawyers be a kind of Reginald Denny character, and that may be as close as television will get: the view of the innocent white victim, in the wrong neighborhood at the wrong time. Do the hyper-documented, ultra-televised L.A. riots defy the docudrama form, because the formulas of mimetic interpretation can't fit even the story of four heroic young black people racing from their home to save a white man's life? While it is standard fare, for instance, for television to produce docudrama reenactments of major disasters such as earthquakes, hurricanes, and violent events, the L.A. riots remain too difficult for TV movie formulas.

However, reenactment is a central aspect of the narrative of the L.A. riots. In the trial for the Denny beating, several witnesses, including Denny, testified to events that happened to them for which they had no memory.[7] Instead, with the prodding of lawyers, they narrated their experience for the jury by watching videotapes of what they could see on the screen that their experience had been. That the video image became the memory was not new, but what was remarkable was that the court provided it legal and experiential status. At the same time, for Reginald Denny, the videotape is the only memory that remains.

In addition, the King video has a new meaning when placed in a contemporary docudrama: Spike Lee's *Malcolm X* (1992). Inserted into the opening credit sequence of the film, the King video represents all of the history of violence against American blacks and, as Malcolm X's voiceover states, the ways in which blacks are still outsiders in America. Thus the videotape is no longer Rodney King's story, but the story of all disenfranchised black men who are not recognized, who have no biographies.

REENACTMENT AND THE TENSION OF MEMORY AND HISTORY

These three images and the biographies that are a part of them indicate in many ways the confluence of image, history, cultural memory, and the making of national myth. Certainly, the image plays an increasingly visible role in the construction of national discourse, the retelling of history and the refiguring of memory. This means that personal memories of "historical" events often become subsumed into the iconic images of those histories.

Yet, at the same time, the primary elements of television and film's histor-ization are repetition, reenactment, and docudrama. The docudrama makes history containable, and subsumes memory into compelling narratives of closure. Contemporary cinematic and television docudramas reenact famous images, such as those from the Challenger, the Vietnam War, and the black-and-white photographs of the Holocaust. They tell biographical stories, and the actors become their subjects, inseparable from their historical images—Ben Kingsley becomes Ghandi, Denzel Washington is Malcolm X, Liam Neeson becomes Oskar Schindler. These docudramas subsume the docu-mentary and contain it for history, and this is in part why their blurring of fiction and fact is a source of public debate. The mimetic becomes the origi-nal; through it the status of the original ceases to have meaning.

But there are also the events that are not reenacted. On the one hand, it is possible to speculate that an event like the Persian Gulf War was never reen-acted because it was already prescripted, it was already a TV movie. On the other hand, the image of the Rodney King video raises the haunting ques-tion of what gets left out of docudrama-as-history. The image of the King beating is a story that cannot fit into the nationalist stories of closure offered by the docudrama. This is an image of injustice that is ultimately not redeemed; it is also an image of the system relentlessly at work, of brutal behavior by police officers, of an America that is racist and violent.

Yet, whether in the form of the docudrama or the relentless repetition of newscasts, the reenactment of nationally-important events is a fundamental aspect of history-making. In the context of postmodernity, the slippage between the real and fiction, between invention and recovery, is a marked one. But it would be a mistake to think that this is a recent phenomenon. In fact, reenactment, forgetting, and invention are essential aspects of memory. When Freud wrote about secondary revision, the process by which the sub-ject revises and narrativizes a dream or memory in order to give it coher-ence, he was referring to the way in which memories are continuously rewritten and transformed over time until they may bear little resemblance to the initial experience.[8] Memory is always about renarratization. Personal memory, cultural memory, and history are all shifting terrains.

Yet certainly there is a tension between individual processes of mourning and the simple closure offered by Hollywood docudramas, between the importance of individual memory of traumatic events and their role as national stories. When someone's biography forms part of the collective text that constitutes the nation's identity, it moves from personal memory to cul-tural memory to history, and the political stakes are quite different in each. I do not think that we can attempt to control these images and stories, which are constantly shifting in meaning through repetition and reenactment, but we can scrutinize their cooptation into normalizing strategies.

An understanding of the importance of biography in postmodernism must acknowledge that the "truth" of biographical stories is as evasive as memory, but their shifting meaning in contemporary social formations is crucial.

There is no original in memory, only its trace, its narrative. To think of memory in the context of postmodernism, we need to acknowledge that memory is claimed and produced in new forms and technologies—sometimes it may even be disguised as forgetting.

NOTES

This essay is from a book on the politics of cultural memory, forthcoming from the University of California Press in 1996.

1. Robert Hennelly and Jerry Policoff, "JFK: How the Media Assassinated the Real Story," *Village Voice* (March 31, 1992), 35.
2. Constance Penley, "Spaced Out: Remembering Christa McAuliffe," *Camera Obscura* 29 (1993), 179–213.
3. David Ellis, "Challenger: The Final Words," *Time* (December 24, 1990), 15.
4. Penley, 193–94.
5. Ulric Neisser and Nicole Harsch, "Phantom Flashbulbs," in Eugene Winograd and Ulric Neisser, eds., *Affect and Accuracy in Recall* (Cambridge: Cambridge University Press, 1992), 25.
6. Neisser and Harsch, "Phantom Flashbulbs," 30.
7. See Seth Mydans, "With Few Witnesses, Videos Are Crucial in Beating Trial," *New York Times* (Sept. 6, 1993), 6; and Jessica Crosby, "Truck Driver Says He Doesn't Recall Beating," *Washington Post* (August 26, 1993), A4.
8. Sigmund Freud, *The Interpretation of Dreams*, [1900], translated by James Strachey (New York: Avon Books, 1965), 526–46.

3

INVENTING AND
INTERPRETING
MALCOLM X

Michael Eric Dyson

In *The Autobiography of Malcolm X* the charismatic black religious nation-alist recalls his momentous 1964 pilgrimage to Mecca, a visit that would alter the course of his life and career.[1] After twelve years in which this minister of the Nation of Islam trumpeted a doctrine of the intrinsic evil of whites, likened the dream of American equality to a "nightmare" for American blacks, and championed a plan to redeem black Americans by saving them from the tide of brainwashing that had drowned awareness of the black race's true superiority, X writes of an incident in Jedda, in which he is treated with great hospitality by a man who, in America, would be considered white:

> That white man...related to Arabia's ruler, truly an international man, ...had given up his suite to me, for my transient comfort.... He had followed the American press about me. If he did that, he knew there was only stigma attached to me. I was supposed to have horns. I was a "racist." I was "anti-white"...everyone was even accusing me of using his religion of Islam as a cloak for...criminal practices and philosophy.... That morning was when I first began to perceive that secondarily; primarily it described attitudes and actions. In America, "white man" meant specific attitudes and actions toward the black man, and toward all other non-white men. But in the Muslim world, I had seen

that men with white complexions were more genuinely brotherly than anyone else had ever been. That morning was the start of a radical alteration in my whole outlook about "white" men.[2]

His life-changing encounters were recorded in letters from Africa to family members and other followers in the United States. The revealing missives detailed Malcolm's view of the color blindness of Muslim society and religion. This series of experiences forced Malcolm to "rearrange much of my thought-patterns previously held, and to toss aside some of my previous conclusions."[3]

Less than a year later, Malcolm X was gunned down by assassins in New York's Audubon Ballroom. By the time of his apocalyptic martyrdom, Malcolm had seceded from the Nation (after bitter disappointment in the moral failures of its leader Elijah Muhammad and the tensions within the Nation concerning his own increased public presence) and begun two organizations, one religious, the other political. Each group reflected Malcolm's transformed perspective about racial and religious matters, especially his belief that broad social engagement permitted blacks their best chance to oppose the lethal legacy of American racism.

It is around Malcolm's increasingly independent political activity during the final fifty weeks of his life, combined with his startling reversal of feeling about the possibility of redemption for white America, that so much controversy and confusion have gathered. Although Malcolm made many overtures to a broader philosophy of human community, he simply didn't live long enough to fulfill the promise of his significant but tentative first steps. While we may conclude with certainty that Malcolm had rejected the whites-are-devils era pronouncements that helped to focus his earlier life and brought him the attention and vilification of a nation, we are brought up short in trying to definitively detail the universal humanitarianism of his later days.

Although his entire legacy until recently has been demonized and dismissed by the traditional academy, Malcolm's popularity never flagged among a cadre of black nationalist activists, journalists, and independent intellectuals who for a quarter century have debated intensely his significance to black politics, black culture, and American society. These debates have had a trickle-up effect; they created the groundswell for the fierce war of interpretation being waged over Malcolm's meaning in our times.

In the face of the grim recurrence of a racism many believed had been greatly diminished, the renewed popularity of Malcolm X—both his image and his ideology—have taken on new importance. The signs of his ascent—from posters, ubiquitous X baseball hats, and sampling of his voice on rap records to the recording of the opera "X" created by Anthony and Thulani Davis; the release of the epic film biography directed by Spike Lee, and the release of his speeches edited to reveal his ideological evolution—are a function of both need and mythology: the current and deeply felt need for a confrontational stance toward America's continuing racism and the seductive mythology of the perfect black man.

Thus it is that Malcolm X's name no longer belongs to him, no longer refers simply to his tall body or to his short life. Like Martin Luther King, Jr., Malcolm has come to mean more than himself. For some Malcolm is an unreconstructed nationalist, while for others he wed his nationalist beliefs to socialist philosophy. Still others subject Malcolm to Marxist and Freudian analysis, while others emphasize his vocation as a public moralist. His stature derives as much from his detractors' exaggerated fears as from his admirers' exalted hopes. He has become a divided metaphor: for those who love him, he is a powerful lens of self-perception, a means of sharply focusing political and racial priorities; for those who loathe him, he is a distorted mirror that reflects violence and hatred.

Malcolm himself anticipated the confusion his views would cause (after all, he confessed that "[e]ven I was myself astounded").[4] At the time, he had not fully gauged the disquiet his new beliefs would cause among supporters already thrown by his earlier break with the Nation of Islam. Among the black religious sect's powerful dramatis personae—its leader the Honorable Elijah Muhammad; the world champion boxer Muhammad Ali; and Louis X, now Minister Louis Farrakhan, Malcolm's associate turned enemy—it was Malcolm who emerged as the major player in the Nation of Islam's dramatic attempts to rescue black Americans from what they viewed as the bankrupt religious and social values of white society.

Yet Malcolm X has received nothing like the intellectual attention devoted to King. As the central figure of the civil rights movement, King justifiably has been the subject of extensive scholarship, but his cultural visibility has also to do with the style, content, and aims of his leadership, which for most of his life were easily translatable and largely attractive to white America. On the other hand, Malcolm's complex leadership, which visited rhetorical scorn on white supremacy and which appealed especially to working and poor blacks, has invited derision, caricature and dismissal, forces which undermine extensive and balanced scholarly investigation.

To be sure, a flood of writings about Malcolm's legacy have been published in alternative and black newspapers, journals, pamphlets and books; they have been vigorously discussed in conferences, rap sessions and panel discussions throughout the black communities of America. Yet with notable exceptions, the literature on Malcolm X has often missed the mark, offering praise where critical judgment is called for, trapping itself in intellectual frameworks that neither illumine nor surprise.

Of course, *The Autobiography of Malcolm X*, as told to Alex Haley, is the Ur-text of contemporary black nationalism. Activists and intellectuals tote it in their back pockets and briefcases in ready reference in debates about black America, while rappers imitate its radical tones and students often quote it as sacred verse. As Malcolm's faithful and creative scribe—he had written two articles about Malcolm and interviewed him for *Playboy*

Magazine when a publisher tapped him to write Malcolm's autobiography in 1963—Haley placed his considerable narrative skills at Malcolm's disposal. It was Haley who brought Malcolm's life to full color, crafting a classic of African-American letters. But as Malcolm opened his life to Haley, he was also reinventing it on the spot. Malcolm was improvising a personal narrative that drew from both the virtues and failures of memory. But the lapses in accuracy that he exhibited were often rooted less in mendacity than in the human need to tell stories in ways that make our lives make sense.

Despite the crucial role of his autobiography in expanding black cultural consciousness, the full meaning of Malcolm X's life inevitably must be judged using more than a story that draws from a single source. Thus it is especially important now to explore a select group of books published over the past two decades that offer widely divergent views of Malcolm X's complex political journey.[5]

In *Malcolm X: The Man and His Times*, the first anthology dedicated to exploring Malcolm's life and thought, the black historian and Hunter College Professor Emeritus John Henrik Clarke has edited a collection of voices that undermine a single understanding of Malcolm's place in history.[6] What many of the essays share is a reverential regard for his black nationalist legacy.

In his contribution to this collection of thirty-four essays, interviews, and organizational statements, the black theologian Albert Cleage (who knew and worked with Malcolm) boldly defends Malcolm's black nationalist reputation by concluding that "if in Mecca he had decided that blacks and whites can unite, then his life at that moment would have become meaningless in terms of the world struggle of black people."[7] Cleage seeks to rebut the beliefs that Malcolm at the end of his life was becoming either an integrationist, an advocate of the internationalization of black struggle, or a socialist.

The activist and political theorist James Boggs criticizes both Malcolm's black nationalist heirs, whom he views as preoccupied with Black Power sloganeering and as bereft of sufficient analytic depth, and "white radicals who lend a grudging support to Black Power," patronizing black revolutionaries as "'unfinished products' who will one day see the light and recognize the superiority of Marxist theory and the necessity of an alliance with the white working class."[8] The writer Charles Wilson insightfully discusses Malcolm's "failure of leadership style and a failure to evolve a sound organizational base for his activities," concluding that Malcolm was a "victim of his own charisma."[9]

Clarke's anthology mattered: in the days following Malcolm X's death, its contributors addressed urban blacks and nationalist intellectuals confronting their deepening social crisis. It argued that black nationalism was an important and thriving alternative to black bourgeois protest, which held out as its goal black integration into white society. Mr. Clarke's book also countered the demonization of a man believed by most whites (and many blacks) to be the embodiment of evil. But its goal of redeeming Malcolm X's legacy rather than evaluating it lessens its value; the collection's tone suggests an exercise in beatification, with cultural interpreters working to preserve fragments of Malcolm's memory against abuse or amnesia.

Fortunately, the books which primarily understand Malcolm in relation to the moral abomination of racism to which his views forcefully responded supply the needed critical attention to his career. Black theologian James Cone's *Martin and Malcolm and America: A Dream or a Nightmare?* treats the religious roots of Malcolm's moral vision; journalist Louis Lomax's *To Kill a Black Man*, addresses the social and political dimensions of Malcolm's moral perspective.[10] But it is in their roles as comparative studies of King and Malcolm that the Cone and Lomax books seize our interest, as they critically pair the defining figures of contemporary black culture. Cone, the widely regarded founder of black theology and a professor at New York's Union Theological Seminary, has been profoundly influenced by both King and Malcolm, and his book is a public acknowledgment of intellectual debt and inspiration.

Most Americans believe that Malcolm and King occupied violently opposed ethical universes, that their positions on the best solution to America's racial crisis led them to a permanent parting of paths. More likely, though, they were the yin and yang of black moral responses to white racism, complementing more than contradicting each other in their last years. Cone even suggests that King and Malcolm were in important ways *converging*, saying that "Malcolm and Martin moved away from the extremes of their original positions and began to embrace aspects of each other's viewpoints."[10] Thus, King began in 1966 to emphasize black pride, explore the virtues of "temporary segregation" to foster the economic health of black communities, and became more radical about the limits of social protest. And Malcolm for his part became publicly political, acknowledged the militancy of integrationists, and even encouraged voter registration.

Although King and Malcolm met only once for a brief moment—resulting in the famed photo of both figures smiling broadly at the U.S. Capitol in 1964—Malcolm did, in 1965, journey to Selma, Alabama, where King was in jail, to speak to civil rights workers before leaving for a speaking engagement in London. His remarks on that occasion to Coretta King—less than a month before his death reveal Malcolm's poignant awareness and acceptance of the distinct roles he and King played in the black freedom movement. "I want Dr. King to know that I didn't come to Selma to make his job difficult. I really did come thinking I could make it easier. If the white people realize what the alternative is, perhaps they will be more willing to hear Dr. King."

In the Lomax book, the author, a friend to both leaders, characterizes each figure more rigidly; the book outlines vividly how distinct Malcolm's openness to violent self-defense was from King's advocacy of non-violence as a strategy of social change. Written in the torturous aftermath of King's assassination in 1968, Lomax's volume has all the virtues of historical immediacy—impassioned narration, proximity to the moment's true feeling, unvarnished insight. What it lacks is the greater virtue of historical perspective, which comes from long and mature reflection upon events. This is the virtue that Cone's book possesses, along with an analytical acumen that explores the development of King's and Malcolm's lives and thought in larger scope and richer detail than many of his nationalist predecessors.

But like them, Cone is plagued by an overreliance on the theme of racial unity as an intellectual principle to explain his twin subject's failure and achievements, limiting his understanding of King and Malcolm and skewing his view of their complex uses (especially King's) of history and culture. Nevertheless, Cone's book is an invaluable aid in comprehending the similarities and differences between the two towering influences on contemporary black culture.

Malcolm X lived for most of his life in opposition to the fundamental assumptions of American moral judgment: that innocence and corruption are on a continuum, that justice and injustice are on a scale, and that proper moral behavior depends on making the right choices between existing options of good and evil. Such a vision of Malcolm is presented in Peter Goldman's *The Death and Life of Malcolm X*.[11] Goldman, senior editor at *Newsweek*, met Malcolm in 1962 and spent hundreds of hours interviewing him. Goldman's book captures with eloquence and imagination the forces of white racial oppression that made life hell for poor Northern blacks, and the minimal resources apparently at their disposal before Malcolm's defiant rhetoric rallied black rage and anger to their defense.

Goldman's Malcolm is one whose "life was itself an accusation," a "witness for the prosecution" of white injustice, a "pubic moralist."[12] With each aspect of Malcolm's life that Goldman treats—whether it is Malcolm's foreshadowing of the Black Power Movement or his withering assaults on white society—Goldman's narrative subtly and skillfully illumines Malcolm's career.

What Goldman fails to do is convey properly the mammoth scope of competing economic, cultural, and historical forces that erupted during the 1940s, '50s, and '60s, and that reflected not only racial antagonism, but class conflict and gender oppression as well. Nor does he present a sufficient analysis of the extreme political limitations placed on black militant men of either religious or secular sensibility. Still, Goldman's book, the first full-scale life of Malcolm, remains an indispensable biography of the enigmatic leader.

If the task of biography is to cast as bright a light as possible on the shadowy areas of human behavior, then psychobiography doubles the effort, using the insights gleaned through psychological theory to illumine the full range of human experience. Over the last decade, several journal articles and two books have notably applied the psychobiographical approach, with varying results. U.C.L.A. social theorist and Marxist psychoanalyst Eugene Victor Wolfenstein's *The Victims of Democracy: Malcolm X and the Black Revolution* is a work of considerable intellectual imagination and rigor that represents the best of this trend.[13]

Wolfenstein takes ample measure of the energies that created Malcolm and the demons that drove him. Recalling Malcolm's "earliest vivid memory"— being awakened in the middle of the night in 1929 because the family house in Lansing, Michigan, was burning to the ground—Wolfenstein contends that Malcolm's "consciousness began in a moment or racist violence."[14] Starting from that point, he brilliantly maps Malcolm's developing awareness both as a black man in a racist culture, and as a member of a violent family. Wolfenstein says that Malcolm's father "made himself, by his own hand, both the defender and destroyer of his family."[15]

In Wolfenstein's scheme, because Freudian theory "provides no foundation for the analysis of interests, be they individual or collective," and Marxism "provides no foundation for the analysis of desires," he uses both to explain Malcolm's life.[16] But his book has deficits; besides his lack of clarity about the importance of religion in providing social cohesion among Northern urban black communities, he focuses exclusively on biological definitions of race. More recent race theorists have maintained that race is not only a biological reality, but carries socially created meanings as well.[17] Such an approach to race might help Wolfenstein explain how Malcolm and other blacks understood and employed race in their defense against white racism, and how rigid views of race held by black nationalists such as Malcolm limited their range of social response. Wolfenstein's major limitation lies in his overuse of Malcolm's autobiography for information about Malcolm. Nonetheless, Wolfenstein's book is the most astute treatment to date of Malcolm's intellectual and psychological roots.

If Wolfenstein's book, despite its flaws, represents the best of the psychobiographical impulse, Bruce Perry's *Malcolm: The Life of a Man Who Changed Black America* may represent the worst.[18] In Perry's eyes, Malcolm's troubled childhood holds the key to his subsequent career as a black leader. According to Perry, the physical abuse of his mother by Malcolm's father; his parent's extra-marital affairs; the breakup of the family after the father's death and the mother's mental collapse; Malcolm's inheritance of his mother's obsession with color; and his hatred of women learned during childhood are all factors that contributed to the mature Malcolm's contorted leadership style.

Perry says Malcolm's "war against the white power structure evolved from the same inner needs that had spawned earlier rebellions against his teachers, the law, established religion, and other symbols of authority."[19] Perry portrays Malcolm's family as besieged by unremitting violence, criminality, and pathology. The mature Malcolm is equally tragic, a man of looming greatness whose self-destructing personality "contributed to this premature death."[20] It is here that Perry's project folds in on itself, its rough edges puncturing the center of its explanatory purpose.

True enough, Perry does unearth new information about Malcolm. For instance, he reveals that in 1961 Malcolm held a secret meeting with the Klan on Elijah Muhammad's behalf, seeking the Klan's aid (since both groups opposed racial mixing) in obtaining land for the Nation of Islam to employ in implementing its separatist philosophy. Perry also discusses Malcolm's alleged homosexual activity, both as an experimenting adolescent and as a hustling young adult "who sold himself, as if the best he had to offer was his body."[21] Perry's discussion of Malcolm's alleged homosexuality taps into an interpretive powder keg, especially since so much of the constituency that supports Malcolm's renewed importance are young, black, and male and are avid participants in a male-driven revival of black nationalism that thrives on the machismo of rap culture. But Perry's revelations are less striking for their threat to Malcolm's image as the quintessential black man than for the pedestrian interpretation he offers of Malcolm's homosexual motivations: absent male role models and a history of tyrannical females.

Since Perry makes a plausible case for their occurrence, a discussion of Malcolm's homosexual alliances might have served Perry as a powerful interpretive wedge beneath the cultural weight of oppressive black machismo, and as a way of exploring and explaining the cruel varieties of homophobia that afflict black communities. Instead Perry's treatment of Malcolm's sexuality is manifestly off the mark; his analysis fails to make a substantive contribution to our understanding of black sexual politics of its relationship to social liberation. Perry fills in details about Malcolm's last year, but again his tendentious reading of Malcolm's career mar his perspective. For instance, he concludes that Malcolm's forays onto foreign soil were an attempt to secure funding for his fledgling organization. But this is only partially true; by his trips abroad, Malcolm was seeking to expand the scope of his views about the black struggle as his philosophy took on international dimensions.

And while Perry convincingly argues that Malcolm had forsaken his views about "devil" whites as early as 1959, during his first trip to the Middle East and long before his trip to Mecca in 1964, he cynically concludes that Malcolm's press conference held at New York's Kennedy Airport after his return from Africa in May 1964 was a "fitting culmination to the public-relations campaign that had begun with his letter-writing campaign."[22] Although Malcolm's last year was undoubtedly a year of sometimes frantic searching for the right road to take, Perry portrays Malcolm's final year as a series of opportunistic ploys to expand his support among nonblack audiences. Further, though Perry concedes Malcolm's "extraordinary capacity for political ambiguity," he more often characterizes Malcolm as a "political chameleon."[23] Perry's book finally impresses as little more than a sniping account that makes a complex figure smaller than life.

To fully grasp Malcolm's complexity, it is necessary to probe his radical shift to a broader base of racial protest during his last year. Perhaps the most prominent and controversial interpreters of Malcolm's last year have been a group of intellectuals associated with the Socialist Workers Party, a Trotskyite group that took keen interest in Malcolm's views after his return from Mecca, and sponsored some of his last speeches. For the most part, their views have been articulated by the social critic George Breitman, author of *The Last Year of Malcolm X: The Evolution of a Revolutionary*, and editor of two volumes of Malcolm's speeches, organizational statements, and interviews he gave during his last year, *Malcolm X Speaks* and *By Any Means Necessary*.[24]

Breitman passionately argues that Malcolm's split with Elijah Muhammad was a major shock, however inevitable. Thus Malcolm needed time to rethink his beliefs and determine his organizational direction. Breitman divides Malcolm's independent phase into two parts: a transition period, lasting the few months between his split in March 1964 until his return from Africa at the end of May 1964, and the final period, lasting from June 1964 until his death in February 1965.

Breitman maintains that this final period marked Malcolm's maturation as "a revolutionary—increasingly anticapitalist and pro-socialist as well as anti-imperialist," though these are labels that Breitman acknowledges Malcolm himself never adopted.[25] But the truth is we have only the bare-bones outlines of Malcolm's emerging worldview, including his views on socialism. Malcolm's speeches throughout these collected volumes showcase a common feature: Malcolm displays sympathy for socialist philosophy without committing himself to its practice as a means of achieving liberation for African-Americans. Malcolm confessed in the *Young Socialist* interview near the end of his life that "I still would be hard-pressed to give a specific definition of the overall philosophy which I think is necessary for the liberation of the black people in this country."[26]

As a speculative study, Breitman's book is fascinating and provocative: as a definitive study of Malcolm's evolving intellectual positions, it is much less convincing. Malcolm left behind fragments of political speech more than systematic social thought, suggestive ideological gestures more than substantive political activity. Breitman is attempting to saddle Malcolm with a set of views he didn't live long enough to clarify or adopt.

The rebirth of black nationalism has sparked renewed interest in Malcolm X's life and thought. With its emphasis on racial pride and self-esteem; its support of black religious, business and educational institutions; and the importance it gives to cultural and racial unity, black nationalism is prominently displayed throughout contemporary black American—witness the popularity of Nation of Islam leader Minister Louis Farrakhan; the broad appeal and controversy of rap music; the adoption of African hairstyles, pendants, and clothing; the expression of Afrocentric ideas by scholars such as Temple University Afro-American Studies Chair Molefi Asante and Rutgers University professor Ivan van Sertima; and of course, the cultural deluge that is Malcomania.

But black nationalism has in the past, as well as in its most recent revival, suffocated the achievements of black women. The same may be said for the civil rights movement, where talented black and white women were often reduced to hewers of pencils and carriers of coffee. That most public interpreters of black nationalism and the civil rights movement are men reflects not only the sexism of these organizations, but the ongoing sexism of our society, which continues to discourage and prevent women from gaining intellectual authority in the debates that shape national perceptions about crucial social movements and public figures. As these facts are more broadly acknowledged and confronted, the number of women who have a voice in these debates should increase. Black feminist perspectives on Malcolm X will only deepen our understanding of a figure who has only recently begun to receive wide reconsideration.

Malcolm X is now a part of the American imagination that once relegated him to its margins; he has become, in death, the source of our constant reinventions of his life. This transcendent status, however, does not free us from the obligation to demand more from our examination of the life that really was his. More than ever, we must forsake uncritical celebrations, not by denying his myth, but by taking it into account, by probing for the continuing wellsprings of his appeal, and in so doing understand our need to romanticize or revile him. Battered by unprincipled opponents, smothered by well-meaning loyalists, Malcolm's past is not yet settled; it never will be. Nonetheless, he must in the end receive what every important historical figure deserves: a comprehensive examination of both word and deed. To do less would be to fail ourselves and the history Malcolm X so boldly helped to create.

NOTES

1. Malcolm X, with the assistance of Alex Haley, *The Autobiography of Malcolm X* (New York: Grove Press, 1965).

2. Ibid, 5.

3. Ibid, 5.

4. Ibid, 5.

5. For a much more lengthy and in-depth discussion of Malcolm's intellectual legacy that extends the work begun in this essay, as well as a crucial interpretation of his revival in contemporary (black) culture, see my *Making Malcolm: The Myth and Meaning of Malcolm X* (New York: Oxford University Press, 1994).

6. John Henrik Clarke, ed., *Malcolm X: The Man and His Times* (1969; Trenton, N.J.: Africa World Press, 1990).

7. Albert Cleage, "Myths About Malcolm X," in *Malcolm X*, ed. Clarke, 15.

8. James Boggs, "The Influence of Malcolm X on the Political Consciousness of Black Americans," in *Malcolm X*, ed. Clarke, 52.

9. Charles Wilson, "Leadership Triumph in Leadership Tragedy," in *Malcolm X*, ed. Clarke, 36–37.

10. James H. Cone, *Martin and Malcolm and America: A Dream or a Nightmare?* (Maryknoll, N.Y.: Orbis Books, 1991); Louis Lomax, *To Kill a Black Man* (Los Angeles: Holloway House, 1968).

11. Peter Goldman, *The Death and Life of Malcolm X*, 2nd edition (Urbana: University of Illinois Press, 1979).

12. Ibid.

13. Eugene Victor Wolfenstein, *The Victims of Democracy: Malcolm and the Black Revolution* (2nd edition London: Free Association Books, 1989).

14. Ibid.

15. Ibid.

16. Ibid., xiii.

17. For a small sampling of such approaches, see Michael Omi and Howard Winant, *Racial Formation in the United States: From the 1960s to the 1980s* (London: Routledge & Kegan Paul, 1986); and Michael Eric Dyson, "The Liberal Theory of Race," and "Racism and Race Theory in the Nineties," in *Reflecting Black: African-American Cultural Criticism* (Minneapolis: University of Minnesota Press, 1993), 132–56.

18. Bruce Perry, *Malcolm: The Life of a Man Who Changed Black America* (Barrytown, N.Y.: Station Hill Press, 1991).

19. Ibid., ix.

20. Ibid., x.

21. Ibid.

22. Ibid.

23. Ibid.

24. George Breitman, *The Last Year of Malcolm X: The Evolution of a Revolutionary* (New York: Pathfinder Press, 1967); George Breitman, ed., Malcolm X, *Malcolm X Speaks: Selected Speeches and Statements* (New York: Pathfinder Press, 1965); George Breitman, ed., *By Any Means Necessary: Speeches, Interviews, and a Letter, by Malcolm X* (New York: Pathfinder Press, 1970), 22–23.

25. Breitman, *Last Year of Malcolm X*, 27.

26. Breitman, *By Any Means Necessary*, 159–60.

(II)

PRIVATE LIVES, PUBLIC FIGURES

Introduction

William S. McFeely

THE FOLLOWING ESSAYS consider the lives of three Americans who led political lives of vital importance to the republic. All three are remembered as
champions of those whom society at large could not bring into its line of
vision; in Bayard Rustin's case, African Americans; in Michael Harrington's,
the poor; in Eleanor Roosevelt's, so wide a range of the ignored that she was
the laughing stock of those guilty of that ignorance.

How does the biographer account for the commitment to reform of these
three activists, all of whom could be thought to have been sheltered (by varying degrees) from the troubles they addressed? Was there something within
their personal lives that might account for their siding with the outsider? The
authors of these essays, who have written or are writing biographies, of
Rustin, Harrington, and Roosevelt, have explored the sexual complexity of
their subjects certain that this aspect of their lives was relevant to their public
activities. The expression of sexuality to which the three public figures were
drawn was, during their lifetimes, deemed by society to be beyond the pale;
perhaps that fact contributed to their understanding of other groups deemed
as outsiders—and hence neglected—by the dominant society.

It is a cause for celebration that homosexuality is now written about with
unabashed candor. But does that mean that both writer and reader approach

explorations of famous people's sexuality with disinterested objectivity? If we are honest we will say no. An author is faced with the fact that everything he or she writes is in some way a reflection of that author as well as of his or her subject. If the biographer identifies explicitly or implicitly with the sexuality of his or her subject, is that writer hindered or helped in understanding that subject? Has the explanation of a public life yielded to the writer's concerns or, instead, been achieved by an emphatic exploration of the subject's private life? Does the examination of sexuality, from any perspective, contribute to an understanding of a political personality, or can we count on a person's political acts being trivialized by the sensationalism that so often accompanies emphasis on sexuality?

If the author does not share the sexual stance of his or her subject, but does share the subject's political commitments, can the author resist offering a disclaimer that no such sexual identity exists? Or can the writer ignore such prissiness in favor of a carefully considered examination of the connection of the subject's sexuality—or religion, or physical condition—to the political stance that is the writer's primary concern? And is the holding of common political views any less of a factor to be skeptically considered by the reader when testing the validity of a biographer's assessment than would be a sexual identification?

And what of the reader? Does he, do we, read solely for edification in the subject's field? Or, more honestly, do we not, when we pick up a book, indulge a rich curiosity about the sexual activities of the rich and/or famous?

All of these questions beg the larger issue: what is the biographer's job? Are we any longer content to have the elements of a biography existing solely to explain public actions? Or is the task, instead of being a straight road of explanation, one that branches into a fundamentally different creative act: the construction, from a myriad of sources, of the rich complexity of a human life?

All of these matters are before us in these essays written by serious but not solemn, interesting rather than disinterested scholars: John D'Emilio, Blanche Wiesen Cook, and Maurice Isserman. As biographers of Bayard Rustin, Eleanor Roosevelt, and Michael Harrington, they have been diligent in their research and responsible in confronting sexuality, which they consider to be of great importance in accurately and fully portraying for us three immensely creative Americans.

4

READING THE SILENCES IN A GAY LIFE
The Case of Bayard Rustin

John D'Emilio

BY ANY REASONABLE STANDARD of measurement, Bayard Rustin should rank as a key figure in the history of twentieth-century American political activism. He was arguably as responsible as anyone for injecting Gandhian nonviolence into the struggle for racial equality. Rustin was at the center of the pacifist circles which sparked the first demonstrations against the arms race and which mobilized against the Vietnam War. He was also fiercely internationalist, working closely with European pacifists and African liberation leaders. Rustin excelled as a tactician and a strategist, and projected a vision of revolutionary change. More than anyone else, he was a bridge linking the black struggle, peace campaigns, and a socialist vision of economic democracy.

Rustin is also a curiously neglected figure. Only one account of the social movements of the postwar years gives Rustin any significant attention. His treatment in memoirs of the era is even less satisfying; figures such as Ralph Abernathy and Roy Wilkins barely mention Rustin at all. Autobiographies by James Farmer and David Dellinger discuss Rustin at length, but use him as a foil: the authors are as visionary, committed, and true to the cause as Rustin is narrow, self-serving, and weak.[1]

When I began work on Rustin, I thought I was leaving gay history behind.

The experience of teaching an undergraduate course on the 1960s made me want to explore further this unusual decade of political and social upheaval. It seemed to me—and to my students—that this was a revolutionary moment if ever there was one, yet the moment passed by. The historical writing—bifurcated into categories such as radical or reformist, national politics or social movements, civil rights or the Vietnam War—dissatisfied me, since those lines made it difficult to apprehend the magnitude of the nation's crisis.[2]

Rustin's life became my vehicle for exploring the revolution that never happened. I was attracted to him because his career confounds many of the dichotomies that characterize the accepted narrative of these years. Coming of age politically in the Old Left of the 1930s, Rustin remained deeply engaged, a source of memory, inspiration, and training for many youthful members of the civil rights movement and the New Left. A non-cooperator who served twenty-eight months in jail during World War II, he was part of a core of radical pacifists who, in the postwar decades, consistently challenged American militarism, provoked the first cracks in Cold War orthodoxy, and stood ready to mobilize when American policymakers escalated the war in Southeast Asia. An African American who played a critical role in the civil rights movement, Rustin spent much of his career working in essentially white organizations and remained unswervingly committed to interracialism. At the height of the black nationalist impulse, Rustin contended that freedom would come only through a class politics that crossed racial lines. Throughout the postwar celebration of capitalism, he never abandoned an economic analysis of America's social ills. And, in a nation too often preoccupied with a sense of uniqueness, Rustin was keenly attuned to the historical significance of decolonization throughout the world, spending stretches of time with African leaders as an adviser on nonviolent strategies of resistance.[3]

Above all, during the critical years from 1963 to 1967, Rustin, who always claimed that revolutionary change was necessary, argued that radical movements had to engage directly the political process. As the line between radical and liberal threatened to open into an unbridgeable chasm, as student radicals, both black and white, teetered on the edge of an eternal romance with street action, Rustin urged a transition "from protest to politics."[4] Having spent two decades in movements marginal to the consciousness of most Americans, Rustin knew that protest was the tool of the powerless. It was not a means but an end, a method to grab attention until the map of politics could be redrawn, and the margin become the center. Rustin believed that the civil rights struggle was on the edge of achieving this, that it had amassed enough strength so that political realignment was a realistic goal. Finally, Rustin thought this strategic shift necessary because otherwise the moment would pass, and the margin would become a permanent home.

And so, in the years after the March on Washington, Rustin fought and argued, schemed and plotted in order to shift the trajectory of protest. But

Rustin's path was the road not taken, and the outcome of these political battles was disastrous for him. Almost without exception, the men and women with whom Rustin had worked closely for upwards of twenty years were appalled by his strategic vision and tactical choices. In interviews, two formulations recur in discussions of Rustin during this period: He took a dramatic turn to the right, and he chose the path of cynicism. He was variously seen as an Uncle Tom, a shill for the State Department, a lackey of the labor union aristocracy, and a prisoner of Cold War liberals. The man who, in the 1940s, seemed to embody perfectly a creative and dynamic politics rooted in Gandhian principle now stood accused of a failure of moral courage.[5]

I was also attracted to Rustin as a subject of study because he was gay. Through his incarceration during World War II and his years as a staff member in Christian-based pacifist organizations, through his association with Martin Luther King and the world of Southern Baptist preachers, through the years of national prominence that came to him as the organizer of the March on Washington, Rustin was undeniably gay. Born in 1912, he stands poised between Langston Hughes, the distinguished poet of the Harlem Renaissance whose sexuality remains ambiguous and contested, and James Baldwin, in whose novels, essays, and public statements will be found an affirmation of homosexual desire. Rustin was not openly gay in the way that the post-Stonewall era has defined coming out. He neither publicly proclaimed his homosexuality nor produced a discourse of sexual self-affirmation. But he never constructed a fraudulent heterosexual life, his associates knew of his sexual interests, and he brought his male partners into the primarily heterosexual political and social world in which he traveled.[6]

To me, this was an added inducement. But I imagined Rustin's gayness tucked into the corner labeled "personal life." The questions it would pose were secondary ones: How did a gay man construct a life of meaning under the pre-Stonewall regime of oppression? What kind of personal networks sustained him? How did he navigate the perils of living not only as a radical but as a gay man in the era of Joe McCarthy and J. Edgar Hoover? Interesting questions, but not essential to the main contours of the story of politics I wished to tell.

From the beginning of my research into Rustin's life, his gayness resisted all efforts of marginalization and insinuated itself at every turn. The opportunities he had, the political choices he made, the response of enemies and colleagues alike to him and to his ideas: none of these can be fully understood without factoring in Rustin's homosexuality and the homophobia of the world he inhabited. Though it would be foolhardy to *reduce* his career to an analysis of sexual identity and gay oppression, I am coming to suspect that his life and work are inexplicable without such an analysis. And, by extension, the histories of social activism and progressive politics in the 1960s are, therefore, much more shaped by gay oppression and homophobia than any of us have dreamed.

To offer such an interpretation, even as a hypothesis in the early stages of research, moves me away from a paper trail of hard, cold evidence into a land of inference and intuitive leaps. For twenty years, gay historians have worked to displace the tropes of silence and invisibility as the organizing frameworks for homosexual experience. To the extent that we have succeeded, we have done so by focusing our gaze on the gay movement, urban subcultures, and medical discourse.[7] But in the essentially non-gay world in which Rustin moved, the silence and invisibility are palpable. In interviews, men and women who worked with him in the post–World War II decades are more than willing to engage the gay issue, but they inevitably frame the discussion by an admission that they never talked about it in those years. Meanwhile, for the 1940s, '50s, and '60s, I have found but one letter in which Rustin writes directly about his sexuality, another in which someone else describes what Rustin has said to him, and a handful of maddeningly coded letters that I haven't yet fully deciphered.[8] This is not the stuff from which to draw indisputable conclusions.

Nonetheless, some things are clear. Over a stretch of twenty years, Rustin's sexuality had a way of erupting into view. In 1944, while he was incarcerated in federal prison as a conscientious objector, officials brought charges of sexual misconduct against him in order to subvert Rustin's efforts to organize an inmate strike against segregation. The tactic worked. A. J. Muste, a mentor and father-figure to Rustin and his boss at the Fellowship of Reconciliation, rushed in to counsel Rustin, and to calm the concerns among other incarcerated pacifists. Muste's advice to Bayard was unambiguous: "If thy right hand offends *thee*, cut it off."[9] Eight years later, when Rustin was arrested in Pasadena and convicted on a sex charge, the Fellowship of Reconciliation promptly cut him loose after twelve years of service, and compounded his humiliation by sending a statement detailing the devastating situation to pacifists around the country. What might have been an incident known only to a few became in this way a matter widely discussed in activist circles and one that would follow Rustin for the rest of his career.[10]

Early in 1956, Rustin traveled to Montgomery to offer his assistance to the leaders of the bus boycott. In a cloak-and-dagger scenario that defies easy summary, pacifist and civil rights leaders in New York met, telephoned, and dispatched letters with dizzying speed—all for the purpose of keeping the contaminated Rustin away from Martin Luther King. Four years later, in 1960, Rustin was orchestrating a campaign involving A. Philip Randolph, King, and the leaders of the student sit-ins, to inject civil rights into the heart of the presidential campaign. This time he fell victim to the maneuvers of Adam Clayton Powell, who threatened to charge that King and Rustin were having a sexual affair—unless Rustin was dismissed as King's special assistant and removed from the convention project. King capitulated without a fight. Interestingly, the only public criticism of King's dismissal of Rustin came from James Baldwin.[11]

Two things seemed clear to Rustin from these incidents: In each case the reactions of others to his sexual desires impressed upon Rustin his contingent status and served to marginalize his influence in movements which, in these decades, were themselves marginal to the centers of power. Muste's response to Rustin's personal crisis forced Rustin to separate sharply his work and his intimate life, driving him toward modes of sexual expression that made the arrest in Pasadena an event waiting to happen.[12] The loss of his position at the Fellowship of Reconciliation, an organization that at least had strong ties with mainline Protestant denominations, led him into the quintessentially marginal War Resisters League, the only radical group which sought his services after the Pasadena arrest.[13] And his dismissal in 1960 as King's assistant meant that Rustin was outside the loop of civil rights leadership during the period from the sit-ins to the Birmingham campaign.

At the same time, none of these incidents spelled an end to his career. Rustin seemed to rise, phoenix-like, from the ashes of each crisis. After his release from prison in 1946, he made the compromises necessary to keep his position in the Fellowship of Reconciliation and, in the succeeding few years, did some of his most courageous organizing for peace and racial justice. After Pasadena, his friends at the War Resisters League came to his rescue by providing him with a secure, if small, base from which to work. While activists in New York sought ways to insulate King from Rustin, Bayard managed to bond with King and became one of his closest advisers. For the next four years, Rustin strategized King's emergence as a national leader; King, for his part, rarely made an important political decision without consulting Rustin. When King succumbed to Powell's demands, Rustin turned his attention back to issues of war and peace, and to the struggles for independence in Africa.

The crises provoked by Rustin's sexuality did more than create an activist career punctuated by fits and starts. It shaped the very way that Rustin worked. He adopted a style characterized by a seamless modesty that never drew attention to himself and that appeared to keep him far from the center of decisionmaking and visible leadership. Throughout the 1940s and 1950s, Rustin's figure remained shadowed, the prototypical representation of gay men in the postwar era. He also developed a tendency to attribute his ideas and his accomplishments to others. Rustin, in other words, affected a pose— his own version of the mask that gay men of that time wore—and his dissembling fooled not only contemporary observers but historians as well for whom Rustin has remained a minor character.

The 1963 March on Washington seemed to mark a decisive turning point in Rustin's fortunes, though it might easily have become a replay of a familiar recording: Rustin and A. Philip Randolph hatch a plan for a march on Washington; Roy Wilkins vetoes Rustin as director (and so Rustin is cast in the role of deputy who does the work but is denied the credit); Strom Thurmond goes public with charges of sex perversion against Rustin. But because Thurmond's charge threatened to wreck an event on which civil rights leaders had banked so much, they were forced to defend Rustin.[14]

The success of the march transformed Rustin's persona. Within a matter of weeks he had been transformed into a leader in his own right with a media profile and public recognition. His picture appeared in the press and in all the major news weeklies, including a *Life* cover photo and a profile in the *Washington Post*.[15] He moved on to other dramatic public roles, such as organizer of a boycott of New York City schools in February 1964, which proved to be the largest civil rights demonstration in history.[16] The relationship with King was repaired for a time, and he was drawn back into King's circle of advisers. In other words, the perversion card had been played and—so it seemed—finally trumped.

In the aftermath of the March on Washington Rustin began to articulate a political strategy that diverged from the purist revolutionary nonviolence on which he had cut his political teeth. He called for the struggle for racial equality to move beyond civil rights and toward a transformation of the American political economy. He argued that this could only happen through the articulation of a full social and economic program, and through forging alliances with other progressives. He believed that civil rights forces had mobilized enough people and enough support that they could conceivably lead a majority movement to capture the Democratic party. And he urged that protest be, not abandoned, but tactically deployed as part of a larger political strategy. All of these ideas came together in an article he published early in 1965, "From Protest to Politics."[17]

At the time, militants in both the peace movement and the black struggle scorned Rustin's ideas. Yet a generation later, they stand up well as a cogent discussion of politics. Perhaps this is simply hindsight: with our retrospective ability to see how the radical war on liberalism helped usher in two decades of conservative hegemony, Rustin's approach seems less suspect. By contrast, many of the manifestos produced in the 1960s by young radicals seem today at best misguided and at worst the rantings of lunatics.[18]

All of this may sound far removed from issues of sexual identity and the problem of reading the silences in a gay life. But there remain in the events of this period certain loose ends, an untidiness that intuition tells me has something to do with Rustin's sexuality. Let me suggest some connections:

First, Rustin's political perspective was unusual among those who shared his political history and credentials—those, in other words, who were self-consciously radical. Rustin, I believe, understood the bankruptcy of radical marginality in a way that few of his peers did. Having suffered repeatedly the stigma of the sexual-pervert label, he had lost all tolerance for left-wing romanticism. His colleagues may also have been marginal to the political system, but many of them returned home at night to intentional communities rooted in heterosexual patterns of sociability. Not Rustin. In 1963, he was fifty-one years old, without a long-term intimate relationship, and, at least politically, he was reaching for something more than a place at the periphery.

Secondly, Rustin argued for his political strategy without an institutional base. Given his level of skill and accomplishment, Rustin's free-floating status can only be attributed to the continuing stigma of his sexual identity.

Even after the March on Washington, the discomfort with Rustin's sexuality lingered. For instance, throughout late 1963 and early 1964, Martin Luther King debated whether to bring Rustin on staff. One senses that King wanted to bring Rustin aboard. But in the end, King backed away, and he did so by revising his own history on the issue. In private conversations, King explained his 1960 dismissal of Rustin not as caving in to Powell's threats, but as a response to Rustin's uncontrolled sexual urges.[19] The outcome left Rustin without a political home and his lack of organizational roots made it harder for him to implement his ideas and easier for others to dismiss him.

Third, even granting the sharp language of leftist debates, there was a level of invective and scorn directed at Rustin that goes beyond political disagreement. For example, soon after Rustin's article "From Protest to Politics" appeared, Staughton Lynd leveled blistering charges against him in the pages of *Liberation*, a magazine that Rustin had helped found. Lynd's criticisms were so far out of proportion to Rustin's proposals and actions that one can not help but wonder what they were *really* about. Rustin's only defender was Dave McReynolds, a younger gay staffer at the War Resisters League, whom Rustin had mentored over the years.[20]

Another example involves Stanley Levison, whom recent writers on King have virtually canonized for his selfless devotion to the civil rights leader. A friend and political associate of Rustin, Levison was introduced to King by Rustin, who continued to provide opportunities for the two men to meet and become close. In a conversation with his brother in September 1963, Levison referred to James Baldwin and Rustin by saying that "the two were better qualified to lead a homosexual movement than a civil rights movement." In 1963, a remark like this could only imply contempt. Coming as it did a month after Rustin's March-on-Washington triumph and from someone best described as an armchair radical, the statement lets us see the hidden homophobia in Rustin's political world.[21]

Rustin did, eventually, make what might plausibly be termed a turn to the right. Without a base, and indeed, without a job, he became the head of a new institute that A. Philip Randolph created for him. Funded by the AFL-CIO, the institute was constrained in its ability to dissent from Cold War liberalism. In the Vietnam era, this involved fateful compromises, which Rustin made. The war had shrunk the political ground which he proposed to occupy, and he sought secure footing by moving to the right, not the left.

The cynicism which others identify in these final choices sits uneasily alongside the profile of the younger Rustin. But should it surprise us? For instance, late in 1964, Rustin coordinated King's trip to Norway to accept the Nobel Peace Prize. Upon his return, Rustin described to two friends an incident in Oslo. One morning in the wee hours, Rustin was called by hotel security to deal with a potentially ugly situation. Apparently, prostitutes were running naked through the halls, in and out of the rooms of King's brother and other members of the entourage.[22] Rustin succeeded in keeping these events out of the papers, but what must have run through the mind of this man, whose sexuality had so often been used against him? The response of others to Rustin's gay identity is deeply implicated in his growing political moderation.

As you can see, once I reach beyond certain facts about Rustin's sexuality, I am left with some evidence and much speculation. I don't know whether my remaining research will uncover mounds of material and talkative informants who will confirm these hunches. But I suspect that no amount of work will free me from the difficulty of reading meaning at the point where words stop and silence begins.

NOTES

1. The only extended treatment of Rustin's career may be found in Milton Viorst, *Fire in the Streets: America in the 1960s* (New York: Simon and Schuster, 1979), 197–231. The memoirs to which the paragraph refers are: Roy Wilkins, *Standing Fast: The Autobiography of Roy Wilkins* (New York: Viking, 1982); Ralph David Abernathy, *And the Walls Came Tumbling Down: An Autobiography* (New York: Harper and Row, 1989); James Farmer, *Lay Bare the Heart: An Autobiography of the Civil Rights Movement* (New York: Penguin, 1985); and David Dellinger, *From Yale to Jail: The Life Story of a Moral Dissenter* (New York: Pantheon, 1993). A forthcoming biography of Rustin by Jervis Anderson will begin to correct the omission.

2. The literature on the 1960s is vast and growing. Some of the better accounts of the political upheavals of the decade are: Godfrey Hodgson, *America in Our Time* (Garden City, N.Y.: Doubleday, 1976); Allen Matusow, *The Unraveling of America: A History of Liberalism in the 1960s* (New York: Harper and Row, 1984); and Todd Gitlin, *The Sixties: Years of Hope, Days of Rage* (New York: Bantam, 1987).

3. Rustin's two books provide some sense of his strategic thinking and his political activities, along with bits and pieces of autobiographical data. See Bayard Rustin, *Down the Line: The Collected Writings of Bayard Rustin* (New York: Quadrangle Books, 1971) and *Strategies for Freedom: The Changing Patterns of Black Protest* (New York: Columbia University Press, 1976). For his influence on youth, see Viorst, *Fire in the Streets*, 350, and Maurice Isserman, *If I Had a Hammer: The Death of the Old Left and the Birth of the New Left* (New York: Basic Books, 1987), 186–187. On the peace movement see Lawrence J. Wittner, *Rebels Against War: The American Peace Movement, 1933–1983* (Philadelphia: Temple University Press, 1984), and James Tracy, "Forging Dissent in an Age of Consensus: Radical Pacifism in America, 1940–1970," Ph.D. dissertation, Stanford University, 1992. On his commitment to interracialism and his class analysis of inequality see Daniel Perlstein, "The Case Against Community: Bayard Rustin and the 1968 New York School Crisis," *Educational Foundations*, 7:2 (Spring 1993): 45–67.

4. Bayard Rustin, "From Protest to Politics: The Future of the Civil Rights Movement, *Commentary*, 39 (February 1965): 25–31.

5. Discussions of the shift in Rustin's politics occur in my interviews with George Houser, Homer Jack, Roy Finch, and David McReynolds, all of whom were associates of Rustin in the peace movement of the 1940s and 1950s. See also Dellinger, *From Yale to Jail*, 216–21; the comments by Stokely Carmichael in Viorst, *Fire in the Streets*, 350, 355; and the interview with Ed Brown in the Civil Rights Documentation Project, Howard University.

6. Rustin was noticeably reticent about speaking for the public record about his sexual identity until relatively late in his life, when he consented to a number of interviews. See George Chauncey, Jr., and Lisa Kennedy, "Time on Two Crosses: An Interview with Bayard Rustin," *Village Voice*, June 30, 1987, 27–29, and Redvers Jeanmarie, "An Interview with Bayard Rustin," *Other Countries: Black Gay Voices*, 1 (1988): 3–16.

7. See, for instance, Jonathan Katz, *Gay American History* (New York: Thomas Crowell, 1976); John D'Emilio, *Sexual Politics, Sexual Communities: The Making of a Homosexual Minority in the United States, 1940–1970* (Chicago: University of Chicago Press, 1983); Allan Bérubé, *Coming Out Under Fire: The History of Gay Men and Women in World War II* (New York: The Free Press, 1990); Elizabeth Kennedy and Madeleine Davis, *Boots of Leather, Slippers of Gold: The History of a Lesbian Community* (New York: Routledge, 1993); Esther Newton, *Cherry Grove, Fire Island: Sixty Years in America's First Gay and Lesbian Town* (Boston: Beacon Press, 1993); and Martin Duberman, *Stonewall* (New York: Dutton, 1993). Note the title of the major collection of scholarly articles on gay and lesbian history: *Hidden From History: Reclaiming the Gay and Lesbian Past*, ed. by Martin Duberman, Martha Vicinus, and George Chauncey (New York: New American Library, 1989).

8. See Rustin to John Swomley, March 8, 1953, Fellowship of Reconciliation Papers, Document Group 13, and David McReynolds to Ben, October 9, 1953, in David McReynolds Papers, Document Group 134: both in Swarthmore College Peace Collection; A. J. Muste to Rustin, June 18, 1945, and July 4, 1945, Bayard Rustin Papers, Reel 20, UPA Microfilms; Rustin to Davis Platt, April 5 and April 20, 1945, in the possession of Davis Platt, New York City.

9. Muste to Rustin, July 4, 1945, Rustin Papers, Reel 20, UPA Microfilms.

10. The F.O.R. statement can be found in Document Group 13, Series D, Box 1, Swarthmore College Peace Collection. For reactions to it see the correspondence in the archives of the American Friends Service Committee: General Administration, Individuals—Bayard Rustin, 1953.

11. James Baldwin, "The Dangerous Road Before Martin Luther King," *Harper's Magazine* (February 1961): 33–42. On Montgomery see the correspondence of Glenn Smiley and John Swomley in the Swomley Document Group, Box 2, Smiley and Rustin folders, Swarthmore College Peace Collection. For a discussion of the Adam Clayton Powell incident, see Rustin Interview, Columbia Oral History Collection, and author's interview with David McReynolds, March 1993. Both episodes are discussed in Garrow, *Bearing the Cross* (New York: William Morrow, 1986; Vintage edition, 1988), 66–69, 138–40, and Taylor

Branch, *Parting the Waters* (New York: Simon and Schuster, 1988), 173–74, 178–80, 313–17.

12. Rustin was arrested on at least one, and perhaps two, other occasions for homosexual activity. The first incident, an arrest for lewd conduct, occurred on October 25, 1946, at 125th Street and Morningside Avenue; the disposition of the case is unknown. A second arrest occurred in Riverside Park, near Columbia University, on the night of September 20, 1947, for being in the park after dark. Information on the first incident comes from a lengthy FBI memorandum on Rustin, dated August 16, 1963, detailing his political affiliations, record of arrests, and foreign travel. Reference to the second incident comes from Rustin to Judge James Lanzetta, 10/28/47, and Rustin to Dear Friend, 10/10/47, both in F.O.R. Papers, DG 13, Series D, Box 1, Swarthmore College Peace Collection.

13. The Fellowship of Reconciliation in 1953 had a staff of more than a dozen in its national office in New York City, as well as several regional offices with paid staff. By contrast the War Resisters League had a paid staff of two.

14. For Thurmond's charges see the *Congressional Record* (August 13, 1963): 14836–44. See also Philadelphia *Sunday Bulletin*, August 18, 1963, sec. 1, p. 30, and New York *Herald Tribune*, August 14, 1963, p. 7.

15. See *Washington Post*, August 11, 1963, p. A6, and *Life* (September 6, 1963). *Newsweek* captioned a photo of Rustin "Out of the Shadows." See *Newsweek* (September 2, 1963): 18.

16. On the school boycott, see New York *Journal American*, February 2, 1964, p. 1 and February 3, 1964, p. 1; New York *Herald Tribune*, February 4, 1964, pp. 1, 7; Milton Galamison interview, Civil Rights Documentation Project, Howard University; and New York City School Boycott Files, Rustin papers, Reels 11 and 12, UPA Microfilms.

17. Rustin, "From Protest to Politics."

18. For criticisms of Rustin by radicals in the mid-1960s, see Viorst, *Fire in the Streets*, 350, 355; David Dellinger, "The March on Washington and Its Critics," *Liberation* (May 1965): 6–7, 31; Staughton Lynd, "Coalition Politics or Nonviolent Revolution?," *Liberation* (June–July 1965): 18–21. As counterpoint to Rustin's call for coalition politics, Lynd proposed that radicals convene a new "continental congress."

19. References to the hiring of Rustin may be found in the following FBI documents: New York Office Memo, 9/11/63, Bureau File 100–106670, Subject: Martin Luther King; New York Office Memoes, January 28, 1964, February 5, 1964, and March 4, 1964, Subject: Communist Party U.S.A., Negro Question, Communist Influence in the Civil Rights Movement; and Special Agent in Charge, New York City, to Director, FBI, 3/25/64.

20. Lynd, "Coalition Politics"; Dave McReynolds, "Transition: Personal and Political Notes," *Liberation* (August 1965): 5–10, 39.

21. Special Agent in Charge, New York City, to FBI Director, September 23, 1963, Stanley Levison FBI File, Martin Luther King Center, Atlanta.

22. Baumgardner to Sullivan, 12/17/64, FBI Memo, Subject: Martin Luther King, Jr.

(5)

OUTING HISTORY

Blanche Wiesen Cook

REMEMBER WHEN ALL BIG BIOGRAPHIES were of famous, scrupulously straight white men? In terms of our national culture that seems epochs ago: a dull, deceitful time before civil rights activism, women's studies (which insists that the personal is political), and the gay and lesbian movement (which airs out the closet) actually triumphed. In terms of biography we have had a significant revolution, and our entire vision has been transformed.

Now after 25 years of feminist biography and criticism and 25 years since Stonewall, our world has changed. Virtually every week there are new biographies that give us more complex, interesting, and accurate versions of the celebrated and creative. New studies of Colette, Glenn Gould, Mary Renault, Janet Flanner, Judy Garland, Benjamin Britten, John Edgar Hoover, Marguerite Yourcenar, and Daphne DuMaurier—to name but a few—change our understanding. Our sense of history, culture, and politics is enhanced in every way. It is not just that some of America's heroes were gay or had gay adventures, but rather that we have the freedom, even the mandate, to ask the most profound questions: How did our subject actually live? What did she think? How did she feel?

Of course, as in all things progressive and good, there is endless backlash. Howls of anguish arise to condemn all complex truths concerning complicated lives. A new word has even been hurled about: *pathobiography*. And so high culture continues to squirm away from the contradictions and textures that actually make humans so interesting. Erasures and denials continue. It is amazing to me that the focus of these denials remains that still explosive area of intimacy. Our great forebearers, especially our foremothers, are simply not supposed to have had interesting or passionate private lives.

During the 1970s, when I began to consider the real lives and relations of admired women, I found the most extraordinary resistance to the idea that behind the pubic facades, tall privets, and stone walls that limited our vision, many of our most esteemed foremothers lived discreet but entirely unconventional lives. Historians and literary analysts preferred to see our great women writers and activists as asexual spinsters, odd gentlewomen who sublimated their lust in various good works.

Many people, including several of my colleagues and contemporaries, wondered why I did this research: Would it not demean and diminish my heroes to discover their true natures, their actual identities? The fact is, we have yet to understand and fully appreciate the marvelous crossroads between sex and power that haunts us all. The purpose of my research was to explore that wondrous place from which so many political women derived their power, their courage, their style. And I learned what our society most hates to admit, that many of our most esteemed foremothers were actually voluptuaries: the very fact of their passion, their love for others, and their ability to express that love and passion sustained them and provided support, strength, and emotional armor. The fact is that our culture has sought to deny the truths and complexities about women's passion because it is a most significant key to women's power.

Moreover, the romance of the closet, the perspective of the fortress, endures with amazing ferocity. I once believed that a great chain of being linked me, my friends in their 60s and 70s, and their friends in their 80s and 90s—the women who might tell me something of how it actually was then. But public women who lived their private lives in the closet, hidden and protected from certainty and scandal, were horrified by my quest. One well-known British journalist, a hearty Sapphist, was outraged: we had much more fun before you young reporters insisted on trotting it all out. Our privacy and our ceremonies were scared; we enjoyed the mystery, and the danger. Now it all seems far less romantic.

For some the closet was lonely and dark. For others it was entirely satisfying—its very secrecy lent additional sparkle to the game of hearts. The romance of the closet had a life of its own. There was, for example, a theater person, a close friend of a close friend; we were told we would like each other. She had much to tell me, yet there was nothing to discuss: "I've been in the closet for sixty years, why the hell should I come out to you?" After three phone calls, appeals to her conscience, to history, the future, her gift to young women, and so on, she agreed: If I would read a play she had written, she would lunch with me. I did, and we made a date for the next week. She died the day before we were to meet.

It seems fantastic now to recall that lesbians of my generation, growing up in the 1950s, had nothing beyond *The Well of Loneliness* to inform us that we were not alone. We thought there was something about Gertrude Stein and Alice B. Toklas, because it looked like there should be. But nothing explicit about Stein had then been published, actually to read. Her own vastly coded and explicit *Lifting Belly* was not available until Yale reissued it in 1980, though it was written in 1917 and once published for the very few in 1958.

As an historian and activist I was originally drawn to Eleanor Roosevelt because of her vision, and the direction of her heat: her capacity to recognize and fight for people without power, to take responsibility and remain courageous in a lifelong struggle against abuse and mockery. None of the issues she faced are settled. The controversies of her time are the controversies of our time.

As first lady-elect, Roosevelt astounded a New York Metropolitan Opera audience when she appeared between the first and second acts of *Simon Boccanegra* to appeal for money for Depression-ruined Americans, saying: "When you come face-to-face with people in need, you simply have to try to do something about it.... After all, this is the richest country in the world. We cannot allow anyone to want for the bare necessities of life."

Eleanor Roosevelt's first public act after the inauguration was a personal inspection tour of Washington's alley slums, where thousands of residents lived in the most appalling circumstances, without running water or sanitation facilities. She initiated a campaign to provide decent housing for all in Washington. Her work on behalf of affordable housing throughout America became a lifelong crusade.

In 1934 she called for indoor plumbing and toilets in every new home, which astounded FDR's advisers. How, one asked, would anyone be able to tell the rich from the poor if ER (as she signed her correspondence) had her way? She replied: In matters of such simple dignity and decency we should not be able to tell the rich from the poor.

During the 1930s Eleanor Roosevelt championed civil rights before any other administration official, and frequently despite her husband's opposition. She made the connection: segregation here, fascism there. Outraged by injustice, her style was personal and direct. But there have been no final victories on the long road to freedom, security, or injustice. Discrimination and fascism remain the determinants of the 20th century.

For her efforts ER was for decades red-baited and reviled. Her FBI file, which John Edgar Hoover kept on her every activity from 1924 (when she campaigned for U.S. adherence to the World Court) until her death on November 7, 1962, eventually numbered over 3,000 pages—perhaps the single largest individual file compiled. The largest single subject in her FBI file involved her efforts on behalf of racial justice, followed by her later efforts against Cold War excesses and nuclear weapons.

In 1940, when she was most fiercely denounced for her activities, ER wrote her friend the novelist Fanny Hurst: "I am sorry that all these attacks against me are causing so much grief to my friends. But in these troubled times I intend to go right on saying and doing what must be said and done. And I intend to provide lots of ammunition for attack in the future."

It is this kind of courage that we long for today. But in mainstream heterosexist culture it is in frightfully short supply. Rather, there is a willingness to mock, trivialize, or despise same-sex love. Ironically, the oddest assortment of people would have us revert to silence, timidity, the degradation of deceit and lies.

Last year at a party for Eleanor Roosevelt's statue (designed by Penelope Joncks for New York's Riverside Park) a writer dedicated to human rights for most people, Jews in particular, was eager to tell me that she would not read such a vile book as mine, which—she said—besmirched her hero, Eleanor Roosevelt. How did it besmirch her? It implied that she was a lesbian, or had lesbian friends, or some such thing. She was not at all sure. But she would not read the book, or touch it. In the summer of 1995, *Entertainment Weekly* ran a screed against the "grisly allegations" biographers make and included Eleanor Roosevelt—simply because she might have had passion in her private life.

The allegation that I "outed Mrs. Roosevelt" is fascinating. It is entirely limited to sex. There has been no expression of concern about the alcoholic swamp that ensnared most of ER's male relatives, no upset about FDR's imbroglios, no mention of the child abuse or wife betrayal from generation to generation. Nobody has protested the information that young Eleanor had to have three locks installed on her door to keep out her endlessly drunk and abusive uncles. Nobody seems bothered by the activities of her father, his lovers, his outside children, or the neurasthenia of her mother. There is only the charge that I have claimed for Eleanor Roosevelt "sexual activity," or even awareness.

How does it serve our culture for that small band of self-appointed custodians of ER's "morality" to insist upon chaste Victorianism? Why are so many wedded to the stereotype of a frigid, sublimating, forever lonely woman? And what is gained by our reluctance to acknowledge that she had the capacity to see and understand all sexual dimensions?

Again, part of the answer concerns power. If women controlled their own lives and lusts, what would happen to the dominant social order? Yes, this is about social control.

Eleanor Roosevelt's love for humanity was rooted in her love for people, the specific individuals she loved. Love is experiential, not an abstraction. To ignore the questions I ask about love and sexuality is to ignore the substance and context of ER's entire adult life. She gave us the gift of that substance and that context by preserving her letters for history. For example, in a 1923 article called "The Women of Tibet" she wrote: "It has been brought to my attention that the wives of Tibet have many husbands. This seems to me a very good thing, since so many husbands have so many wives."

Eleanor Roosevelt loved more than once in a lifetime dedicated to passion and experience. After 1920 many of her closest friends were lesbian women. She shared their confidences, joys, and sorrows. She honored their relationships, and their privacy. She protected their secrets and kept her own. Women who love women and women who love younger men have understood for generations that it was necessary to hide their love lest they be the target of vicious slander and cruelty. Historically, the romance of the closet and the perspective of the fortress have been necessary barricades against bigotry and pain.

Our culture's ongoing romance with the Victorian closet is a curious thing. By Victorian standards the Victorians themselves were wicked beyond belief. Yet that cloak of purity and prudery has draped Anglo-American culture for over a century. The fact is that that burdensome and disfiguring legacy of false rectitude was precisely what Eleanor Roosevelt and her friends worked so hard to discard; in their daily lives they challenged it again and again.

6

MICHAEL HARRINGTON
An "Other" American

Maurice Isserman

THIRTY YEARS AGO the "Other America" entered the nation's social vocabulary, a phrase as recognizable today as a synonym for poverty as "how the other half lives" was in the Progressive era. In 1962 Macmillan published an earnest and plain-spoken study of poverty in the United States by a hitherto obscure young socialist activist named Michael Harrington. Harrington's expectations for *The Other America* were modest; he would be pleased, he told a friend in 1961, if it sold 2,500 copies. He left the country soon after its publication, using his small advance to finance a long-planned year's sabbatical from politics in Paris. But when Harrington returned to New York at the end of 1963, he found himself nationally acclaimed as "the man who discovered poverty." President John Kennedy had read the book and recommended it to his policy advisers. JFK's successor, Lyndon Johnson, geared up for a "war on poverty"; some of his most controversial guiding assumptions would reflect *The Other America*'s discussion of "the culture of poverty." In the decades since, Harrington's book has sold 1,300,000 copies, and remains a benchmark for contemporary social concern.[1]

That part of Michael Harrington's story is well-known. Less known, however, is how Harrington came to his identification of—and with—"the other America." His explanation in his 1973 memoir *Fragments of the Century* embraces the conventions of the classic conversion narrative. As a social worker in the St. Louis slums in 1949, he recalled how he was overcome one day by the "stench from the broken stopped up toilets" of a rickety tenement, and vowed "that somehow I must spend the rest of my life trying to obliterate that kind of house...."[2] It may have happened that way, but none of Michael's surviving friends or family can remember any such dramatic social awakening; his decision shortly afterwards to give up social work in St. Louis for a position in New York as a writer-trainee for *Life* magazine, seems an oddly indirect way of setting out on such a mission.

Harrington offered another explanation for his eventual life's work in a television interview on the occasion of the 20th anniversary of *The Other America*'s publication: "I grew up in [the Catholic Church], and from the time I was a little kid the Church said your life is not something which you are supposed to fritter away; your life is in trust to something more important than yourself."[3] The Church in which Harrington was baptized, served as an altar boy, and whose schools he attended from kindergarten through his graduation from the College of Holy Cross in 1947, was an institution whose followers were deeply conscious of their minority status in the United States. Defensively nursing the wounded sensibilities of preceding immigrant generations, Michael's elders exhorted his generation of young Catholics to remain apart from and embattled with the individualist/materialist/modernist values of the dominant culture. When Harrington attended the prestigious Jesuit-run St. Louis University High School, its yearbook proclaimed that the goal of Jesuit education was to instill its graduates with "the necessary fortitude and enthusiasm to...strive towards the urgent conversion of a perverted, pagan universe."[4] Harrington's sense of personal mission, in part, grew out of the seriousness with which, in this formative period of his life, he took his Church's teachings. At least that in itself was enough to give him some sense of being separate from and "other" than the mainstream. Still, something else is required to explain Harrington's subsequent vocation since, after all, relatively few Catholics of his background and generation chose to devote their lives to righting the wrongs of the poor.

Psychological interpretations of the sources of radical activism have proven liable to partisan abuse. Some conservative commentators dismiss any kind of left-wing commitment as a species of psychological maladjustment. Sympathetic accounts of the lives of political activists, on the other hand, can easily shade into hagiography, with biographers insisting that their subjects were motivated solely by a selfless love for humanity.[5] Michael Harrington deserves better. After all, he discovered Freud long before he read a word of Karl Marx (a sympathetic Jesuit at Holy Cross would smuggle him copies of Freud's works from the section of the library forbidden the undergraduates in the 1940s). Sympathetic references to Freud continued to dot his writings throughout his socialist years. And in his autobiography, he candidly discussed the nervous breakdown he suffered in the 1960s, and the four years of psychoanalysis which followed.[6] (I like to think he would be sympathetic to an account of his own life which balanced an assessment of his political convictions with at least some attention to psychological dynamics.)

Michael Harrington seems to have been an outsider, twice over. He was encouraged to think of himself standing outside the dominant culture by virtue of his Catholicism. But the "otherness" he inherited from his religion was only part of the story. More significantly, within the Church he also chose an outsider's perspective. By the time he was an adolescent, Harrington had forged an identification with an undergraduate Catholic subculture populated by self-styled rebels—aesthetes, bohemian misfits, and even, although discreetly, sexual outlaws—a grouping considerably broader if more diffuse than the institutionally-oriented elites whose beliefs James Fisher has so ably analyzed in his recent book on the "Catholic counterculture."[7]

Harrington liked the phrase "the Other America," and 1962 was not the first time he used it. In May of 1960 he published an article with that title in the liberal Catholic weekly *Commonweal*. Subtitled "Beyond the Neon Signs and the Coke Bottles, Another America Still Survives—as of Now," Harrington's *Commonweal* piece drew on his experiences criss-crossing the United States as an itinerant socialist agitator in the 1950s. The triumph of "mass culture" bemoaned by the New York intellectuals since the end of the 1930s, was not complete or secure, Harrington contended. An alternative America, a nation not "dominated by gadgets and mass media," lay just beneath the surface of mainstream America. In Seattle, for instance:

> the people live in the presence of Mount Rainier.... Driving in the city, one never knows when the turning of a corner will reveal the aspect of beauty. On a clear day, each hour, each period, is given a special definition by the mountain. And this geography enters into a culture. It is, of course, intermingled with the history of the region: logging, the IWW, the Seattle General Strike of 1919…the weatherbeaten and brawling tradition of a port. Thus the coffee cups in many restaurants in Washington are bigger than they are in the East. Their shape developed out of an outdoor, working world and they are part of the texture of life in the area. At the trucker's stop in the Cascade mountains where breakfast is ten strips of bacon, four eggs, and a pile of home fries, these coffee cups are one of the forms defining a history and a way of living. They are related to the towering fact of the mountain.[8]

As an apprentice revolutionary in the 1950s, Harrington had come to pride himself on his rigorous scientific socialism. But no stretch of dialectical materialism will get you from Mount Rainier, to oversized coffee cups, to the Wobblies. There is instead a kind of unabashed lyricism in the passage reflective of Harrington's earliest career aspirations, to be a poet. As early as age ten he had chosen a nom de plume suitable for a poet laureate, "Sir John Michael"—an interesting choice for a student still in parochial school.[9] Long after abandoning his poetic aspirations, he retained the habit of viewing his possibilities and surroundings through a literary lens, a sometimes romantic projection of what a world in which he might play a role commensurate to his talents could be and should be like. Harrington first learned that there was such a thing as "the Left" by reading about it in the novels of John Dos Passos' *USA* trilogy.[10] His weatherbeaten Seattle longshoremen are in fact literary brothers to the "husky boilermaker from Frisco" who, in *The Big Money*, hopped a freight car to join the protest against the execution of Sacco and Vanzetti (an event which led Dos Passos to declare "all right we are two nations") Harrington's radicalism was hopeful, generous, and expansive. Although steeped in European intellectual theory (both Catholic and Marxist), his cultural impulses reflected a distinctly indigenous tradition of radical individualism. By the 1960s he had come to envision a powerful, redemptive political coalition of two "other Americas"—the excluded America and the alternative America joining hands—and it was to the realization of that vision that he devoted the remainder of his life.

Harrington grew up the only child of a prosperous middle class household in St. Louis. His mother, ashamed of her own origins as the daughter of an immigrant saloonkeeper, was socially ambitious. An intelligent woman, frustrated in her own professional aspirations, she took deep satisfaction in her son's intellectual gifts. "Once, when Michael was seven years old," she recalled to an interviewer after her son became a political celebrity, "we were both reading in bed. He was reading Dickens and he turned to me and said, 'My this author expresses himself well.' …I gave a great deal of thought to selecting books, a child's history book, a history of art book and so on, and building a children's library as he grew up." She also enrolled him in classes in ballroom dancing and packed him off to cotillions where he could mix with the daughters of the St. Louis Catholic elite.[11]

Catherine Harrington's investment in her son's intellectual advancement would not prove in vain. Having enrolled in kindergarten at the age of four and skipped the eighth grade, he was a precocious twelve years old when he began his freshman year at St. Louis University High School in 1940. But Catherine Harrington's social ambitions, and those of her son, soon diverged. Michael Harrington was set apart from his high school classmates by being "a little chubbier, a little more of a boy" than his peers.[12] He also chose to set himself apart. "We had some of the wealthiest kids in St. Louis at the high school," a classmate recalled, "and some of them looked like the cover of *Esquire*, with matching argyle sweaters and socks. [Mike] was never like that. I remember him with a big sloppy sweater. He didn't care about a lot of things that other kids cared about."[13] In high school Harrington began to assert his own standards against those of his formidable mother (dubbed "the Czarina," and "Lady Harrington" by his schoolmates).[14] He successfully fended off her attempts to dress him up. When asked by a friend why he didn't bother to wash his face more often, he replied earnestly, "Poets don't."[15]

The remarkable thing about Harrington's high school experience is that, for all his seeming social disadvantages, he wasn't unpopular. He created an identity for himself that allowed him to stand out from the crowd, (a "gentle scoffer," as one of his classmates put it) while making his mark within the community. He excelled academically, and in many other ways. Too small to compete on the athletic field, he became sports editor of the school newspaper. The 1941 yearbook commented that freshman Harrington "seems to be in about every organization he could find at school." He even marched around with the band one year carrying a French horn, although he couldn't actually play the instrument. He particularly excelled in debate, as one of his partners recalled:

> Many a time in high school, I saw Mike win a debate by standing there with his open Irish face, and blinking at the judges, and quoting brilliantly from a purely fictitious authority to prove his point. In one debate he even had the nerve to quote from "Dr. Dingbat Fu," and they bought it. He was very, very good.[16]

There were rewards for Harrington to garner, despite—or perhaps because of—the fact that he took a stance outside the mainstream. The pattern repeated itself at Holy Cross, which he entered at the age of 16, and where many of his classmates were considerably older veterans of the Second World War. Again he excelled academically, and in his senior year was chosen as class salutatorian. Again he was an editor of the student newspaper. His political views in college were conservative, and his editorials for the newspaper bristled with a defense of Church doctrines on such issues as the "abominable...infamous...loathsome...and hideous practice" of birth control.[17] For that time and place, his ideas were utterly conventional, but he sometimes found surprising ways of expressing them. Emulating the Catholic essayist G. K. Chesterton, Harrington developed a fondness for paradox, notably expressed in an editorial entitled "For the Radicals," arguing:

> he is a radical who argues against divorce, he is a dissenter who argues against birth control...a rock in a swirling ocean of conflicting ideas, the Catholic Church stands out as the last stronghold of the radical.... A system which is two thousand years old, is the only radical in a world of conformists.[18]

At once earnest, provocative, ironic, and playful, "For the Radicals" was an accomplished piece of writing for an undergraduate. It anticipated the style of the writer who, a quarter century later, would begin his autobiography with the phrase "I am a pious apostate."[19] And it signaled its author's disdain for "a world of conformists," even if that meant embracing the then suspect identity of "radical."

Holy Cross had its own standards of conformity. The seniors in Harrington's class in 1947 listed Norman Rockwell as their favorite artist, Dinah Shore as their favorite "songstress," and the religious potboiler *The Robe* as their favorite novel.[20] Harrington's literary circle rebelled by reading Joyce and Eliot. And when Evelyn Waugh's *Brideshead Revisited* was published in 1946, Harrington eagerly sought out the novel and passed it clandestinely on to others. The novel's dubious reputation among the Jesuits enhanced its literary appeal. "The act of rebellion of reading *Brideshead* was part of the charm," according to one of Harrington's classmates.[21] Although Waugh was a Catholic, his faith was too fervent (too much the unreliable enthusiasm of a recent convert) for Jesuit tastes. Moreover, Waugh's casually tolerant treatment of homosexuality in the novel—particularly that of the spiritually troubled but appealing aristocratic wastrel Sebastian Flyte—raised an explosive issue at this single-sex institution.

Harrington's closest friend at Holy Cross and fellow editor of various publications was Bill L., a gay man who in his undergraduate years was painfully coming to grips with his own sexual identity. He confided his secret to Harrington, who was sympathetic despite his own heterosexuality. "Michael was not attracted to men," Bill recalled, "and he was not attractive to men." But along with Bill and some others in their circle, Harrington was "thoroughly exposed at Holy Cross to the whole subject of homosexuality." He and Harrington "almost made a study of it," instructed by two senior editors on the school publications. Their mentors were military veterans, one of whom had spent considerable time exploring the gay gathering places of wartime London. According to Bill, "they liked to talk about it." Behind closed doors, they held court. There was no seduction or physical initiation involved. The thrill here was not the physical act of sex—it was the illicit discussion of an outlaw subculture.[22]

Harrington was not gay, but he still was intrigued by the notion of the gay lifestyle, and this in an era when it was condemned by the Church as a threat to morality, and by the government as a threat to national security.[23] He could not have been oblivious to the risks of even this casual association with homosexuality. The revelation of this little group's existence could have brought scandal, disgrace, and expulsion—not to mention the horror it would have provoked at home.[24] But notwithstanding Harrington's unshaken devotion to Church doctrine, and his flirtation with political conservatism, his curiosity about and affinity for an outlawed and dangerous subculture, won out.

From Holy Cross Harrington went on to Yale Law School where, as usual, he excelled. But towards the end of his first year he wrote to his parents to say he would not be continuing:

Dear Mom and Dad,
...In keeping with our rule of not keeping anything back, I want to tell you what I've decided in the last few weeks. I'm quite sure now that I don't want to come back here next fall—that I don't want to go on with law. When I came up, the agreement was that I was to mature for a year, think it over, get away from the bohemian atmosphere and make a choice. I think I'm the only person who can make the choice, and the answer I've reached is that its [*sic*] not for me.[25]

Instead of returning to Yale in the fall of 1948, he enrolled as graduate student in English at the University of Chicago. From there (with a brief stopover as a St. Louis social worker) he moved on to New York City, then to the *Catholic Worker*, and finally to the socialist movement.

The emergence of Harrington's political radicalism was bound up in some fairly intimate ways with issues of personal identity. He found satisfaction in the mastery of arcane and forbidden cultural and, eventually, ideological folkways. He simultaneously fulfilled and rebelled against the expectations of a domineering mother (it is probably significant that his first involvement in organized radicalism was under the auspices of another powerful maternal figure, Dorothy Day, a woman the same age as Catherine Harrington). None of this is meant to trivialize the political choices Michael Harrington would make, by reducing them to the acting-out of a psychologically-charged personal agenda. The concerns Harrington expressed in *The Other America* and throughout his career were significant in and of themselves, apart from whatever gratification he took in voicing them. The fact that Harrington was sometimes a little unworldly, "literary," and self-created turned out to be an advantage at a critical moment in his career and in contemporary American history. Identifying with outcasts and outsiders, he was temperamentally as well as politically inclined to look beyond the conventional wisdom and beneath the surface complacency of "mass culture" and the "affluent society." He was himself an "other American."

NOTES

1. Irving Howe discusses the reception and significance of *The Other America* in his introduction to a new paperback edition of the book, Michael Harrington, *The Other America: Poverty in the United States* (New York: Collier Books, 1994).

2. Michael Harrington, *Fragments of the Century* (New York: Saturday Review Press, 1973), 66. Jane Addams describes a comparable conversion experience in her 1909 memoir *Twenty Years at Hull House*, an account which her biographer finds equally suspect. See Allen Davis, *American Heroine: The Life and Legend of Jane Addams* (New York: Oxford University Press, 1973), 48.

3. CBS Sunday Morning News, January 10, 1982.

4. St. Louis University High *Dauphin*, 1942. For Harrington's account of the influence of his Catholic education, see *Fragments of the Century*, 8–17.

5. As examples of the former, see Morris Ernest and David Loth, *Report on the American Communist* (New York: Holt, 1952), Gabriel Almond, *the Appeals of American Communism* (Princeton: Princeton University Press, 1954), or Stanley Rothman and S. Robert Lichter, *Roots of Radicalism: Jews, Christians, and the New Left* (New York: Oxford University Press, 1982). As an example of the latter, see Arthur Zipser, *Workingclass Giant: The Life of William Z. Foster* (New York: International Publishers, 1981).

6. Harrington, *Fragments of the Century*, 183–94. Gail Sheehy used Harrington's

account of his breakdown as one of her "Predictable Crises of Adult Life" in *Passages* (New York: E.P. Dutton & Co., 1976), 298–302.

7. James Terence Fisher, *The Catholic Counterculture in the United States, 1933–1962* (Chapel Hill: University of North Carolina Press, 1989).

8. Michael Harrington, "The Other America," *Commonweal*, Vol. 72, May 27, 1960, 222–24.

9. Interview with Peggy Fitzgibbon, November 3, 1990.

10. Interview with Marty Corbin, October 30, 1992.

11. "Once Known for Her Own Record, Now She is Michael's Mother," *St. Louis Post Dispatch*, January 20, 1971.

12. Interview with Richard Dempsey, May 16, 1992.

13. Interview with Msgr. Jerome Wilkerson, May 13, 1992.

14. Interview with Bill Loftus, July 20, 1993.

15. Interview with Bill Loftus, July 20, 1993.

16. Interview with Bill Loftus, July 29, 1993.

17. Holy Cross *Tomahawk*, April 30, 1947, 2.

18. Holy Cross *Tomahawk*, May 8, 1946, 2.

19. Harrington, *Fragments of the Century*, 3.

20. Holy Cross *Purple Patcher*, 1947.

21. Interview with Bill L., April 12, 1993.

22. Interview with Bill L., September 27, 1991.

23. On popular and official attitudes towards homosexuality in the late 1940s and 1950s, see John D'Emilio and Estelle B. Freedman, *Intimate Matters: A History of Sexuality in America* (New York: Harper and Row, 1988), 292–29.

24. Harrington "still smiles," an interviewer wrote in 1987, "remembering the household horr[or] when he announced that he intended…to become a poet…. In those days," he grins, "being a poet meant just one thing, you had to be gay—or, as they called it then, a faggot." Bella Stumbo, "The Lonely Fight of Last Old Leftist," *Los Angeles Times*, April 4, 1987.

25. Letter from Michael to Catherine and Edward Harrington, April 18, 1948, in author's possession.

CHANGING
THE SUBJECT

◯ Introduction

Betty Sasaki

"I am alternately pleased, puzzled and perturbed...by this, by the alterity that is perpetually thrust upon African-American women, by the production of black women as infinitely deconstructable "othered" matter. Why are black women always already Other? ...Why have we—black women—become the subjected subjects of so much contemporary scholarly investigation, the peasants under glass of intellectual inquiry in the 1990s?"[1]

—Ann duCille, "The Occult of True Black Womanhood"

WHEN SOCRATES SAID that "the unexamined life is not worth living," did he also mean the lives of others? The recent rise in popularity of biographies in general, and of biographies about "non-traditional" subjects in particular, raises questions concerning the changing value, both economic and ethical, attached to examining the life of another.

This chapter points to specific—and potentially problematic—issues surrounding the "multicultural biography," namely, that to change the subject is to shift attention from one subject to an "other." Who is the "changed" subject? Who is "changing" the subject? And, finally, whose changes are projected upon the new subject in the process of writing that subject's biography?

As more and more emphasis is placed on recognizing those subjects and voices previously excluded from traditional curricula across the disciplines, these questions take on enormous weight. The current enterprise of multicultural education, while expanding the theoretical terrain of subjective authority, must also come to terms with the problematic and often contradictory aspects of its own good intentions. In its commitment to respond to the very real problem of exclusion, the multicultural project runs the risk of overlooking the new questions it generates. At what point do efforts toward inclusion become acts of appropriation? To what extent is the multicultural project placed at the service of, or subordinate to, institutional agendas, educational commodification, and individual self-promotion? To what extent do biographies of the Other simply change the subject, through elision, reduction, or amplification, reshaping differences to better fit into existing paradigms of selfhood? As Robert Carr observes, the seduction of testimonial literature, which bears a close kinship to the multicultural biography, is that it gives its readers a false sense of access to the Other.[2] The possible result of this pseudointimacy is that the life of the Other can only be valid as "an index to someone else's experience subject to a seemingly endless process of translation and transference."[3]

While the biographical endeavor aspires to what this collection's editors claim as the construction of "the multiple cultures in which we live," it also carries the implicit motive of justifying itself. The multicultural biography, in particular, is positioned at a cultural crossroads of conflicting claims as to the significance, and "value" of the lives it purports to tell (and implicitly wants to sell). Thus, even as scholars and new biographers claim to reshape and revise established cultural history, they are, themselves, inescapably shaped and envisioned by that same history, by the "biography" of our own culture. Out of this multidimensional exchange of influences there emerges a continuum of critical perspectives and positions from which to approach and represent the life of the Other.

The different ways in which the three essays of this chapter deal with the questions of how and for whom they speak place them along this continuum at points as various as the subjects they treat. In the process, each author composes a different biographical portrait of the changed subject by grappling with and, at times, problematizing the seductive potential of previously excluded or marginalized life stories. Not surprisingly, biographers ground their narratives in a variety of sources, and thus redefine the boundaries of the biographical genre even as they appropriate that genre's popularity (and, to a certain extent, its increasing academic legitimacy as a vehicle for changing social, historical, and ontological concepts about the Self and the Other). Claiming the controversial figure of Madam C. J. Walker as a representative "race woman," Jeffrey Louis Decker analyzes her business success as central to both black uplift and black womanhood at the turn of the century. Underscoring the particularities of Walker's status both as a poor woman fighting against the sexism and classism of her male business peers, and as a woman of color struggling toward financial success in a segregated America, Decker argues that Walker's "conspicuous presence" at this juncture of American history must be included in any serious discussion of turn-of-the-century black uplift. In the absence of any direct or unified autobiographical material, Decker attempts "to reconstruct her life piecemeal," locating her voice in annual business reports, product advertisements, and public statements.

Hayden Herrera's essay on Frida Kahlo, a Mexican painter whose career was long overshadowed by the fame of her husband, Diego Rivera, reconstructs the life of her subject by reading Kahlo's self-portraits as "a kind of diary." In contrast to Decker, who represents Walker's personal rags-to-riches story as an integral part of the larger historical narrative of racial and gender oppression and uplift, Herrera interprets Kahlo's work through the psychological lens of the artist's tragic and painful personal experience. Foregoing discussions of Kahlo's participation in and influence by larger artistic and political movements such as surrealism, and subordinating Kahlo's relationship with Rivera to Kahlo's primary relationship with herself, Herrera composes a portrait of a singular woman engaged in a struggle to define and transform herself through her art.

Richard J. Powell also takes an artist as his biographical subject, the African-American painter William H. Johnson. Rather than place his subject's life story at the center of his essay, as Herrera does, Powell's biographical narrative frames his discussion of Johnson's work. In his analyses of *Moon Over Harlem* and *Fighters for Freedom*, paintings which portray the conflicted historical events of Johnson's time, Powell problematizes his own position as both art historian and biographer—a position from which he must critically negotiate the elements of individual and biographical specificity and the social and historical universals that necessarily come into contact in a work of art and the life of the artist.

As each of these essays illustrates, to "change the subject" is to make a choice, not only about the subject, but also about the perspective from which that subject's life is written. As more and more scholars cross over to write about the lives of non-traditional subjects, it should encourage us, as biographers and readers of biography, to pause and examine the values we both place and practice upon the life of the Other.

NOTES

1. Ann duCille, "The Occult of True Black Womanhood: Critical Demeanor and Black Feminist Studies," *Signs* 19:3 (1994), 591–92.
2. Robert Carr, "Crossing the First World/Third World Divides: Testimonial, Transnational Feminisms, and the Postmodern Condition," in *Scattered Hegemonies: Postmodernity and Transnational Feminist Practices*, eds. Inderpal Grewal and Caren Kaplan (Minneapolis and London: University of Minnesota Press, 1994), 153–72.
3. duCille, op. cit., 622.

7

TWO PAINTINGS BY WILLIAM H. JOHNSON

Richard J. Powell

My aim is to express in a natural way what I feel, what is in me, both rhythmically and spiritually, all that which in time has been saved up in my family of primitiveness and tradition, and which is now concentrated in me.

—William H. Johnson, 1932

In all my years of painting, I have had one absorbing and inspiring idea, and have worked towards it with unyielding zeal: to give—in simple and stark form—the story of the Negro as he has existed.

—William H. Johnson, 1946

THROUGH THE AEGIS of a 1991 artist monograph and a major traveling exhibition, the art and life of the important but little known American painter William Henry Johnson (1901–1970) was rescued from almost complete obscurity. What made this act of cultural retrieval all the more noteworthy was the introduction into the modern American art canon of over one hundred oil, tempera, and watercolor paintings that epitomize a provocative merging of World War II–era modernist aesthetics with African-American cultural sensibilities. As suggested in the biographical components of these endeavors, Johnson's "invisibility" to the contemporary, art–viewing public (even in light of his artistic contributions) had just as much to do with his lengthy residency in Europe as it had to do with American racism and the art world's unwillingness to recognize and/or celebrate more than a few gifted black artists at any given moment. In spite of these historical circumstances and institutional roadblocks, a reconstruction of his career has been possible, as is the recounting of the melodramatic and, at times, seductive biography of the artist.[1]

William Henry Johnson was born poor and black in South Carolina at the turn of the century. Although there were few artistic opportunities in the segregated South for someone like Johnson, he realized that he wanted to be more than a common laborer. He left South Carolina around 1917 and migrated to New York City, where he was eventually accepted into the prestigious School of the National Academy of Design. His artistic talents, first honed and perfected by copying the *Mutt and Jeff* and *Bringing Up Father* comic strips, were soon polished and brought towards academic perfection by teachers such as Charles Louis Hinton and George Willoughby Maynard. But these instructors were eventually superseded by less conservative ones, like Charles Webster Hawthorne and George B. Luks, who encouraged Johnson to experiment with gesture and color, and to rely on inner feelings for his renderings of landscapes and still lifes. These lessons in protomodernist approaches to art found an even greater outlet when, in 1926, Johnson went to France on a private art scholarship. There, the example of the School–of–Paris legends Chaim Soutine and Amedeo Modigliani pushed Johnson's painterly academism into more expressionist territories. When Johnson briefly returned to the United States in 1929 (where he won a gold medal and a cash prize from the Harmon Foundation), his brand of modernist portraiture prompted the critics in *Art Digest* to ask "Is William H. Johnson, Negro Prize Winner, Blazing a New Trail?"[2]

But before the art critics had a real chance to ponder this question, Johnson had indeed blazed another new trail, this time settling in a small fishing village in Denmark, where he married a weaver and ceramist fifteen years his senior, whom he had met only a little over a year earlier on the French Riviera. His new wife, Holcha Krake, her sister, Erna Voll, and his brother–in–law, the German sculptor Christoph Voll, introduced Johnson to Northern European expressionism and primitivism, which, ironically, was just then being maligned by many critics and deemed "degenerate" by people sympathetic to the increasingly influential National Socialist Party in Germany. Still, William Johnson and Holcha Krake jointly exhibited their art throughout Denmark, Norway, and Sweden for much of the 1930s.[3]

In 1938, the rumblings of war in Europe and the growing sense that the United States was the place to be at this "period in [his] artistic development" prompted Johnson to return with his Danish wife to America. Living in a loft in the Chelsea section of New York City, and securing a Works Progress Administration job as an art instructor at the Harlem Community Art Center, Johnson embarked on yet another phase of painting. The results—bold, brilliant, jigsaw–like compositions of generic black farmers, black couples dancing the jitterbug, the urban street play of children, guitar- and tambourine–toting street musicians, and other African–American subjects—are a curious amalgam of cubist/expressionist strategies, American abstractionist techniques, and African–American aesthetic principals, all marshalled together in service to what Johnson once described as "his family of primitiveness and tradition."

But on the heels of these works, several personal misfortunes occurred that, in tandem with Johnson's career, created a marked change in his paintings. A fire in his New York loft, his wife's succumbing to the ravages of breast cancer, and his own psychological isolation from the artistic community all coincided with this new body of work. These paintings—crude, colorful, and ecstatic renderings of family members in South Carolina, illuminations of Negro spirituals, historical subjects, and political figures from current world events—ironically represent both the decline in his more cultivated talents and the culmination, of sorts, of his more spiritual and polemical powers as an artist.[4]

In 1946, Johnson again crossed the ocean and settled in Denmark. Tragically however, he soon suffered a complete mental breakdown, was diagnosed with an advanced stage of syphilis, and was shipped, under the auspices of a U.S. State Department escort, back to New York. There, his works and possessions were placed in a Hudson River storage facility and he was committed to the Central Islip State Mental Hospital, where he remained, in a virtually vegetative state, until his death in 1970. In response to a court–appointed attorney who, in the mid–1950s, was going to destroy the contents of Johnson's rented storage space, family friends stepped in and saved over 1,000 of Johnson's works of art. In the 1960s, when the works were again threatened with dispersal and/or destruction, the Smithsonian Institution's National Museum of American Art became the final repository for the collection.

In response to signs of urban unrest during the summer of 1943, Johnson painted *Moon Over Harlem*. This riot was precipitated by an altercation in a Harlem hotel between a white police officer and a black soldier. During a scuffle between the two, the soldier allegedly hit the policeman with the policeman's own nightstick and ran. The policeman pulled out his revolver and shot the soldier, wounding him in the arm. While the soldier was being operated on at a nearby hospital, a crowd, which had gathered outside, grew in numbers and emotional frenzy. After someone erroneously shouted, "A white cop shot and killed a black soldier," angry people began streaming onto the adjoining avenues, demanding that justice be done, gathering momentum and soon, in their outrage, breaking windows, looting stores, turning over cars, setting fires, and turning Harlem into a site of violence and destruction. On Monday, after the police had restored some semblance of normalcy to the community, reports showed that six people had been killed, over one hundred people injured, several hundred arrested, and loss of property estimated in the millions of dollars incurred.[5]

In Johnson's circa 1943–44 version of the riot, he visually presents this incident by means of a painted frieze showing concrete brown pavement, an inky black sky, a purple Manhattan skyline, ten human figures in various positions, and a reddish, ominous, full moon. The ten people in the picture— six uniformed policemen and/or militia men and four people being arrested—are depicted by Johnson in a stark, minimalist manner: linear, angular, and more sign–like than life–like. The central figure in *Moon Over Harlem*—a black female rioter, bloodied, with one breast exposed, turned upside down by three uniformed men—commands our attention. Her tethered and humiliating position is the very embodiment of the 1943 Harlem riot: an oppressed and debased community, whose frustration and self–destruction prompted an authoritative abuse of power.

Soon after completing *Moon Over Harlem*, Johnson began painting a series of historical and current event subjects. Entitled *Fighters for Freedom*, this series portrayed famous men and women from African–American history, contemporary politicians on the world front, World War II military figures, opposition leaders from third world countries, and selected grassroots activists, all of whom were recognized for their key roles in liberating people from various forms of political and social oppression. Inspired, no doubt, by the end of World War II and the international community's discussions about the creation of a United Nations Charter, Johnson saw his *Fighters for Freedom* series as having to do with the broad, historical scope of "freedom," ranging from nineteenth-century abolition movements in the U.S. to mid–twentieth-century democratic movements on the international scene.

Nat Turner, one of the paintings from Johnson's *Fighters for Freedom* series, concerns itself with the well–known leader of the equally infamous (and ill–fated) 1831 slave revolt in Southampton, Virginia. Rather than illustrating the rebellion itself, Johnson chose to depict Nat Turner just after his execution: hanging from a crude, magenta–colored gallows/tree, placed in front of a stark landscape of yellow, orange, and red skies and a cemetery of racially–variegated and segregated grave markers. Although removed from the actual events surrounding Nat Turner and his slave revolt by over one hundred years, Johnson supplied viewers with enough symbolic ammunition (i.e., the bloody sky, the crucifix–like tree, the weapons in the lower right corner, and the African, Caucasian, and mulatto crosses) to tell a convincing and harrowing story of violent insurrection and human sacrifice.

Both *Moon Over Harlem* and *Nat Turner* can also be interpreted in the context of Johnson's personal ordeals during those tumultuous years in which he created these paintings. Almost simultaneous with the making of *Moon Over Harlem* was Johnson's discovery that his wife was suffering from breast cancer. The central figure in this painting of a displaced, assaulted, and exposed woman must have resonated with Johnson's real-life predicament in learning that his wife was seriously ill and might die. The black woman's exposed breast, seemingly detached and floating against a yellow field of orange and white flowers, is in the center, so to speak, of painted matters. Although it might be presumptuous to make a simple analogy between this painted black breast with his own wife's breast cancer, it is conceivable that this painted black woman, with her body turned upside down and caught up in inextricable, brutal forces, had a kindred sister and brother in the life–and–death ordeals of Holcha Krake and William H. Johnson, circa 1943–44.

While the *Nat Turner* painting does not share *Moon Over Harlem*'s special, biographical circumstances, it does share the former painting's genesis in difficult, trying times. By 1945, Johnson had more or less separated him-self—both physically and psychologically—from friends, family, and the greater New York art community. Although still sporadically exhibiting under the curatorial eye of supporters like Betty Parsons at the Wakefield Gallery, Johnson painted alone in his East 10th Street loft, earning a living as a common laborer in Brooklyn's Naval Yard, and assiduously saving his money in order to buy a one–way boat ticket back to a post–war Denmark. Feeling misunderstood by several critics concerning this new, sign–like, "primitivist" direction that his art had taken, Johnson likened himself to an art maverick, a seer, and a martyr, of sorts, to the creative cause that he and his late wife believed in throughout their romantic, relatively idyllic existence in pre–World War II Europe. Around the same time, Johnson made other paintings with lynchings and crucifixions (*Mount Calvary*, ca. 1944; *Lamentation*, ca. 1944; and *Let My People Free*, ca. 1945) which also dis-played magenta crosses and/or gallows and, in several instances, representa-tions of a black Jesus which recalled Johnson's own facial features. If this aligning of himself with such martyrs as Jesus Christ and Nat Turner were not enough, in Johnson's circa 1944 *Self-Portrait* he portrayed himself, in the manner of Van Dyck's portrait of *Charles the First in Three Positions*, as a self–conscious, subtly religious, Johnson–in–three–persons format.

The title of this collection of essays, *The Seductions of Biography*, implies a ruse has been perpetrated when authors succumb to biography's irresistible bait. In the often conservative discipline of art history, there is suspicion and concern when scholars seem to focus too heavily on the personal affairs and other "extraneous" biographical aspects of their subjects. Although most art historians would concede that a nominal measure of the biographical (such as birth and death dates, descriptions of artists's work sites) is useful in one's art history research, for many in the field you have crossed the proverbial line of propriety when you start delving into sexual territories, political affiliations, and other personal matters. Biography, as the title of this volume suggests, is frequently viewed as a "tempter" or a "temptress," leading scholars down a thorny path of vague speculations, unfurled imaginings, or outright fantasies.[6]

William H. Johnson's biography, like those of many other artists of the modern and postmodern periods, is a seductive, fascinating entity in its own right. But because Johnson's biography encircles the artistic production, as well as the solid, creative accomplishments in his lifetime, the scholarship does not depend alone on the subject's good looks, exotic world travels, the tragic deaths of him and his wife, and insane asylums which Johnson knew all too well. Ideally, artist biographies, as the designation indicates, concern, first and foremost, acts of artistic production, which are the rationale for looking further and deeper into artists's lives. Biography is only capable of taking over art history when the investigator is not, in the final analysis, really interested in the art but, rather, uses art as a ploy for talking about sex-uality, politics, illnesses, and personal shortcomings.

Yet it is equally the case that *without* the personal and political factors (as distracting and overwhelming as they can sometimes be), a discussion of William H. Johnson's artistic output and his extraordinary career would amount to little more than a narrow, thinly constructed study, bereft of background, frame and, yes, color. The challenge, of course, in making use of this personal information is being able to ascertain exactly what kinds of personal data will support the ongoing art historical research and, conversely, what personal information, ultimately, is not useful to the process. Alas, the answer can only be found through a careful study of the particular artists and/or art works under consideration, with those specific circumstances determining the applicability and potential emphasis of a so–called seductive biography.

Given the scarcity of well-written, thoroughly researched biographies on black artists, one can hardly resist the prospects of being "seduced," especially if it means transcending the tired, hagiographic treatises which often parade under the objective guise of many black biographies. Those works that avoid the controversial, occasionally messy, and often unflattering sides of their subjects do a disservice both to the artists/subjects and to their life's work. By looking selectively at aspects of the lives under investigation, these works offer very little in the way of complete, complex, and/or integrative analyses of important works and lives.

Of course, the flip side of this Pollyanna–ish, "feel good" approach to black artists biographies is, unfortunately, the standard "I–was–impoverished/I–had– a–hard–life/I–was–mistreated" formulae, which often precludes any altering or editing of that sorry, "hard luck" script. Fortunately, a new generation of biographers of black artists and other black achievers are presently at work, and they have introduced into the genre a perspective which sees neither sin nor race betrayal in being black *and* middle–class, affluent, privileged, or educated.

Recent art historical and biographical studies on black visual artists like Robert Scott Duncanson, Henry Ossawa Tanner, Horace Pippin, and William H. Johnson have rectified some flagrant omissions in the study of modern and world art history. Still other major figures in African–American art and visual culture, such as Edmonia Lewis, Aaron Douglas, Archibald Motley, Beauford Delaney, Charles White, Elizabeth Catlett, Roy DeCarava, Lois Mailou Jones, and Bob Thompson, are without rigorous, in depth, challenging studies of their lives and careers. Even the legendary, iconic figures of Romare Bearden and Jacob Lawrence, though widely written about and regularly exhibited, lack penetrating, critical examinations of their work, and of the associations, encounters, and other personal affiliations which surrounds their work.[7]

Does William H. Johnson's biography (or any artist's biography, for that matter) actually help one to better understand the art? This question could perhaps be posed in other ways: Does Quincy Troupe's collaborative auto/biography of/with the late Miles Davis, replete with scenes of violence and abuse towards women, help listeners to better understand such musical masterpieces as *Kind of Blue* and *Bitches' Brew*? Does Hayden Herrera's biography of Frida Kahlo, filled with revealing accounts of her many affairs and medical problems, help viewers to better understand her art, both in a performative and pictorial way? Does Martin Duberman's biography of Paul Robeson, layered with reference after reference to ties with communist sympathizers and political operatives, shed any meaningful light on his multi-faceted life in the arts? Or do these biographical detours impede our under-standing, throwing up Salome's veils of innuendo and titillation, ultimately getting in the way of analyzing the artists themselves and their works?

The answer, for the present, is yes, these biographies do help one to bet-ter understand the creative acts of these artists, but only insofar as the writ-ers of biography are able to situate the lives of their subjects within the modes and measures of each artist's creative templates. And in the case of the readers of these lives, biographies help one to understand the art only inso-far as the readers will allow themselves to embrace the whole of an artist's life and work. Only with these curbs and curfews in effect can writers and readers avoid the big, easy trap of being seduced *and* abandoned by biogra-phy's allure.

Returning to William H. Johnson, one can take in the sights and sources of such paintings as *Moon Over Harlem* and *Nat Turner* and uncover layer upon layer of history, narrative, and biographical material, both about the sub-jects and the artist. Yet also evident in these and other paintings by Johnson are the telltale signs of artistic license and invention, which transform histor-ical and biographical truths into artistic ingredients that Johnson adds to his own, special, creative gumbo. In fact, one could argue that much of what makes the biographical "seductive," especially in the case of a painting like Johnson's *Nat Turner*, is his embellishing on both historical facts (i.e., Johnson's rendering of Turner's prophetic execution site amongst the black, white, and mixed–blood deceased) and biographical "truths" (i.e., Johnson's self–identification with martyrdom and his self-projection into an African–American historical past). William H. Johnson's uncanny self–incor-poration into art and history, as well as his protopostmodern critiques of the convention–laden historical narrative, make him and his art fitting and even key subjects for a discussion about the various attractions and hazards con-tained within the biographical. What one discovers in the process of differ-entiating between artistic invention, social history, and personal biography, are not so much polarities and methodological oppositions from one category to the another, as much as forged commonalities and, as in the case of William H. Johnson, the communal goal of bearing witness to art *and* life.

NOTES

1. Richard J. Powell, *Homecoming: The Art and Life of William H. Johnson* (New York: Rizzoli, 1991), and the exhibition, *Homecoming: William H.*

Johnson and Afro–America, 1938–1946. Beginning in the fall of 1991, and to date, this traveling exhibition has appeared at the following venues: National Museum of American Art, Smithsonian Institution, Washington, D.C.; the Whitney Museum of American Art, New York, NY; the Addison Gallery of American Art, Phillips Academy, Andover, MA; the Amon Carter Art Museum, Fort Worth, TX; and the Herbert F. Johnson Museum of Art, Cornell University, Ithaca, NY. All biographical and art historical references to William H. Johnson and his work, unless otherwise noted, are from Richard J. Powell, *Homecoming: The Art and Life of William H. Johnson* (New York: Rizzoli, 1991).

2. "Is William H. Johnson, Negro Prize Winner, Blazing a New Trail?" *Art Digest* 4 (15 January 1930): 13.

3. Johnson's encounters with northern European expressionism and the primitivist agenda in modern art are chronicled in Richard J. Powell, "In My Family of Primitiveness and Tradition: William H. Johnson's Jesus and the Three Marys," *American Art* 5 (Fall 1991): 20–33.

4. For a discussion of Johnson's late, more primitivist works, see Richard J. Powell, "William H. Johnson's *Minde Kerteminde*," *Siksi: The Nordic Art Review* 1 (1986): 17–23.

5. Jervis Anderson recounts the circumstances surrounding the 1943 riot in Jervis Anderson, *This Was Harlem* (New York: Farrar, Strauss and Giroux, 1982).

6. A glaring example of biography's ability to elicit heated criticism from the more traditional, art historical rank and file was the vehement response from art historian Francis V. O'Connor to a 1989 artist biography (and a Pulitzer Prize winner for nonfiction) of Abstract Expressionist painter Jackson Pollock. Steven Naifeh and Gregory White Smith, *Jackson Pollock: An American Saga* (New York: Clarkson N. Potter, Inc., 1989); Francis V. O'Connor, "An Undeserved Pulitzer for a Pop Biography?" *New York Times*, 12 May 1991, section 2, p. 37, 40.

7. For several exemplary biographical treatments of African–American artists, see Joseph D. Ketner, *The Emergence of the African–American Artist: Robert S. Duncanson, 1821–1872* (Columbia: University of Missouri Press, 1993); Dewey F. Mosby, Darrel Sewell, and Rae Alexander–Minter, *Henry Ossawa Tanner* (Philadelphia: Philadelphia Museum of Art, 1991); Judith E. Stein, *I Tell My Heart: The Art of Horace Pippin* (Philadelphia: Pennsylvania Academy of the Fine Arts, 1993); and Richard J. Powell, *Homecoming: The Art and Life of William H. Johnson* (New York: Rizzoli, 1991).

It is important to note that, while Bearden and Lawrence have been the subjects of numerous biographical treatments, exhibition catalogues, journal articles, and the like, neither of these artists have been a) placed in a biographical context that sufficiently explores their relationship to their respective times and cultural moments; or b) thoroughly scrutinized from the position of African–American moderns who, unlike their Euro–American counterparts, employ specific visual and thematic strategies in service to alternative, culturally–engendered aesthetics. Two exceptions to this observation, perhaps, can be found in Myron Schwartzman, *Romare Bearden: His Life and Art* (New York: Harry N. Abrams, Inc., 1990); and *Jacob Lawrence: The Migration Series* (Washington, D.C.: Rappahannock Press, 1993).

8

RECONSTRUCTING ENTERPRISE

Madam Walker, Black Womanhood, and the Transformation of the American Culture of Success

Jeffrey Louis Decker

AT THE THIRTEENTH ANNUAL CONVENTION of the National Negro Business League, held in late August 1912 at the Institutional Church on Chicago's South Side, the organization's founder and president, Booker T. Washington, refused to interrupt the second day's schedule in order to yield the floor to a little-known, forty-four year old black woman named Madam C. J. Walker.[1] On the third and final day, with outside temperatures hovering at 90 degrees, inside the convention hall even the sage of Tuskegee would not deny Madam Walker the chance to speak. Once again unable to gain recognition from Washington, Walker shouted from her seat in the audience: "Surely you are not going to shut the door in my face. I feel that I am in a business that is a credit to the womanhood of our race."[2]

In order to legitimate a female voice within the institutional apparatus of segregated enterprise, Madam Walker developed a unique if contradictory expression of African-American women's agency, one which appropriated and transformed the myth of Horatio Alger uplift—according to the gospel of Booker T. Washington—in a manner that pointed to the moral efficacy of entrepreneurial endeavors for black womanhood. Walker thus opened her intervention at the 1912 NNBL convention by asserting that she was indeed "a credit to the womanhood of our race," and proceeded to testify to her remarkable, if not unfamiliar, rags-to-riches story. She began: "I am a woman who started in business seven years ago with only $1.50."[3]

Walker's extemporaneous story of discipline and determination takes a page out of Booker T. Washington's popular *Up From Slavery* (1901). Washington's autobiographical voice authorized black entrepreneurship for segregated America largely through its appropriation of white, middle-class models of turn-of-the-century success, such as Horatio Alger's moralist "luck and pluck" formula. As Washington's biographer, Louis R. Harlan, suggests, the wizard of Tuskegee presented himself to his readers "as the American success hero in black."[4] Rather than emphasize the significance of slavery and its legacy for blacks in industrializing America, Washington followed in the tradition of Benjamin Franklin by embracing the idea of virtuous uplift founded on the solid rock of character-based merit.

Unlike traditional purveyors of the myth of success from Franklin to Washington, Walker never formally composed an autobiography. Recent studies of autobiography demonstrate the genre's complicity with the Enlightenment project of establishing the subject of history as white, male, and middle-class.[5] For this reason, life stories written by women and minorities are more likely to reveal the conventions of individuated self-making. But what if, as in the case of Madam Walker, no autobiography exists? Academic multiculturalism has gone a long way toward addressing this limitation by opening the field of autobiography to sources ranging from slave narratives to *testimonios*. In an effort to locate the voice-agency of the nonconventional entrepreneur, I have found it necessary to delimit the genre to include annual business reports and newspaper advertisements, where an enterprising individual might exploit her success story as a means of peddling her product to consumers.

Walker left only autobiographical fragments, forcing her biographers to reconstruct her life piecemeal from public statements made within very specific institutional sites. She did not compose her life in a room of her own but on the convention floor of Washington's National Negro Business League. The wizard of Tuskegee had organized the League at the turn of the century, and it became overnight the single most powerful institution promoting entrepreneurial uplift within segregated America. Not surprisingly, his imprint is visible upon Walker's August 1912 intervention into the male dominated NNBL. Consider the way she concludes her speech from the convention floor:

> Now my object in life is not simply to make money for myself…. Perhaps many of you have heard of the real ambition of my life, the all-absorbing idea which I hope to accomplish, and when you have heard what it is, I hope you will catch the inspiration, grasp the opportunity to do something of far-reaching importance, and lend me your support. My ambition is to build an industrial school in Africa—by the help of God and the cooperation of my people in this country, I am going to build a Tuskegee Institute in Africa! (prolonged applause)[6]

By linking business success in segregated America to the uplift of Africa by blacks in America, Walker raises a story of individual self-making to the level of nation-building. It is important to remember that Walker's efforts on behalf of Africa were largely circumscribed by the Tuskegee machine. Today Washington is rarely remembered as a proponent of black nationalism. However, just after organizing the NNBL, Washington went into partnership with European investors in order to experiment with Tuskegee-style industrial education in Germany's African colonies. This was black nationalism in its "civilizationist" tradition.[7]

"DOWN IN THE WASH-TUB": REVISIONS OF BLACK ENTERPRISE

The most severe restraint placed on black entrepreneurship at the turn of the twentieth century was marketplace segregation, a limitation which left African-American leaders wondering whether or not Jim Crow truly had the opportunity to become a self-made man in America. This issue was at the heart of an 1899 publication titled *The Negro in Business*, the first systematic investigation of black enterprise in the United States. The book's editor, W. E. B. DuBois, opened the Atlanta University study by insisting that it was impossible "to place too great stress on the deep significance of business ventures among American Negroes. Physical emancipation came in 1863, but economic emancipation is still far off."[8] Statistics amassed in *The Negro in Business* point to approximately 5,000 black Americans engaged in private businesses during the last decade of the nineteenth century.[9] Few of these black enterprises manufactured industrial goods. Most, like Madam C. J. Walker's cosmetics company, were concentrated in the service and retail sectors of the segregated economy. "These enterprises," Du Bois concluded, "are peculiar instances of the 'advantage of the disadvantage'—of the way in which a hostile environment has forced the Negro to do for himself."[10]

In order to generate the conditions under which black business could flourish, African Americans actively incorporated the imposition of segregation into the very fabric of their entrepreneurial schemes. Black businesses exploited preassigned color-coded markets, a strategy of economic survival supported by the majority of black intellectuals and race leaders. The Atlanta University study, for example, adopted the following resolution: "The mass of the Negroes must learn to patronize business enterprises conducted by their own race, even at some slight disadvantage."[11] A year after *The Negro in Business* was published Booker T. Washington created an institutional mechanism—the National Negro Business League—by which this resolution might be realized.

Madam Walker's intervention before the 1912 NNBL convention stages how "the advantage of the disadvantage" extended to a marketplace segregated not merely by the color line, but along gender lines as well. Before demonstrating further the monetary success of her "Wonderful Hair Grower" products by citing impressive increases in annual gross revenue over the previous six years, Walker interrupted her impromptu success story by stating: "I went into a business that is despised, that is criticized and talked about by everybody—the business of growing hair." While it may be true that male barbers were venerated within segregated America for the myriad tasks they performed, Walker's occupation was disparaged by a black middle class who were not only prone to class and gender bias but uneasy about the moral efficacy of the massification of consumer culture. Specifically, the black bourgeoise perceived hairdressing and straightening as menial work performed solely by lower-class black women. And hair-growing was simply the province of conmen.

Pausing before an NNBL audience now held captive by her audacious behavior, Walker coupled her frustration at gaining recognition on the convention floor with her prior attempts "to abandon the wash-tub for more pleasant and profitable occupation."

> I have been trying to get before you business people and tell you what I am doing. I am a woman that came from the cotton fields of the South; I was promoted from there to the wash-tub (laughter); then I was promoted to the cook kitchen, and from there I promoted myself into the business of manufacturing hair goods and preparations.[12]

Walker suggests that her public sphere identity was largely defined for her until she became self-employed and, hence, self-promotable. Her public testimony is remarkable for its assertion of agency through black enterprise (from "I was promoted to" to "I promoted myself"). Nevertheless, by reading Walker's story of self-promotion next to more conventional Progressive Era narratives of success, we begin to see the degree to which patriarchy defined the meaning of the black female enterprise.

Walker's gender-coded uplift story forced her audience to confront the plight of poor black women who had little choice but to accept menial domestic employment as laundresses, maids, and cooks.[13] Walker, attempting to seize the narrative authority of entrepreneurial self-making before an NNBL membership that was both awestruck and amused, pleaded: "Please don't applaud—just let me talk!" Walker's exclamation drew more laughter, but she pushed forward.

> I am not ashamed of my past; I am not ashamed of my humble beginning. Don't think because you have to go down in the wash-tub that you are any less a lady! (prolonged applause)[14]

At stake for Walker was not just establishing her lowly start in life. She conveys to her audience that, despite the prevailing stereotype which labeled black women who labor in the fields or as domestics as unnaturally masculine, black womanhood is not sacrificed at the alter of the washtub. There is no shame, Walker insists, in work of any kind.

Madam Walker rose from being a sharecropper's daughter to becoming black America's most notable millionaire at a time when black businessmen were struggling to maintain a precarious foothold in the segregated marketplace. She had gone public with her rags-to-riches story prior to her unannounced appearance before the NNBL convention in 1912. An extensive biographical sketch of her life was published in the 11 November 1911 edition of the Indianapolis *Freeman*, a nationally circulated black newspaper which just happened to have its base of operation in Madam Walker's recently adopted hometown.[15] This is the most complete contemporary account of her life on record. The newspaper biography reports Walker's birth, as Sarah Breedlove, to ex-slaves during the first days of Reconstruction. Her early years were spent on a Louisiana sharecropping farm. At seven, she was orphaned. Seven years later she wed a man named McWilliams; the *Freeman* puts it plainly: "She married at the age of fourteen in order to get a home."[16] A hard life in Vicksburg, Mississippi, was made more difficult when, at twenty, she was widowed and left to care alone for her only child.[17] Walker and her daughter, like many African Americans living in the Black Belt during the post-Reconstruction era, left the South by following the Mississippi River north to St. Louis. She found employment as a domestic in St. Louis and, during this period, developed her miracle hair treatment formula. She migrated west to Denver, Colorado, in order to make a business of her cosmetic discovery. In Denver she met and married her second husband, C. J. Walker, a black journalist who initially helped market her product. Despite the considerable potential for developing a profitable enterprise, the *Freeman* reports that C. J. Walker "discouraged" his wife from expanding her business because "he could see nothing ahead but failure."[18] Apparently ignoring the advise of her husband, Madam Walker pursued her entrepreneurial ambition alone.

This early biographical sketch is notable for how it situates Walker's first husband as outside of and her second husband as an obstacle to her quest for entrepreneurial success. When Walker finally told her narrative of entrepreneurial self-making before a live audience—as she did every year at the NNBL (with one exception) between 1912 and 1916—she made only a passing mention of her widowhood and no reference at all to her second husband, whose initials and surname she made famous. The strained marriage ended in divorce. The absence of domestic life from Madam Walker's uplift story (whether told by the *Freeman* or by herself) suggests the degree to which narratives of enterprise excluded married women, regardless of race, from autonomous public sphere success. Like other enterprising women of the period, Walker was best-equipped to make her mark in the business world when she was not wedded to the restricted expectations of a woman's role within the home. Still, Walker's entrance into the marketplace was energized by if restricted to the emerging field of consumer-oriented manufacturing.

BETWEEN BOOKERISM AND GARVEYISM

The *Annual Report* of the 1912 NNBL indicates that Washington was, at least publicly, unmoved by Walker's unscheduled address before his organization. Despite both the sensation her speech created on the floor and her nod to the important work of the wizard of Tuskegee, Washington apparently ignored Madam Walker by avoiding comment on her testimony and moving immediately to the next item of business on the agenda. This was no doubt due, in large part, to the fact that the NNBL (like all American entrepreneurial organizations of the time) was a men's club. Black women almost always attended these conventions as wives, if they attended at all.[19]

At the 1912 convention Madam Walker forced open the door of the NNBL not just for black women, but for working-class women who labored in occupations considered less than respectable by the black bourgeoisie. The following year, Washington formally invited Walker to speak before the NNBL in Philadelphia on the practical subject of "Manufacturing Hair Preparations." She opened her first officially sanctioned address by announcing that she had decided that "it would be more interesting and profitable for me to tell how I have succeeded in the business world, in order that other women of my race may take hold of similar work and make good." As a capitalist, Walker's primary concern was with profits. As a self-promoter, she was interested in the art of the sale. She understood that the best way to sell her goods was to advertise herself through the language of virtuous uplift familiar to her customers.

Yet Walker also viewed her own success as inextricably bound to uplifting the race. More specifically, she argued before the 1913 NNBL that her efforts to dignify the cosmetics industry would profit other black women too. Thus, prior to repeating the narrative of her triumphant plight from sharecropper to entrepreneur before the convention audience, Walker spoke to the unique obstacles facing black women in business.

> [T]he girls and women of our race must not be afraid to take hold of business endeavor and, by patient industry[,] close economy, determined effort, and close application to business, wring success out of a number of business opportunities that lie at their very doors.[20]

Walker touts her own achievement in giving many women of her race the opportunity for employment as sales agents for her products. "I have made it possible," she concluded, "for many colored women to abandon the washtub for more pleasant and profitable occupation."[21] It was fast becoming a widely known fact that hundreds of black women were gainfully employed as Walker agents, and, as such, instructed in the civic virtues of business success as well as cosmetics application.[22]

With Walker's 1913 NNBL address finished, Washington rose in order to direct the convention towards its next item of business. Yet, before doing so, he gave Walker a compliment, one which might be considered patronizing and even back-handed given the context in which it was uttered and the considerable laughter it drew from the floor: "You [fellow entrepreneurs] talk about what the men are doing in a business way, why if we don't watch out the women will excel us."[23] Indeed, Walker was excelling in every way. Her business was booming. Furthermore, as she toured the country giving lectures on "The Negro Woman in Business," she was hailed in the black press as both black America's first millionaire and "America's Foremost Colored Woman," who displayed a "philanthropic prominence classing with Helen Gould, John D. Rockefeller and Andrew Carnegie."[24]

The following year, Washington invited Walker—now considered the most famous entrepreneur in black America—to the NNBL's Fifteenth Annual Convention in Muskogee, Oklahoma. We might speculate that he learned a lesson from his prior encounter with her, for on this occasion Washington simply announced: "We are going to give [Madam Walker] five minutes' time in which she can talk about anything she chooses." Not surprisingly, Walker reiterated themes familiar to her audience—including references to her personal rags-to-riches story, to what she called "the struggle I am making to build up Negro womanhood," and to her philanthropic efforts at home and in Africa. In another audacious and thoroughly self-promoting gesture, Walker took the opportunity to request that the NNBL officially "endorse" her as the leading business woman in black America. Never one to play it safe, she concluded her 1914 address by seeming to have returned the favor of Washington's back-handed compliment from the year before: "[E]verything that [Booker T. Washington] and his League are trying to do deserves and gets my warmest sympathy and support, and," she added, "if the truth be known there are many women who are responsible for the success of *you men.*" When the laughter and applause ceased, the NNBL immediately gave Walker their endorsement as "the foremost business woman of our race."[25]

Walker's command over Washington's business league was now complete. Washington died prior to the following year's convention, which was devoted to eulogizing the Progressive Era's most prominent race leader. This makes Walker's apparent absence from the 1915 NNBL conference (her name never appears in the annual report) seem almost conspicuous. At the next year's 1916 annual meeting, Walker made a triumphant return to the League by declaring in her scheduled address: "I have now built up the biggest business owned and operated by Negroes anywhere in America."[26] No black entrepreneur, male or female, could challenge this boast. Soon thereafter, Walker symbolically backed her colossal assertion by building on the Hudson River her Xanadu, a spectacular mansion dubbed Villa Lewaro by Enrico Caruso.

The evidence strongly suggests that, even prior to her outspoken debut at the 1912 NNBL gathering, Walker had already mastered the conventional paradigm of the self-made man. Two and one-half years earlier she used her success story to advertise her make-over products in the local and national black media. On April 16, 1910, Walker publicly announced the new location of Walker Manufacturing Company by running her first advertisement in her hometown Indianapolis *Freeman*, one of the most widely read and respected black newspapers in the country. The ad for her Wonderful Hair Grower covered a full two-thirds of the newspaper's second page. About half the ad space was covered by letters (eleven in all) from satisfied customers. One letter, for example, testified to the Walker product's unequaled merits in "the art of growing hair." Walker also used her own likeness to promote her business. Atop the page for this ad was a "Before and After" photo of Madam Walker, a visage which became a trademark when she put her face on the labels of her products. The text of the ad conveyed Walker's eighteen years of frustration at losing her hair "[u]ntil she made this wonderful discovery, which is now known to people throughout the country." Walker balanced her pitch for her product's ability to improve one's external appearance with the story of a divinely ordained discovery of her miracle hair-grower. It is important to remember that mainstream spokesmen for the gospel of American success had long promoted the partnership of God and Mammon, just as the nation became increasingly secularized during the late nineteenth century. As one prominent historian of the self-made man in America suggests: "The doctrine of the secular calling provided the foundation for the religious defense of worldly success."[27] A shrewd saleswoman and self-described "Hair Culturist," Madam Walker was no stranger to this doctrine, which she exploited to gain the confidence of potential customers:

> During my many years of research, endeavoring to find something to improve my own hair, in preparations manufactured by others I was always unsuccessful, until through the Divine Providence of God I was permitted in a dream to discover the preparation that I am now placing at the disposal of the thousands who are today in the same condition that I was in, just three years ago.[28]

Not once, but at four separate moments in the Wonderful Hair Growing ad of April 1910, Walker explicitly credits God for bequeathing the magical hair care formula to her and for inspiring her to share it with others.

But she also altered the convention of divinely ordained success to meet the expectations of the black American consumer. For example, in an interview with the Kansas City *Star* (circa 1915), Walker repeated her story of entrepreneurial inspiration, but placed an African medium between herself and God—and suggested that the entire scenario appeared to her within a dream.

> He answered my prayer, for one night I had a dream, and in that dream a big black man appeared to me and told me what to mix up for my hair. Some of the remedy was grown in Africa, but I sent for it, mixed it, [and] put it on my scalp.[29]

Walker's recollection is embedded in the Ethiopian dream-life of black American culture in the first decades of the twentieth century. The motherland also played a more tangible role in Walker's affairs. By 1914 she could claim before the NNBL annual convention that, among her other philanthropic endeavors, she was currently financing the education of five African children (three boys and two girls) at Tuskegee "for the purpose of founding and establishing a Negro Industrial School on the West Coast of Africa."[30]

Within a year before her own death in May 1919, Madam Walker's political and economic agenda for racial uplift at home and abroad took on a pan-Africanist look that would soon be associated with Garveyism. She gladly offered her Hudson mansion as the site of at least one 1919 meeting of the International League of Darker Peoples (ILDP), a small group of activists whose members included A. Philip Randolph and Marcus Garvey. The ILDP, in rejecting President Wilson's proposal at Versailles that Europe continue to oversee Germany's African colonies, demanded that German Africa be replaced by a governing body composed of "enlightened sections" of the African diaspora.[31] Thus, while the demand for African self-rule marked a turn away from Booker T. Washington's limited partnership with European colonization, it nevertheless remained within the "civilizationist" legacy of black nationalism in America.

On the home front, Madam Walker, like many race leaders of her day, opposed social equality, a phrase associated with racial integration. "We don't want social equality with white folks," she was heard telling the delegates at the July 1918 Association of Colored Women convention in Denver, a year before her death. "We do want equality of opportunity" within segregated America.[32] Walker's speech before the Association of Colored Women captures the considerable scope of Walker's enterprise: it manifested a self-promoting marketing strategy for her hair care products; it appealed to a type of race pride which both recalled the Age of Booker T. Washington and anticipated the coming of Marcus Garvey; it also helped expand the terrain for enterprising women who sought entrance into America's segregated marketplace.

MADAM WALKER IN THE "WOMAN'S ERA" AND BEYOND

While Walker's ambition allowed her to elude many of the obstacles placed in front of her by the male-dominated NNBL, she never issued a systematic critique of the organization's expectations in regard to black womanhood. The League's annual reports suggest that explicit criticism was not heard on the convention floor until 1917, when Mrs. D. Lampton Bacchus spoke unexpectedly (i.e., "at her request") on the topic "Woman—A Factor in Business." Elaborating on the type of obstacles confronting black female entrepreneurs, Lampton Bacchus states:

> Today she occupies a unique place in the world, being confronted by a woman question, a business and a race question, and yet, she is almost an unknown and an unacknowledged factor in each. We often find ourselves hampered with a

very, very conservative attitude from those whose opinions we seek and respect most. This is not true of all our men, for had we not the support of them, no woman could succeed in business or be employed in the different occupations of men.[33]

Lampton Bacchus's own business experience—and her invitation to address the NNBL convention on this topic—was largely circumscribed by her father's influence. Bishop E. W. Lampton of Greenville, Mississippi, had appointed his daughter to administer his considerable estate after his death. The means by which Lampton Bacchus entered the public sphere of business—that is, a family inheritance—was by far the most common avenue to entrepreneurship for women of any race. Moreover, her appeal on behalf of black womanhood should be placed within the legacy of African-American women reformers that emerged at the end of the nineteenth century. This tradition included intellectuals and activists such as Frances Harper, Ida B. Wells, and Anna Julia Cooper. As Hazel Carby demonstrates, black women reformers in the late nineteenth and early twentieth centuries challenged the racist assumptions behind conventional notions of authentic femininity.[34] In doing so they articulated the unique predicament of black women, who were consistently denied access to the social authority and influence assigned to white women better able to fulfill the expectations prescribed by the cult of true womanhood.

Madam Walker, however, does not fit neatly into the tradition of black women intellectuals and activists. While self-taught, she was not an intellectual; although a philanthropist, she cannot rightly be called a middle-class reformer. Neither, as suggested throughout this essay, can Walker simply be assigned a role as disciple of Booker T. Washington's ethos of character-based and producer-oriented success. For these reasons discussions of black uplift after the turn of the twentieth century are inadequate without accounting for Madam Walker's conspicuous presence in segregated America. Even by 1912, the year of her memorable if unexpected appearance before the National Negro Business League, the black press reported that Walker trained as sales agents nationwide "not less than 1,600 people, women mainly."[35] At the following year's NNBL convention, Walker made the slightly more modest claim of having given "employment to more than 1000 women." Nevertheless, she could boast that her agents "are now making all the way from $5, $10, and even as high as $15 a day."[36] These numbers are put into perspective when it is understood that, at this time, unskilled white workers earned under $2 per day and few black women made more than $1.50 *per week*.[37]

Madam Walker was a race woman of the first order. In this regard, her uplift story is not her own. Conventional notions of American success, based on the individuated rags-to-riches story, fail to account for the impact of Walker's example on her community prior to desegregation. As a black American and as a woman, her ambition was bound to the progress of others attempting to work an advantage from the disadvantage. This is illustrated in the fact that, after her death, Walker's place within the popular memory of black America continued to climb. Prior to desegregation she was memorialized as a folk hero. In black newspapers and magazines she was cited repeatedly for her accomplishments as a Negro and a woman, a millionaire and a philanthropist. The readers of *Ebony*, for instance, in celebration of Black History Week during February of 1956, chose Madam Walker as their first inductee into the monthly magazine's Hall of Fame.[38]

Thirty years earlier journalist George S. Schuyler, writing in regard to Madam Walker but without his signature flair for satire, prophesied: "Undoubtedly history will record her as one of the great women of her time without regard to race or color." The only irony in the article appears unintentional: Schuyler sang the praises of the late, great capitalist in the socialist monthly *The Messenger*. His eulogy went so far as to exploit the enterprising language of rugged frontier individualism. Regarding her philanthropic efforts, "Madam Walker blazed the trail...among the members of her race." Regarding her entrepreneurial acumen, "she was the pioneer big business woman in the United States."[39]

Finally, however, Schuyler sounded the utopian impulse of socialism in his concluding remarks on Walker's legacy. "She was the herald of a new social order in which women will be independent and the oldest form of property will vanish forever."[40] Not merely a self-made millionaire and notable philanthropist, Madam Walker left future generations of women an inspirational inheritance. The paradox of her heritage was that it might inspire women to be less satisfied not only with their lot as wives but also as wage-earners within the Walker Manufacturing Company.

NOTES

1. A debt of gratitude is owed to A'Lelia Perry Bundles, the great-great-granddaughter of Madam C. J. Walker, who, at a crucial juncture in my research, provided me with valuable information regarding Walker's life. Bundles's biography, *Madam C. J. Walker* (New York: Chelsea House, 1991), published in a young reader's series called "Black Americans of Achievement," is the only book-length treatment of Walker's life to date.

2. *Report of the Thirteenth Annual Convention of the National Negro Business League* (Nashville: Sunday School Union Print, 1912), 154.

3. Ibid.

4. Louis R. Harlan, *The Booker T. Washington Papers: The Autobiographical Writings*, vol. 1 (Urbana: University of Illinois Press, 1972), xv.

5. See, for example, Felicity A. Nussbaum, *The Autobiographical Subject: Gender and Ideology in Eighteenth-Century England* (Baltimore: Johns Hopkins University Press, 1989).

6. *Report of the Thirteenth Annual Convention of the National Negro Business League*, 155.

7. Louis Harlan provides a discussion of Washington's limited role in the development of colonial Africa in *Booker T. Washington: The Wizard of Tuskegee, 1901–1915* (New York: Oxford University Press, 1983), 266–94. For an account of the "civilizationist" tradition within black nationalism, see Wilson Jeremiah Moses, *The Golden Age of Black Nationalism, 1850–1925* (New York: Oxford University Press, 1988).

8. W. E. B. DuBois, "Results of the Investigation," *The Negro in Business: A Social Study Made under the Direction of the Atlanta University by the Fourth Atlanta Conference*, ed. W. E. B. Du Bois (Atlanta: Press of Atlanta University, 1899), 5.

9. Ibid., 6.

10. Ibid., 15.

11. "Resolutions Adopted By the Conference," in *The Negro in Business*, 50.

12. *Report of the Thirteenth Annual Convention of the National Negro Business League*, 154.

13. For an analysis of black women's employment in the South at the turn of the century, see Jacqueline Jones, *Labor of Love, Labor of Sorrow: Black Women, Work, and the Family from Slavery to the Present* (New York: Basic Books, 1985).

14. *Report of the Thirteenth Annual Convention of the National Negro Business League*, 154–55.

15. The Indianapolis *Freeman* provided Walker extensive press coverage from the time she moved her business operations to Indiana in 1910 until her death in 1919. On this day, the newspaper ran three separate stories on Walker: the aforementioned front-page biography, which both opened by erroneously giving the day of her birth as December 25, 1867, and included a flattering photo of Walker over the caption: "The best known Hair Culturist in America"; a page-two photo-journalist piece depicting the operations of the Walker Manufacturing Company, Inc.; and, a page-four lifestyles article titled "Mme. C. J. Walker. A Review of a Remarkable Business Woman and her Brilliant Career."

16. Indianapolis *Freeman*, November 11, 1911, 1.

17. Decades after Madam Walker's death, rumors circulated concerning the belief that her first husband, Moses McWilliams, was the victim of a lynching. There is no factual evidence to support this claim. As A'Lelia Bundles suggests, given Walker's vocal support for the NAACP's antilynching campaign in the mid-teens, "one would think that she would have capitalized on such a life-defining event to help the cause." Nevertheless, the lynching of McWilliams is, Bundles remarks, a "plausible fiction given the era" (personal correspondence).

18. Indianapolis *Freeman*, November 11, 1911, 1.

19. Conventional gender assignments at NNBL gatherings are indicated in a 1909 open letter signed by Washington and addressed to black newspapers which advertised the upcoming tenth annual convention. While Washington "urge[d] the attendance of men and women of our race engaged in business throughout the country," he made a special plea to businessmen: "We hope that the men will not only be present in large numbers but, if possible, they will bring their

wives and other members of their families." See Indianapolis *Freeman*, July 3, 1909, 3.

20. *Report of the Fourteenth Annual Convention of the National Negro Business League* (Nashville: Sunday School Union Print, 1913), 210.

21. Ibid., 211.

22. During the same year, for example, one woman wrote her: "You have opened up a trade for hundreds of colored women to make an honest and profitable living where they make as much in one week as a month's salary would bring from any other position that a colored woman can secure." Cited in A'Lelia Perry Bundles, "Madam C. J. Walker—Cosmetics Tycoon," *Ms.* 11 (July 1983): 93.

23. *Report of the Fourteenth Annual Convention of the National Negro Business League*, 212.

24. Indianapolis *Freeman*, December 26, 1914, 1.

25. *Report of the Fifteenth Annual Convention of the National Negro Business League* (Nashville: Sunday School Union Print, 1914), 153.

26. *Report of the Seventeenth Annual Convention of the National Negro Business League* (Nashville: National Baptist Publishing Board, 1916), 134.

27. See Irvin G. Wyllie, *The Self-Made Man in America: The Myth of Rags to Riches* (New Brunswick, NJ: Rutgers University Press, 1954), 60.

28. Indianapolis *Freeman*, April 16, 1910, 2.

29. Cited in Bundles, "Madam C. J. Walker—Cosmetics Tycoon," 92.

30. *Report of the Fifteenth Annual Convention of the National Negro Business League*, 152.

31. ILDP quoted in Judith Stein, *The World of Marcus Garvey: Race and Class in Modern Society* (Baton Rouge: Louisiana State University Press, 1986), 50.

32. Denver *Post*, July 11, 1918, 13.

33. *Report of the Eighteenth and Nineteenth Annual Sessions of the National Negro Business League* (Nashville: Baptist Publishing Board, n.d.), 77.

34. Hazel V. Carby, *Reconstructing Womanhood: The Emergence of the Afro-American Woman Novelist* (New York: Oxford University Press, 1987).

35. Indianapolis *Freeman*, December 28, 1912, 16.

36. *Report of the Fourteenth Annual Convention of the National Negro Business League*, 210.

37. Bundles, *Madam C. J. Walker*, 15.

38. *Ebony* 11 (February 1956): 25.

39. George S. Schuyler, "Madam C. J. Walker," *The Messenger* 6 (August 1924): 257–58.

40. Ibid., 266.

9

FRIDA KAHLO
Life into Art

Hayden Herrera

BEGINNING IN 1926 when she painted her first *Self-Portrait* at the age of nineteen, and ending shortly before her death in 1954 with *Marxism Will Give Health to the Sick*, the Mexican painter Frida Kahlo produced some 66 self-portraits plus about 80 paintings of other subjects, mostly still lifes and portraits of friends. Her self-portraits record her birth, her childhood, her marriage to the muralist Diego Rivera, divorce and reconciliation, miscarriage, her sadness over not being able to bear children, and finally the misery of numerous surgical operations that never cured the injuries to her leg and spine from a bus accident that nearly killed her when she was eighteen.

It was the accident that made Kahlo take up painting. She was, as she put it, "bored as hell in bed," and she needed a way to help support her family. Pain and illness prompted a long dialogue with herself. To the extent that she painted for private purposes and that she was her principal audience, Kahlo's self-portraits form a kind of diary. "I paint my own reality," she once said. "The only thing that I know is that I paint because I need to, and I paint whatever passes through my head without any other consideration." Yet Kahlo had a public purpose as well: she wanted to make herself and her predicament known.

Her self-portraits demand our attention in subtle and manipulative ways.

They single out the viewer as the person who must share Kahlo's feelings. Yet, though they are sometimes shockingly personal, they do not offer a full confession. Gripped by Kahlo's intensity, the viewer comes to realize that the painter keeps her secrets. In addition, Kahlo's self-portraits express a need for connection and affirmation that recalls the feelings of rejected lovers and the long-term patients. Kahlo's first self-portrait, for example, was made in 1926 while recuperating from the accident and as a gift for her boyfriend, who was at that time trying to distance himself from her. It shows that painting herself was a way of attaching people to her, of holding their love. When she sent him this self-portrait, she wrote to her boyfriend, "I implore you to hang it in a low place where you can see it as if you were looking at me." Feeling isolated by illness, Frida Kahlo painted substitute Fridas that extended her being out into the world.

Self-portraits also served to confirm what Kahlo felt to be her tenuous hold on life. "Death dances around my bed at night," she wrote to a friend from the hospital after her accident. And as her body disintegrated over the years, the death embrace tightened. Perhaps Kahlo's motive for painting herself was not unlike that of many journal keepers and autobiographers: perhaps she wanted to give the fragmented, the chaotic, and the ephemeral a wholeness, order, and permanence, and to defy the meaningless abyss of lived time.

"I paint self-portraits," Kahlo said, "because I am so often alone, because I am the person I know best." The confinement of semi-invalidism led to a narrow focus. In practical terms, too, Kahlo's most accessible subject was, of course, herself. Her self-portraits reveal a self-fascination and a fixation on the body that often comes with illness. They also show a raw, gut-shuddering loneliness. Even when Kahlo appears with her husband, with herself, or with her pet monkeys, she presents herself to the viewer as a person who has no relationship to anything or anyone besides the viewer. Whether she situates herself in a desert landscape or in an empty room, Kahlo is cut off from her surroundings. There is nothing to which she is attached, except the object of her gaze, which is both us, the viewer, and Kahlo, since looking in the mirror or at her self-portraits in progress made Kahlo her chief viewer.

No doubt Kahlo's childhood experience with sickness had much to do with her aloneness: she never forgot her fear when witnessing her father's epileptic seizures which no one explained to her. Nor did she forget her struggle with polio at age seven. It left her with a deformed leg that made her the butt of other children's teasing. As a girl, Kahlo invented an imaginary companion. When she grew up that imaginary companion became herslf in self-portraits. In one of the loneliest paintings even painted, *The Two Fridas* (1939), Kahlo holds her own hand. Her world is self-enclosed. Her extracted hearts—a straight-forward symbol of pain in love—are linked by a vein; she is connected only to herself.

As the two Fridas stare down at us, they insist, almost angrily, that we share their suffering. Yet they are withholding, for even as Kahlo displays her wounds, she keeps her mask of stoic reserve. The rage in this self-portrait, and in many others, comes from a mixture of physical and emotional pain. Much of the emotional anguish was caused by Rivera's frequent philanderings and desertions. *The Two Fridas*, for example, was painted the year Rivera divorced Kahlo before remarrying her in 1940.

Kahlo recorded the twists and turns of her marriage beginning with *Diego and Frida Rivera* (1931), a wedding portrait painted two years after she married. Even at this early and relatively happy time, body language suggests Rivera's immense egotism and his unpossessability. Frida extends her arms to him: she had to play the constant seductress. Years later she said, "Being the wife of Diego is the most marvelous thing in the world…. I let him play matrimony with other women. Diego is not anybody's husband and never will be, but he is a great comrade."

Six years later in *Memory* (1937), she recalled her feeling of dislocation when Rivera had an affair with her favorite sister. Then came a great series of self-portraits from the year she was divorced, paintings like *Self-Portrait with Cropped Hair* (1940), in which she has taken out her rage by cutting off the long hair which Rivera adored. Even after she placed her marriage on a basis of mutual independence when she remarried Rivera in 1940, Kahlo's self-portraits show that she continued to want to possess her husband. In 1949 he left her again, this time because he wanted to marry her friend, the film star Mariá Félix. Now, in *Diego and I*, Kahlo depicted herself in tears. But later that year, when she and Rivera were reconciled, she painted her own rather desperate vision of marital contentment in a painting in which she and Rivera are sustained by a series of what she called "love embraces," and in which she revealed her discovery that the best way to hold on to Rivera was to indulge him as if he were a baby.

Being married to Rivera affected Kahlo's art in another way: Since he was the older and more famous artist, she chose an artistic identity that was the opposite of his. While he painted huge murals with broad historical and political themes on public walls, she painted self-portraits on small sheets of masonite or tin. Painting on a smaller scale, convenient for an invalid, also enhanced the intimacy of her subject matter.

Although she painted a few self-portraits in the first five years of her career, Kahlo's concentration on reproducing her own image really began in 1932 when, after a miscarriage, she decided to alleviate depression by painting the important moments in her life. Having recorded the horror and helplessness of miscarriage in *Henry Ford Hospital*, she then painted *My Birth*, which likewise reflects her despair over losing her child, this time by showing both herself and her mother as dead. Later Kahlo said that her childlessness was a force behind her art: "Painting completed my life. I lost three children…. Painting substituted for all of this. I believe work is the best thing." In *Roots* (1943), she painted a childless woman's dream in which her body opens up to give birth to a vine that extends her life sap into the parched Mexican earth. It may not be too far-fetched to suppose that, in part, Kahlo made self-portraits instead of making children. It was her way of recreating her self, of ensuring her physical continuance.

Kahlo went on with her life story with *My Nurse and I* (1937), which shows her as a baby held in the arms of her Indian wet nurse. Even as she declares her pride in her native roots, Kahlo's sense of separation is apparent in the nurse's unloving embrace. In *Girl with Death Mask,* painted the following year, Kahlo looks even lonelier and less protected. Possibly the skeleton mask alludes to her brush with death through polio.

Another reason to paint self-portraits was to create an alternate self, Frida the heroic sufferer as opposed to Frida the victim, Frida the flamboyant, beflowered, and beribboned creature—Rivera's beautiful foil—as opposed to Frida the ruined and abandoned one. As the years went on, Kahlo's self-image became one of fierce strength. Perhaps painting this strong woman was a kind of self-fortification: like whistling a happy tune to convince oneself that one is not afraid. Beyond that, communicating her suffering through bodily wounds rather than facial expression might have been a primitive way of exorcising pain by projecting it outward, visualizing it on the canvas rather than inside her own skin.

In the 1940s and 1950s Kahlo painted her response to surgery. *The Broken Column* (1944), presents her as a kind of Saint Sebastian, an idol for herself and others to worship. In *Tree of Hope*, painted two years later, she appears twice, Frida the savior and Frida the to-be-saved. This painting, she said, "is nothing but the result of the damned operations"—a spinal fusion which did not stop the gradual collapse of her spine. After a year in the hospital from 1950 to 1951, during which time she had some seven back operations, she produced *Self-Portrait with the Portrait of Dr. Farill*, made as a gift of gratitude to her surgeon. She painted it directly from her heart, she seems to say, for her very pigment is her heart set on a palette. "Dr. Farill saved me. He gave me back the joy of life," she wrote in her journal.

She clung to that joy, but her will to live was nearly broken when her right leg was amputated at the knee in 1953. "Feet what do I need them for if I have wings to fly?" she wrote in her journal below a drawing of her severed leg. Beside a drawing of herself toppling from a column she wrote, "I am disintegration." The last drawing in her diary is of a *black angel* and then the words, "I hope the exit is joyful and I hope never to come back." Kahlo's death in 1954 at the age of forty-four was reported as a pulmonary embolism. It is more likely that she died of an intentional drug overdose.

The story Kahlo told in self-portraits is powerfully moving, but has no movement; narrative is paralyzed, flicked on and off in a sequence of iconic stills. Kahlo does not act; she is acted upon. She is the victim of things done to her body, the victim and object of her own piercing regard. Yet, for all their stasis, Frida Kahlo's self-portraits seem to shake with life. That life is in Kahlo's eyes: they look into us and at her own image in the mirror in order to know it more.

WHOSE LIFE IS IT, ANYWAY?

○ Introduction

Barbara Johnson

Miss Rose thought she was writing a book about a writer dead thirty years and seems to have overlooked, as I say, the plain fact that she has ended up writing a book largely about me.

> —Ted Hughes, concerning Jacqueline Rose's book
> *The Haunting of Sylvia Plath*

Those words struck me like a blow. So I was *sold* at last! A human being *sold* in the free city of New York!

> —Harriet Jacobs, *Incidents in the Life of a Slave Girl*

Le desir de l'homme, c'est le desir de l'Autre.

> —Jacques Lacan

THERE ARE ALWAYS at least two people competing for control over the story of a life. Sometimes they are the biographer and the subject, sometimes the biographer and the guardians of the subject's estate. Even in autobiography, there is struggle between the retrospectively narrating self and the person, now gone, who once lived. And of course, the autobiography of a former slave offers the story of a life that has literally—or rather, legally—belonged to someone else.

Twenty years ago, the question of literary biography was marginalized in literary studies by a tendency to focus on the practice of reading the internal workings of literary texts. Freed from the control of origins and authorial intentions, the text became a playground for readers' ingenuity. As Roland Barthes famously proclaimed, "The birth of the reader must be at the cost of the death of the Author." Yet as recent biographers have come to discover, the death of the author sometimes results in the birth, not of the Reader, but of the Estate. One of the most fascinating cases of the struggle of an estate to control the rights to an author's life has recently been chronicled by Janet Malcolm in her book *The Silent Woman: Sylvia Plath and Ted Hughes.* (With at least five full-length lives of Plath published to date, the Plath case seems to illustrates the old adage that the number of biographies varies inversely with the cooperativeness of the estate.)

The interpretive freedom granted by Barthes to the reader is precisely what is bitterly resented by the survivors of Sylvia Plath, particularly her husband, Ted Hughes, from whom Plath was separated at the time of her suicide. Hughes complains:

> Critics established the right to say whatever they pleased about the dead. It is an absolute power, and the corruption that comes with it, very often, is an atrophy of the moral imagination. They move onto the living because they can no longer feel the difference between the living and the dead.[1]

In other words, to interpret is to treat as dead, perhaps even to kill. Barthes was right.

Yet the living go on claiming the right to control the story. "I hope each of us owns the facts of her or his own life," protests Hughes, to which Janet Malcolm responds:

> But, of course, as everyone knows who has ever heard a piece of gossip, we do not "own" the facts of our lives at all. This ownership passes out of our hands at birth, at the moment we are first observed. (p. 8)

To be observed is to be dispossessed: our lives are precisely what we can never own. Knowledge of them is always already the other's. Yet Janet Malcolm goes on to compare biography to burglary, which suggests that, whoever owns the life, the biographer always seizes it transgressively. What this implies is that the biographer does indeed steal, but what is stolen is something not owned. That is perhaps why there is so much struggle around it.

The papers in this section offer fascinating versions of this struggle to control life stories. Whether the subject is "exorbitantly forthcoming" like Anne Sexton or "rebuffing and rebuking" like Jesusa Palancares, the biographer is forced to confront her own desire in the making of the text. Diane Middlebrook analyzes the ethics of disclosure both in the case of Anne Sexton, a woman with no sense of privacy, and in the case of Billy Tipton, a woman who passed as a man for more than fifty years. Doris Sommer analyzes the politics of cross-class curiosity in Elena Poniatowska's testimonial novel, *Till We Meet Again, Dear Jesus*. Jean Yellin meticulously proves that Harriet Jacobs was the author of *Incidents in the Life of a Slave Girl*, and, in the process, discovers that Jacobs's original public knew perfectly well who she was, that ignorance of Jacobs' authorship was caused by historical forgetting, not authorial reticence. While Yellin constructs the biography of an autobiographer, Phyllis Rose creates the autobiography of a biographer, revealing the ways in which, in writing the lives of others, she was processing her own life struggles, coming to grips with her desire as political and her politics as desire. Indeed, all of these essays suggest that in biography, the life you steal may be your own.

It is no accident that these narratives in which the question of the owner-ship of life is raised with such acuity should all be narratives about the lives of women. It is as though it is unimaginable *not* to ask who owns a woman, whether she can be penetrated, whether she can be known and by whom. The words "embarrassment" and "guilt" occur in all four essays in conjunc-tion with the politics of women's bodies and women's knowledge, particu-larly in cases of cross-race and cross-class curiosity and resistance. In very different ways, these subtle and provocative essays explore the politics of embarrassment and the embarrassment of politics in the desire to "take a life."

NOTES

1. Ted Hughes, letter to Jacqueline Rose, quoted in Janet Malcolm, *The Silent Woman* (New York: Alfred A. Knopf, 1994), 46–47.

(10)

TELLING SECRETS

Diane Wood Middlebrook

THE PUBLICATION of my biography of Anne Sexton in 1991 prompted a controversy, surprising to me, about ethical obligations of biographers toward their subjects. The precipitating event was a news story announcing that one of Anne Sexton's psychiatrists had provided me access to over 300 hours of taped psychotherapy sessions.[1] The journalist interviewed a number of medical ethicists who claimed that the doctor had violated a fundamental ethical principle governing the conduct of psychiatry: the necessity of protecting doctor/patient confidentiality. A formal complaint was then filed by a colleague in the American Psychiatric Association, a complaint that was considered by the profession's ethics committee for two years before the charges were dropped. The defining issue was whether Sexton had given informed consent to disclosure of her records.

This was not a lawsuit; far from it: the Sexton estate had agreed in advance to provide me, as biographer, with every sort of documentation of Sexton's medical treatment, including the therapy tapes in Sexton's own possession at the time of her death. The doctor had simply complied with the estate's policy. Moreover, when the book was ready for publication, the two parties (doctor and estate) developed a written agreement concerning eventual deposit of the tapes in a research archive. All legal issues in the case were settled with exemplary cooperation in advance of the publication of the biography. But that did not prevent the doctor from becoming embroiled in very severe charges of ethical misconduct. Ethical disputes are not the same as legal disputes.

I was not personally charged with ethical misconduct, but it seems that not much by way of ethical conduct is expected of biographers anyway. Or so I gathered from an editorial in the *New York Times*, in which the biography of Anne Sexton was held up as an cautionary example. The psychiatrist was condemned for releasing the tapes, but allowances were made for the author. "Middlebrook did what any biographer would do," said the *New York Times*; "[she] rose to the opportunity as the trout to the fly...."

The barb of truth prompted some self-examination. What ethical considerations had guided my decisions about what to say in that book, and what not to say? Would the same moral reasoning apply in the context of my new project, the biography of Billy Tipton, a female jazz musician who had passed successfully as a man for fifty years? Prior to the publicity I had not thought about this in the abstract, and I am not sure that my retrospective insights can in fact be generalized. All ethical conflicts, like all politics, are local. Moreover, I speculate that the ethical perspective in a biography is largely an aspect of its rhetorical mode, part of the constructed eloquence of its appeal to a community of peers.

But instructed by my proximity to the professional ordeal of Sexton's psychiatrist, I find some analogies between questions posed by medical ethicists and the questions that rise from the work of producing a biography. Chiefly, does a version of the principle of informed consent extend to biography? That is, suppose a biographer knows the subject's wishes in the matter of disclosure: is the biographer ethically obliged to respect those wishes? And is there any biographer's equivalent to the firm rule of doctor/patient confidentiality, any kind of information that is always unethical for a biographer to disclose?

That first question has to do with the ethics of the relationship between biographer and subject—or better, since we are speaking about disclosure—to the subject's secrets. The case of Anne Sexton offers a nicely complicated set of issues for ethical contemplation in this regard. She was classified, somewhat scornfully by critics, as one of the American postwar "confessional" poets, artists who wrote candidly about experiences of the kind many people thought should be kept entirely private. She described her mental illness, hospitalizations, and addictions; just as unusual in those days of the early 1960s, she wrote about women's experiences of intimacy with men, with other women, and with children. A short list of titles can convey the kinds of embarrassment Sexton's poetry caused: "For John, Who Begs Me Not to Enquire Further," "The Abortion," "Housewife," "For the Year of the Insane," "Menstruation at Forty," "Wanting to Die," "Cripples and Other Stories," "The Addict," "In Celebration of My Uterus," "For My Lover Returning to His Wife," "The Ballad of the Lonely Masturbator," and so forth.

Though Sexton's poetry conveyed a life of catastrophes and melodramas, she managed her professional life very purposefully. She won large audiences for her work, and also received all the major literary prizes available to American poets. And during the year preceding her suicide at age 45, she carefully organized her literary estate. She employed a secretary to organize her manuscripts and other personal papers; she consulted literary scholars about appointing an executor, and she wrote a will specifying her intentions. She named her elder daughter Linda as the executor of her will; I speculate that Sexton delayed committing suicide until Linda was twenty-one so that her daughter could step immediately into that role.

Young as she was, Linda Sexton proved to be very businesslike in handling the estate. She oversaw the publication of the books left in manuscript; edited a collection of letters, then sold the papers to the Harry Ransom Humanities Research Center at the University of Texas; and undertook a search for a biographer. Linda Sexton wished to be proactive in the matter of encouraging a serious book to be written about her mother's messy life; she intended to appoint an academic critic with the credentials to evaluate Anne Sexton's place in literature and she wished to appoint someone who had never met Anne Sexton.

These were reasonable criteria but they also reflected personal agenda of Linda Sexton, for Anne Sexton had already appointed a biographer, eleven years before her death. This was Lois Ames, a psychiatric social worker. At the time Sexton met her, Ames was under contract to write a biography of Sylvia Plath, with the promise of cooperation from the Plath estate. That book was never written. Instead, Ames became a close friend, traveling companion, helpmeet, and confidant of Anne Sexton. But as literary executor Linda was under no legal compulsion to carry out her mother's wishes. When she offered the project to me, I knew nothing about Lois Ames's prior claims.

Sexton's biography—a dream project for someone who had recently undergone an intellectual resocialization by feminist scholarship—was an opportunity that I would not have passed up in any case. Anne Sexton did not claim to be a feminist herself, but she was a leader of the pack nonetheless, as one of the first American poets whose bold art made feminist issues accessible to middle-class white women. And Linda Sexton guaranteed me that no aspect of her mother's life would be off-limits. Our contract granted me not only full editorial autonomy over the book, but exclusive access to every scrap of material in the archive, including the materials pertaining to Sexton's psychotherapy that later became so controversial: Sexton's own reels of therapy tapes and her transcriptions of them; copies of hospital records; letters to and from Sexton's doctors; and other documentation of medical treatment. Sexton had placed these materials among her literary papers with the apparent intention of putting them on record. While Linda Sexton reserved the right to withhold permission to quote unpublished materials, she believed the biographer should be able to consult these confidential papers for background and, where they had explanatory power, to make use of them. "My mother had no sense of privacy," Linda told me, "and I don't believe it's my place to construct one on her behalf."

By this remark Linda Sexton meant me to understand, among other things, that she herself did have a sense of privacy and intended to exercise it on behalf of the survivors, including her sister, her father, and her children; but that she respected the difference between her mother and herself in this regard, and meant to honor it. So I had in Anne Sexton an unusually cooperative estate and an exorbitantly forthcoming subject. As a consequence, the ethical problems that the Sexton material presented lay mostly in the field of feelings that psychoanalysis labels countertransference: how to deal with the intense disapproval I often felt precisely because of the predilection for self-exposure so prominent in her character?

Sexton's attitudes toward privacy, I found, had been greatly influenced by the sense of bodily shame she carried from childhood. One of the symptoms of her illness was a pathological self-disgust; one of the cures was unidealizing self-acceptance, which she gained through many years of hard work in psychotherapy. Dismantling an exaggerated aversion to her body was liberating to Sexton, and she carried her insights into poetry.

Writing Sexton's biography required a moral re-education: I learned to recognize the temptation to interpret as pathology behavior I didn't like. Then I could distinguish from her follies Sexton's achievements as a disciplined artist who believed that the whole purpose of art is the disclosure of what is REAL—a word she often wrote in capital letters. As she said once to an interviewer who was shocked by the autobiographical content of her play, "I can invade my own privacy. That's my right. It's embarrassing for someone to expose their body to you. You don't learn anything from it. But if they expose their soul, you learn something. That's true of great writers. They expose their souls; then suddenly I am moved, and I understand my life better."[2]

Nonetheless, I discovered that there were limits even to Sexton's investment in self-exposure. While organizing her papers back in 1973, Sexton had taken pains to mark on a green cardboard file, in large letters in bold black pen, NEVER TO BE SEEN BY ANYBODY BUT LOIS AMES. NEVER TO BE PUBLISHED; then she signed and dated the folder. When Linda Sexton sold the papers to the University of Texas in 1980 she held back this one file. In 1985 she changed her mind, sent the file to Texas, and placed it under restriction: no one may look at the file without her written permission. Of course she had looked in it first; and what she found had made her think twice about what the inscription meant. "Never to be published" was easy enough to understand, but what about the reference to the eyes of Lois Ames? By 1985 Ames had become generic, so to speak; there was now little likelihood that Ames would undertake a book about Sexton, and if she did, she would now need Linda Sexton's permission to read this very file inscribed with her name. So Anne Sexton's written instructions could be interpreted as referring not to the person but the role she had assigned Ames, the role of biographer—that was me!

In my next visit to the Sexton collection in Texas, armed with a note from Linda, the thing I most wanted to see was this tatty green file. After spending six years of intermittent drudgery in that familiar room, I fully savored the drama of the moment. Sitting with the file unopened in my hand, the only piece of forbidden fruit in the entire archive, I took my time, speculating about what it could possibly contain.

Like Linda, I had no intention of obeying the wishes Anne Sexton wrote down, signed and dated in 1973. This is my reasoning: the dead cannot have wishes, they can only have wills, and wills delegate the responsibility for making decisions. I shared Linda Sexton's view that her mother apparently wished to withhold nothing from her biographer. But I do not believe that such a conception of one's subject constitutes an ethical justification—quite the opposite. Claiming to know what the dead would have wanted is usually a self-serving ploy of interested parties, I have found. Thus what Sexton's attitude might have been toward my use of any materials whatsoever—including the therapy tapes—is a meaningless question, in my view, because the dead cannot be asked to make contextual judgments as the living can. And though the dead cannot be consulted, they can also not be shamed or in any way hurt by disclosures about what really happened to them, as the living can. What the biographer owes the subject is very like what the psychoanalyst owes the analysand upon encounter with hidden material: not judgment, but insight. I read the green file, and I wrote about what I found in it, on page 66 of the biography.

Similar issues inhabit the estate of my current subject, Billy Tipton. Salient facts can be summarized very quickly: As a teenager, Dorothy Tipton began cross-dressing in order to get a job with a band. She cut her hair, bound her breasts with torn sheets, put on men's clothes and re-christened herself Billy. The customers in the clubs didn't know that the saxophone player was actually a girl, but the other band members did—this was 1934, the Depression, everybody needed a job; and this was jazz, too. In her mid-twenties, Tipton went on the road and, while she stayed in touch with her brother and her cousins who continued to think of her as Dorothy, to everybody else and for the rest of her life, she was Billy—and Billy was "he."

Tipton established himself as the leader of a trio that traveled constantly: to Kansas City, Joplin, Amarillo, Santa Barbara, Portland, Seattle, and finally Spokane, Washington, where he settled down. Eventually he took over a booking agency and stopped playing music. During his twenty years as an itinerant musician—1935 to 1955—he appears to have made at least four successful common-law marriages. After he settled in Spokane, he legally married a stripper named Kitty whom he met in the night club where his trio played. She quit the business and they adopted three children, and became utterly conventional good citizens, active members of the PTA and the Boy Scouts. Everybody—band members, clients, wives, and sons—was amazed to discover, only after Tipton was dead and the corpse examined, that Tipton had a woman's body. As one of his sons put it in a TV interview, however, "He'll always be Dad to me." After interviewing a number of people close to Tipton, including three of the wives, I have found no cause to doubt their claims that they really believed he was a man.

Billy Tipton too left a will, naming his divorced wife Kitty as executor. In it he disclosed none of his secrets. But if I should ever find a document in which Tipton left an explicit request not to publish any of the sorts of information my research has uncovered, I believe that my proper and ethical relationship to that document would be, not to carry out the instructions, but to figure out where they fit into the puzzle of Tipton's character and into the social conditions that made possible this lifelong masquerade. I think of my files on the life of Billy Tipton, filling up slowly as a cistern, as a catchment area for investigating contemporary society's deeply held ideas about sex difference.

I believe that all records left by the dead, whether intentionally or unintentionally, are a legacy with absolute value of the kind that might best be understood under the legal definition of "cultural property." This definition holds that culture has an interest in the products and documentation of human activity, and that individual ownership claims recede with the passage of time. Once a person's lifework is terminated by death, the circumstances surrounding the life and the work can be asked every kind of question.

Then is there any kind of information that is always unethical for a biographer to use? The answer is yes, two kinds. One is the kind frequently found today in genres that blend historical writing with fiction, and offer speculation disguised as information. Possibly the most egregious example ever published is Joe McGinniss' *The Last Brother*, a life of Senator Edward M. Kennedy. McGinniss never interviewed Kennedy; instead, he composed and quoted as direct discourse a number of interior monologues commenting on family tragedies. A journalist whose previous métier was the so-called "true crime story," McGinniss claimed to be expanding the resources of biography by "novelizing" the genre. This is the biographical equivalent of glow on the face of the fashion model bestowed by the Scitex computer retouching system: art undetectably intervening where actuality is claimed.[3] But McGinniss' book was a dud, possibly because genre works like a default system in the reader's contact with a book. In a work of fiction (remembering Aristotle), we want to hear about things happening the way they ought to have happened. With biography, we want to know that these things happened even when the life reads as if it had been conducted in a novel.

The other thing biographers should not do is invade the privacy of the living, remembering that what is ethical is not the same as what is legal. Nonetheless, biographers are often brought to reflect upon ethical questions by taking hard knocks from legal ones; legal guidance is especially helpful in the question of rights to privacy. The U.S. Supreme Court articulated a useful concept for biographers in its 1965 finding that the Bill of Rights provides citizens a "penumbra of privacy" protecting relationships in which the privacy of communication is an essential element. This ruling applied to professional confidentiality, but the principle extends to ethical ground as well, in my view. Citizens give up some of their privacy rights when they enter into relationships with public figures of the sort that biographers tend to write about, and yet I believe any biographer is ethically obliged to bear in mind the notion of the penumbra of privacy when writing a representation of any living person. When biographers discover information compromising to the living, they should take pains to avoid inflicting harm. They should ask for permission to use the information; if permission is refused, they should disguise identities; if they cannot disguise identity they should forebear to disclose hurtful findings until the person's death has made them harmless.

Having drifted this from the excruciating particulars of real choices, the only kinds of conflict that can decently be labeled ethical, I will now go all the way, and end thumpingly with a motto. Too witty to sound entirely high-minded, too general for application in specific instances, the following motto nonetheless captures a view essential to ethical conduct in the practice of biography as I understand it: "We must respect the living," says Voltaire, somewhere, "but only truth is good enough for the dead."

NOTES

1. Alessandra Stanley, "Poet Told All; Therapist Provides the Record," *New York Times*, July 15, 1991, 1.
2. Anne Sexton, quoted by Beatrice Berg, "Oh, I Was Very Sick," *New York Times*, November 9, 1969, D7.
3. See Mary Tannen, "That Scitex Glow," *New York Times Magazine*, July 10, 1994, 44–45.

CONFESSIONS OF
A BURNED-OUT
BIOGRAPHER

Phyllis Rose

I AM SORRY to say that I want to write about myself. That is the mark of the burned-out biographer. The burned-out biographer is no longer willing to suppress herself in the service of another. She no longer wants to express indirectly in terms of the narrative of another's life the burning issues of her own. That interrogation by the self of another which animates a good biography no longer works. The self wants center stage, the whole enchilada.

If you believe the myth of objective fact and objective biography, the self is not supposed to be in biography at all. Journalists and other positivists who turn to biography tend to regard any uncertainty about truth, any concern with subjectivity, as academic waffling. Of course the truth can be known! Of course it exists apart from the perceiving self! It exists in hard little nuggets which are to be dug up from the surrounding matter, arranged in chronological order, and presented in as great numbers as possible. This is the ideal of one school of biography, what I'd call the objective school. Another, which I call the school of literary biography, whether or not the subject is a literary figure, tends to see all facts as artifacts and to see context and argument as co-partners of fact. But this school does not have the public's respect. This is not what biography *is*, popularly understood. The public—as we have seen in various legal decisions—distrusts artfulness in nonfiction and sees little difference between arranging and condensing and outright lying.

What I want to talk about is not so much the subjective nature of biography as the cost to the biographer of that subjectivity. And since I don't want to implicate anyone else, I will talk about my own case.

My first biography was *Woman of Letters: A Life of Virginia Woolf*. This book began with a love of Virginia Woolf's novels and a fascination with the connections between them and her life. At the time I began the book, around 1970, not so much was known about Virginia Woolf's life. I worked with her unedited and unpublished diaries, which had recently been acquired by the Berg Collection of the New York Public Library. I took her feminism seriously, as almost no previous writer had done. My very simple idea was that being a woman was important to Virginia Woolf and that this had affected the writing of her novels. For example, my take on Mrs. Ramsay of *To the Lighthouse* was different from that of most previous critics because how I saw her was influenced by what I knew about Woolf's ambivalent feelings towards her mother, on whom Mrs. Ramsay was based.

I had not really set out to write a biography, but a series of readings of the novels framed by biographical material that would support my argument. When people started reading the manuscript, however, they called it my biography of Virginia Woolf. I was surprised to find that what I had been writing was biography, but I immediately decided this was a good thing. I liked the field I had backed into so unknowingly, I could see the advantages. Principally, at a time when literary criticism in the academy insisted that attention to anything outside the text itself was illegitimate, biography gave me permission to invoke a context for literary works. It was as though I had been given a Pass Go Free card. I could bypass New Criticism. I could bypass deconstruction. I could bypass theory. I had no temperamental affinity for the various orthodoxies which have prevailed in English Departments for the past twenty-five years, and biography was my excuse for avoiding them. Biography, in fact, saved my professional life. I was grateful and became a proselytizer for it, urging other people to use biography as a way of doing scholarly work.

As I was writing *Woman of Letters* I was unaware of my theme, and I did not—except fitfully—identify with Virginia Woolf. I only knew that I was writing with urgency and passion. The work meant something to me, even if I didn't know what. Later, when the book was in the past, I understood that I had used Virginia Woolf to work out issues that were urgently important to me at the time—issues of autonomy, selfhood, independence, and their relationship to gender. The book that established my professional viability and identity was itself about identity and viability. I believe now that identification with my subject provided the motive and force needed to write the book which, like all projects that take years to complete, required powerful motivation. I believe now that every biography in some way provides psychic food for the biographer, probably by allowing the biographer to float in and out of the fantasy that she is her subject, allowing the biographer in fantasy to appropriate parts of the subject's life.

By the time *Woman of Letters* was published, I had been divorced for three years after a ten-year marriage. I was obsessed with marriage as a formative institution and decided to write a book about marriage, using Victorian writers for my examples because I had been a specialist in the nineteenth-century British novel. My model was Lytton Strachey's *Eminent Victorians*, extended portraits of individuals in the service of a vision of Victorian culture. My book, *Parallel Lives*, focused on the marriages of five Victorian writers—Carlyle, Ruskin, Mill, George Eliot, and Dickens—and it suggested that parallels exist between the marriages of my Victorians and marriages today. What exactly these parallels were I left up to readers to discover for themselves, but throughout, in my telling the story of these marriages, I emphasized the shifting current of power between a man and a woman tied by marriage. That power was an issue in marriage was the underlying message of *Parallel Lives*.

With this book I *was* aware of the connection to my own life. I congratulated myself on how discreetly I was telling the story of my own marriage and divorce. I thought frequently of Oscar Wilde's aphorism, "Criticism is the only civilized form of autobiography," amending it just a bit to "Biography is the only civilized form of autobiography." If Flaubert said, "*Mme. Bovary, c'est moi,*" I could say, "*Jane Carlyle, c'est moi. George Eliot, c'est moi. Harriet Taylor, c'est moi. Et Charles Dickens, c'est moi aussi.*"

About then, I started getting asked from time to time to speak on panels about biography. Often I felt spurious in such gatherings: a little voice inside me said the kind of biography I did was not *real* biography. Real biography went to the Hall of Records and the cemetery, while I went to the library. Real biography did more interviews than I did. Real biography discovered that So-and-so was born in 1906 rather than 1912, or that X was hospitalized for depression in the 1950s, despite his public air of equanimity, or that Y couldn't face the day without drinking a half bottle of gin before noon, or that Z had left his wife and family every Sunday night to frequent gay bathhouses. Whereas I merely found new contexts—Virginia Woolf in the context of her feminism, Dickens et al. in the context of their marriages. It occurred to me that the little voice inside my head saying "You're not a real biographer" had to be a cousin of the angel in the house Virginia Woolf imagined, who stood behind women writers saying, "You can't write," an internalization of patriarchal ham-stringing. But this realization didn't help.

Soon after *Parallel Lives* was published in 1983, I began work on a biography of Josephine Baker, the African-American dancer born in St. Louis in 1906, who took Paris by storm in 1925 and went on to become the first international black superstar. The idea for this book was born when I saw a travel poster in the Paris Metro advertising the glories of New York City by the image of a large black man on roller skates carrying a portable stereo. He was not African American, I felt sure, but African, Senegalese probably, and the image—so little likely to serve as an ad for New York in the United States—crystallized for me, with mingled rue and pleasure, how much fantasy there was in the French fascination with American blacks. My book about Josephine Baker was to be as much about the racial ideologies that lay behind and prepared for her triumph in Europe in the twenties—both enthusiastic primitivism and proto-Nazi racism—as it was about her individual life. Biography's bias toward the individual life increasingly frustrated me. I was more interested in representative lives, lives that resonated because of issues of class, race, or gender. Josephine Baker gave me a chance to talk about the way France had functioned as a place of escape for African-Americans and the way the French in turn had mythologized the black American experience. I had used biography as a cover for literary criticism in the Virginia Woolf book; now I was using it as a cover for cultural history.

My material for this book was radically different from the material I had used to write about Virginia Woolf or the Victorians. To me, this was part of the appeal of the project. No diaries, no vast and many-sided correspondence existed for Josephine Baker as for my literary subject. Photographs became primary texts—not just for the information they gave me about her performances and her packaging, but also because of the psychological revelations contained in these records of her self-presentation. I spent a great deal of time, for example, looking at pictures of her cross-eyed mugging, which seemed to me at the heart of her personality. I read that gesture as exhaustively as one might read a poem. I saw it as part of a tradition of blank comedy that was simultaneously ingratiating and subversive. I saw in it the clowning of kids who have low self-esteem and goof their way to popularity. I saw in it the attempt of someone who was used to being an object of sexual attention to deflect the erotic gaze of her audience, sort of a hex sign. I saw it as part of a strategy of identifying with the aggressor, coopting face-making rages, turning them into a joke—the characteristic gesture of an expatriate, someone who leaves before she can be kicked out, someone who makes faces before faces can be made at her.

In every book, for me, there is a personal involvement, some kind of psychic nurturing, the nature of which is sometimes not clear until after the book is finished. But even now I find it difficult to say plainly what was, at a deep level, in it for me in writing about Josephine Baker: not because I don't know, or at least suspect, but because I find it so embarrassing. I'll say it allusively. I wanted to prove and to explore my own freedom. On one level, the assertion of freedom is clear in the very choice of Josephine Baker after literary figures like Virginia Woolf and Charles Dickens. In writing about Baker, I was saying that I do not want to be categorized. I want to prove that I can write about other than literary figures. But the freedom I wanted to explore was more specifically a sexual freedom. At the deepest level Baker appealed to me because she seemed, in a dated phrase I can't seem to improve on, to be a liberated woman. If *Woman of Letters* was the book of my twenties and autonomy, if *Parallel Lives* was the book of my marriage, this was to be the book of my mastery. Like Josephine Baker arrayed in ostrich feathers and rhinestones, it was to be celebratory.

At the time I was aware only that I wanted change. My life felt too predictable, and I longed for a spontaneity I felt I had lost. In concrete ways, writing about Baker brought me new interests and new sources of vitality. I took tap-dancing lessons. I started listening to jazz. I did research at the Schomburg Center, in what for me was a new and exciting part of New York—Harlem. Later, my research took me to Paris for half a year. Here I got something new in a big way, and I met the man who's now my husband. All thanks to Josephine Baker! Such are the payoffs of biography!

But since I was as much concerned with the European racial mythologies that prepared her success as I was with Josephine Baker, it did not take me long to realize that in appropriating what I saw as the spontaneity and even the sexuality of my subject, since I am white and she was black, I was reenacting in my own person the phenomenon I had set out to describe. The awareness made me rigid with self-consciousness and self-accusation. Only the most dire financial necessity kept me going, the knowledge that I could not afford to waste two years of work and that I had accepted an advance I could not afford to repay. I proceeded and completed the book only through willpower and a sense of responsibility, the qualities I had set out to short-circuit. For a long time after I could look at the book with no pleasure: it seemed to me the best that intelligence and discipline could produce, but what I had intended was something different, something more explosive.

I have come by my own route to a point Janet Malcolm makes brilliantly in her *New Yorker* piece "The Silent Woman," which moves from examining biographies of Sylvia Plath to an allegorical vision of the transgressive nature of biography:

> The biographer at work is like the professional burglar, breaking into a house, rifling through certain drawers that he has good reason to think contain the jewelry and money, and triumphantly bearing his loot away. The voyeurism and busybodyism that impel writers and readers of biography alike are obscured by an apparatus of scholarship designed to give the enterprise an appearance of banklike blandness and solidity. The biographer is portrayed almost as a kind of benefactor. He is seen as sacrificing years of his life to his task, tirelessly sitting in archives and libraries and patiently conducting interviews with witnesses. There is no length he will not go to, and the more his book reflects his industry the more the reader believes that he is having an elevating literary experience, rather than simply listening to backstairs gossip and reading other people's mail. The transgressive nature of biography is rarely acknowledged, but it is the only explanation for biography's status as a popular genre.[1]

What Malcolm says is intentionally harsh and extreme. There are other ways to explain biography's status as a popular genre—solace, for example, narrative appeal, and even perhaps a disinterested desire for information. And to say biography is *like* theft is not to prove it is theft. But there is a largely unacknowledged truth at the heart of what she says.

You may have noticed that the kind of biographer Janet Malcolm describes is not my kind of biographer. He or she is the person who finds out that the devoted family man spent every Sunday night at the gay bathhouse or that he drank a pint of gin before lunch. This is the biographer as miner (if not thief), one who is out to dig up facts, preferably scandalous. But if what I've been saying is true—that at the heart of the biographer's motivation is some act of personal appropriation, some sort of psychic exploitation—then the enterprise of the literary biographer is equally transgressive, equally a metaphoric theft, equally suspect. In some sense each biographer in a different way exploits his or her subject. Which does not mean we should close down biography, but it means that some of us, perhaps too aware of the morally tenuous nature of our enterprise, will pay the price of our art in guilt. Some of us may even close ourselves down.

NOTES

1. Janet Malcolm, "The Silent Woman," *The New Yorker* 69 (23–30 August, 1993), 86.

Incidents IN THE LIFE
OF HARRIET JACOBS

Jean Fagan Yellin

CONCEIVING AN AUTOBIOGRAPHY marks an era in a writer's life; the decisions involved in writing that autobiography present the author with multiple possibilities. When Harriet Ann Jacobs, the slave narrator of *Incidents in the Life of a Slave Girl: Written by Herself*, decided to tell her story in 1853, the decision signalled a major change in her life. The process of writing her life presented new challenges—especially concerning the creation of herself as a literary subject, and the negotiation of the private and the political aspects of her experience. In *Incidents*, Jacobs presents a version of her life in the words of a first-person pseudonymous narrator "Linda Brent," whose story argues a unique perspective on race, condition, and gender in nineteenth-century America. Like the conception of an autobiography, its publication also marks an era in a writer's life. For Jacobs, the appearance of *Incidents* in 1861 signalled her open participation in public discourse. Throughout the Civil War and the early years of Reconstruction, Jacobs used her new public voice to engage in journalistic debate concerning the major political issues of the day.[1]

Harriet Ann Jacobs was born in Edenton, North Carolina, about 1813, the grandaughter of Molly Horniblow (slave of Elizabeth Horniblow), the daughter of Elijah (slave of Dr. Andrew Knox) and of Delilah (slave of Margaret Horniblow). Although as chattel, Harriet became the property of Margaret Horniblow at birth, she was permitted to live at home with her parents, and in early childhood she did not know herself to be a slave. When she was six, her mother died and she was taken in by her owner who treated her kindly and, despite the laws, taught her to read and spell. When Harriet was twelve, Horniblow died. Instead of being freed as she had expected, Harriet was willed to Horniblow's three-year-old niece and sent into the little girl's home, where she was sexually harrassed by the child's middle-aged father, Dr. James Norcom. At sixteen, in a desperate effort to prevent Norcom from forcing her into concubinage, she became pregnant by a neighbor, the young white attorney Samuel T. Sawyer. Norcom's wife, who apparently thought Norcom had fathered Harriet's baby, threw her out of the house. Worse, Harriet's recently-freed grandmother Molly Horniblow, the emotional and moral center of the teenager's life, also condemned her. Although grandmother and granddaughter were soon reconciled and Harriet moved into Molly's house, the older woman offered her pity, but not forgiveness.[2]

Over the next few years, Harriet Jacobs bore a son and a daughter by Sawyer. In her early twenties, she was again threatened with concubineage by Norcom, and she again rejected him. To punish her, he sent her from town to a nearby plantation. In June, 1835, learning that he planned to move her children from Grandmother's house to the country and to "break them in" as plantation slaves, Jacobs devised a plan. She would run away, Norcom would want to rid himself of her troublesome children, and their father would buy and free them. Some parts of her scheme worked. She did run away, Norcom did sell the children, and Sawyer did buy them. But while he permitted the children to live with Jacobs's grandmother, he did not free them, and with the town under close watch by Norcom and the town constable, Jacobs was unable to escape North. Over the summer, she hid with friends. Her family then concealed her, first in a swamp and later in a tiny attic in Grandmother's home. Not until 1842, almost seven years later, did Jacobs reach the North, where she was ultimately reunited with her daughter and her son. Even in New York, however, she was hunted by the Norcoms. Especially after passage of the 1850 Fugitive Slave Law, she feared kidnapping both for herself and for her children, particularly for her daughter, now a young woman. In 1852, after yet another threat from slavecatchers, Jacobs was bought by her Northern employer, Cornelia Grinnell Willis. She and her children were finally safe.

Harriet Jacobs was a nineteenth-century woman, and in her America, women did not routinely write their sexual history. Jacobs's treatment of this taboo subject in *Incidents in the Life of a Slave Girl* is extraordinary. She breaks the silence surrounding women's sexual experience, and she chronicles a sexual history that does not conform to social norms. In doing so, she presents an unique analysis and critique of women's sexual roles in nine-teenth-century America.

In a set piece in *Incidents*, "Linda," Jacobs's pseudonymous narrator, describes two socially constructed patterns of female sexual behavior in the South. Showing that these patterns are linked and that they are mirror images of each other, she makes clear that they are race-specific and condition-specific:

> I once saw two beautiful children playing together. One was a fair white child; the other was her slave, and also her sister…. The fair child grew up to be a still fairer woman…. Scarcely one day of her life had been clouded when the sun rose on her happy bridal morning.
>
> How had those years dealt with her slave sister, the little playmate of her child-hood? She, also, was very beautiful; but the flowers and sunshine of love were not for her. She drank the cup of sin, shame, and misery, whereof her persecuted race are compelled to drink. (p. 29)

In this passage, the free white woman who conforms to society's demand that she be virginal before marriage and monogamous afterward, and the enslaved black women who is denied both virginity and marriage by that same society, are seen as sisters.

How did Harriet Jacobs come to make this analysis? How did she decide to write her sexual history, which centers on the forbidden topic of the rela-tionship of the institution of chattel slavery to women's sexual roles? In *Incidents*, "Linda" reports that she had learned to be silent about her sexual experiences not only in the slave South, where she was condemned by both Grandmother and Mrs. Norcom, but also in the free North. She writes that upon reaching Philadelphia in 1842, she reacted strongly after being cau-tioned by a sympathetic male black abolitionist with whom she had shared her past:

> "don't answer every body so openly. It might give some heartless people a pre-text for treating you with contempt."
>
> That word *contempt* burned me like coals of fire. (pp. 160–61)

Jacobs determined to tell no one of her past. After seven years in the North, however, she tearfully revealed her sexual history to her Quaker-abolitionist-feminist friend, Amy Post. Post urged her to publish her story for the good of the cause but, Post later recalled, Jacobs "shrank from publicity. She said, 'You know a woman can whisper her cruel wrongs in the ear of a dear friend much easier than she can record them for the world to read.'"[3]

Not until 1852 did Jacobs, now free, begin seriously to consider Post's sug-gestion that she write her life. She expressed her conflicting feelings to her friend:

> your proposal to me has been thought over and over again but not with out
> some most painful rememberances dear Amy if it was the life of a Heroine with
> no degradation associated with it.[4]

Jacobs here implies that she could write her life if her sexual experiences had
been those of a free white woman whose actions society condoned, and not
the experiences of an enslaved black woman whose actions society both
mandated and condemned. A few months later, however, she told Post she
was again considering telling her story to help the antislavery cause: "Dear
Amy since I have no fear of my name coming before those whom I have
lived in dread of, I cannot be happy without trying to be useful in some
way."[5]

What changed her mind? Jacobs reversed her earlier decision to keep her
life private at least in part, perhaps, as a response to the way her freedom had
been achieved. Like many principled abolitionists, she thought that freedom
by purchase involved a compromise with the slave system, and when her
Northern employer had proposed to buy her, she had rejected the offer.
Nevertheless, over her objections and without her knowledge, Cornelia
Grinnell Willis had purchased her from the Norcoms. In a letter to Post
commenting on her new status as a free woman, which was published as an
Appendix in *Incidents*, Jacobs voiced her conflicting feelings by signifying
on her name:

> I thank you for your kind expressions in regard to my freedom; but the free-
> dom I had before the money was paid was dearer to me. God gave me *that* free-
> dom; but man put God's image in the scales with the paltry sum of three hun-
> dred dollars. I served for my liberty as faithfully as Jacob served for Rachel. At
> the end, he had large possessions; but I was robbed of my victory; I was obliged
> to resign my crown, to rid myself of a tyrant. (p. 204)

In *Incidents*, Jacobs's "Linda" expressed her mixed feelings at being freed
by purchase: "The bill of sale is on record.... I well know the value of that
bit of paper; but much as I love freedom, I do not like to look upon it" (p.
200). In light of this, it seems to me that Jacobs's decision to write her autobiography—like the decision of many other autobiographers—was motivated by a determination to take back her life, to gain her "victory" and
finally to win her "crown."[6]

Nevertheless, when Jacobs first imagined her book, her notion was not to
attempt to compose her narrative herself, but to find help producing an "as-
told-to" biography. After a disastrous effort to convince Harriet Beecher
Stowe to act as her amanuensis, however, she began to write—not her life,
but comments on current events framed as pseudonymous correspondence
to the newspapers.

Then, in the fall of 1853, Jacobs sent an extraordinary letter to Post. She
begins by reporting Molly Horniblow's death:

dear Amy I have lost that Dear old Grandmother that I so dearly loved oh her
life has been one of sorrow and trial but he in whom she trusted has never forsaken her her Death was beautiful may my last end be like hers.

Immediately following this passage, she shifts to a new topic: "Louisa
[Jacobs's daughter] is with me I dont know how long she will remain I shall
try to keep her all winter as I want to try to make arrangements to have some
of my time[.]" Jacobs needs this time because she has decided to write her
book herself, and she announces her intention in a self-consciously literary
style:

> I must write just what I have lived and witnessed myself dont expect much of
> me dear Amy you shall have truth but not talent God did not give me that gift
> but he gave me a soul that burned for freedom and a heart nerved with deter-
> mination to suffer even unto death in pursuit of...liberty...only let me come
> before the world as I have been an uneducated oppressed Slave.[7]

This letter, written in the wake of Jacobs's earlier expressions of her extreme
reluctance to write her story for publication, suggests that on some level,
Grandmother's death has freed her to write her life.

In *Incidents*, the relationship between "Linda" and Grandmother is
extremely complicated. Grandmother had condemned "Linda's" sexual
behavior, then pitied, but not pardoned, her; had opposed her escape, but at
the risk of being reenslaved herself, had hidden "Linda" for years; and she
had raised "Linda's" children while competing with her for their love. It
seems likely that in and through the process of conceiving and writing the
story of her youth, at middle age Jacobs is finally freeing herself from the
heavy burdens of silence and of guilt that she has carried since her teens—a
silence and a guilt occasioned, at least in part, by Grandmother's disapproval.

Supporting this interpretation is the passage in Jacobs's autobiography
where—after "Linda" condemns her youthful sexual actions—she shifts
ground and writes, "Still, in looking back, calmly, on the events of my life, I
feel that the slave woman ought not to be judged by the same standard as
others." (p. 56) She ought not be judged, that is, by the corrupt social norm
that mandated the behavior both of the "pure" free women it praised, and
also of the "impure" slave women it reviled—the same corrupt social norm
that Grandmother apparently had used to condemn Jacobs when she was sixteen. Also supporting this interpretation is the book's conclusion, where sur-
rounded by "gloomy recollections" of her past, "Linda" evokes her "tender
memories of my good old grandmother, like light, fleecy clouds floating over
a dark and troubled sea" (p. 201). In these final lines, which read as an
homage to Grandmother, "Linda" frees herself of the shame, anger, and dis-
tress she has voiced intermitantly in her text. In these lines, Harriet Jacobs
finally signals her peace with her grandmother Molly Horniblow.

Deciding to write her life, Jacobs constructed an alter-ego, the pseudonymous first-person narrator "Linda Brent," whose version of her life Jacobs apparently thought was publishable in antebellum America. The invention of "Linda Brent" enabled Jacobs to tell the story of her deviance from sexual norms, and it also enabled her to edit that story. Although the version of Jacobs's life that "Linda" presents conforms neither to approved standards of female sexual behavior nor to approved standards of female writing concerning sexual behavior, it does not utterly reject these norms. In *Incidents*, the notion of "sexual purity" is not opposed, and the treatment of sexuality is not prurient. Further, while on the one hand "Linda's" story is made immediate by being told in the first person, on the other it is distanced by being told pseudonymously.

In her Author's Preface, "Linda" promises: "Reader, be assured this narrative is no fiction. I am aware that some of my adventures may seem incredible; but they are, nevertheless, strictly true" (p. 1). As far as I have been able to discover, this promise is kept. But it is a promise to tell the truth, not to tell the whole truth. And indeed "Linda" does not tell the whole truth of Harriet Jacobs's life.

For example, Jacobs devotes an entire chapter to her aunt Betty, whom "Linda" calls "Aunt Nancy." She describes her aunt as a heartbroken, childless mother who is so overworked by her mistress that she gives birth prematurely six times and who, when her workload is lightened, finally bears two children, neither of whom survives. "Linda" does not, however, write that her aunt's last pregnancy coincided with "Linda's" first. Yet research reveals that on October 5, 1830, the Sheriff of Chowan County was ordered to sell property belonging to James Norcom in order to repay money that he had borrowed from the State Bank of North Carolina, and that the property to be sold was a group of slaves, including five members of Jacobs's family: "Harriett & child—boy John—woman Betty & child [Jacobs's aunt and baby]."[8] This document does not state whether it was Dr. Norcom who proposed that these slaves be sold to pay his debt, or whether it was the Court that singled them out. It does reveal, however, that the teenaged Harriet and her aunt, both slaves in the Norcom household, had living children in October 1830. Because we know that Jacobs's son Joseph was born in 1829 or 1830, and because she tells us that her aunt's last baby lived only four weeks, this document establishes that she and her aunt went through pregnancy and childbirth at approximately the same time.[9]

With this information, we can speculate that it was, perhaps, the fact that Jacobs shared with her aunt the experience of pregnancy, childbirth, and motherhood—and the fact that with their babes still at the breast, niece and aunt shared the danger of being sold away—that caused Jacobs's closeness to this aunt and prompted her decision to construct a memoir in *Incidents*. "Linda" does not tell us this, but she does present her aunt as a bereaved mother. It is, we recall, the childless "Aunt Nancy" who fuels "Linda's" determination to free her children against all odds.

Further, Jacobs suppressed another major aspect of her life in "Linda's" account. It appears that, after the death of Jacobs's mother (circa 1820), Jacobs's father remarried. This marriage, apparently to a free woman, produced a son named Elijah, born when Harriet Jacobs was about nine years old. It would be very strange if she did not know this half-brother while she was a girl in Edenton. There is evidence that, many years later in the North, Jacobs's daughter Louisa was in touch with her mother's half-brother and his children. Yet nowhere does Jacobs's "Linda" mention the existence of this branch of her immediate family.[10]

What "Linda" does present is a carefully crafted version of Jacobs's life. Simplifying her personae, she chooses to present herself as a "Slave Girl" and, in terms of family, as "Grandmother's child." Stripping down her story, she tells enough, perhaps, but surely not everything, about her sexual history in slavery. And she is always careful, in telling that history, to reject the role of sexual victim that, by mid-century, was routinely assigned slave women in writings by male slave narrators and free abolitionists. Jacobs's narrator controls her text—and her reader—not only with her words but also with her silences, which she chooses just as carefully. She represses much. Her silences, like her words, are an assertion of agency.

In 1861, after *Incidents* was published, Harriet Jacobs again transformed herself, this time into a public figure with her own name. While her invention of "Linda Brent" can be traced from her "Dear Amy" letters, her invention of her public personae can be traced from her early letters to the editor, which she signed "Fugitive."

Those familiar with the recent history of *Incidents* are aware that I worked for years to establish Harriet Jacobs as its author and to document her claim that the life of "Linda Brent" was her own. Hence to me, it was doubly surprising to learn that Jacobs's first audience was well aware of her identity. But know it they did. The standard nineteenth-century bibliographical reference, Cushing's *Initials and Pseudonyms*, identifies "Linda Brent" as Harriet Jacobs—a piece of information that was apparently lost in the early twentieth century (although librarians of African-American collections like the Schomburg and The Library Company of Philadelphia routinely identified Jacobs as the author of *Incidents*).[11]

When *Incidents* appeared early in 1861, Jacobs's first reviewers did not immediately identify her as "Linda." But private correspondence from the period testifies that Jacobs's authorship was known not only to William C. Nell and L. Maria Child, both of whom were involved in the publication of *Incidents*, but also to an entire circle of Garrisonian reformers. Shortly after *Incidents* was bound between covers, Jacobs went to Philadelphia, where she openly sold her book to activist women. One of these, the Quaker abolitionist Sarah Pugh, noted in her diary that she had met its author: "spent an hour with Linda."[12] That summer, Jacobs's editor L. Maria Child, visiting in Boston, wrote that she saw Harriet Jacobs among a group of activists returning from their annual celebration of West Indian emancipation. "Among the friends I met at the A.[nti] S.[lavery] office was the author of Linda whom everybody agreed in declaring to be a very pre-possessing person."[13] Far from hiding her authorship of *Incidents*, Jacobs identified herself as "Linda" as soon as it was published.

Had the Civil War not broken out, it seems likely that—following in the footsteps of other slave narrators—Harriet Jacobs would have mounted the platform as an abolitionist lecturer. Instead, with the onset of the hostilities, she began to use her celebrity as "Linda" to create a new role and to invent a new personae in antislavery circles. Signing herself "Linda," in September 1862, she wrote a long letter to William Lloyd Garrison's newspaper *The Liberator* about her relief efforts among the "contraband"—the fugitive Southern slaves crowding behind the lines of the Union Army in Washington, D. C., and in Alexandria. Garrison published her piece along with a note:

> A very interesting and touching account of the condition of the contrabands in Washington and its vicinity, by Mrs. Jacobs, the author of "LINDA," may be found on the last page. We trust its perusal will stimulate philanthropic spirits to do something in their behalf, in addition to what has already been so kindly done by a few others, through the agency of Mrs. Jacobs.[14]

This announcement proclaimed Jacobs's new public identity. Her efforts among the black refugees now provided her with credentials as a relief worker and Harriet Jacobs, the creator of "Linda," had become Harriet Jacobs, the humanitarian.

Throughout the remainder of Civil War and the beginning years of Reconstruction, the reformers—and in particular, the women abolitionists—commented on Jacobs's work among the Freed People. To them, she was something of a celebrity. "Did you see [Harriet] Jacobs, 'Linda'?" one refugee worker at a Southern outpost eagerly queried a colleague, recently returned from Washington.[15]

Writing in the Northern reform press and in African-American newspapers, Jacobs used her public presence to urge readers to send money and supplies for her relief efforts, and to keep up their political pressure for full citizenship rights for the Freed People. In the refugee camps of the South, she openly confronted civilian and military officials, demanding just treatment for the Freed People. As a consequence of her activism and of her steady stream of private and public letters, Jacobs became well known in relief circles. In 1867, when she undertook a fund-raising trip to Great Britain on behalf of the black community in Savannah, Georgia, the New York Society of Friends reported that the British National Freedmen's Aid Union gave her carte blanche, voting to donate one hundred pounds sterling "for use in the benevolent objects of Harriet Jacobs."[16]

In *Incidents in the Life of a Slave Girl*, the newly-freed fugitive slave Harriet Jacobs took control of her life by writing her story as "Linda Brent." Later, after publication of her book, Jacobs used her personae as "Linda" to become a public figure in her own right. While a century later both Jacobs and her book had been forgotten, today we are witnessing another transformation: *Incidents* is becoming established as a valuable text and its author is being judged both a significant historical figure and an important nineteenth-century autobiographer. In her Author's Preface, Jacobs's "Linda" had voiced high hopes for her book: "May the blessings of God rest on this imperfect effort in behalf of my persecuted people!" (p. 1). More than a century later, it appears that her prayer is being answered.

NOTES

1. *Incidents in the Life of a Slave Girl: Written by Herself*, ed. L. Maria Child (Boston: For the Author, 1861). Throughout, citations are to the edition edited by Jean Fagan Yellin (Cambridge: Harvard University Press, 1987).

2. For biographical information, see *Incidents*.

3. Post, October 30, 1859, Rochester, New York. Isaac and Amy Post Family Papers, Department of Rare books, Manuscripts, and Archives, University of Rochester Library, Rochester, New York. Unless otherwise noted, all references to Jacobs's correspondence are to items in this collection, hereinafter designated as IAPFP.

4. Harriet Jacobs to Amy Post, Cornwall, Orange County [October? 1852?], IAPFP.

5. Harriet Jacobs to Amy Post, February 14 [1853], IAPFP.

6. See *Incidents*, xviii–xix.

7. Harriet Jacobs to Amy Post, October 9 [1853], IAPFP.

8. Chowan County Civil Actions Concerning Slaves, item dated October 5, 1830, North Carolina State Archives.

9. Within a month of the writing of this document, "Aunt Nancy's" baby must have died; "Linda" tells us that the infant lived only four weeks, (*Incidents*, 144).

10. Concerning Elijah Knox, I have learned the following: He was born ca. 1824. In June 1846, and at "about 22" years, he completed his apprenticeship to Robert Warren of Hertford County, North Carolina. He first appeared in the *City Directory* in New Bedford in 1867. Elijah Knox died in New Bedford on January 12, 1907. Louisa Matilda Jacobs's will, dated August 2, 1907, leaves $100.00 to William and Elijah Knox of New Bedford, sons of her half-uncle Elijah Knox. See "Harriet Jacobs's Family History," *American Literature*, December 1994, 192–95.

11. For my announcement of the authorship and genre of *Incidents*, see "*Written by Herself*: Harriet Jacobs's Slave Narrative," *American Literature* 53 (November 1981): 479–86. For the standard citation, see William Cushing, *Initials and Pseudonyms: A Dictionary of Literary Disguises* (New York: Thomas Crowell, 1885).

12. *Memorial of Sarah Pugh. A Tribute of Respect from her cousins.* (Philadelphia: J. B. Lippencott 1888), 100.

13. L. Maria Child to Lucy [Searle], August 22, 1861, Wayland, Cornell Anti-Slavery Collection.

14. *The Liberator*, September 5, 1862.

15. C. M. Severance to Elizabeth P. Peabody, April 1, 1865, Port Royal, Antioch College Library.

16. *Eighth Report of the Committee of Representatives of New York Yearly Meeting of Friends Upon the Condition and Wants of the Freedmen, 1869*, 4. Haviland Records Room, New York Yearly Meeting, Religious Society of Friends.

13

TAKING A LIFE
Hot Pursuit and Cold Rewards in a Mexican Testimonial Novel

Doris Sommer

"Now FUCK OFF. Go away and let me sleep." That's the way Jesusa Palancares cuts off her story and shuts out the persistent interrogator who has been asking for it. This dismissal is her final word, after more than 300 very full pages of the most detailed and boldly narrated life, a picaresque life of careers ranging from combat soldier in the Mexican Revolution to factory worker, cabaret dancer, hairdresser, and laundress. And just to make sure we're impressed, the story is embellished by real or imaginary brushes with historical characters like Emiliano Zapata and old "Goat-Beard" Carranza.[1]

The apparent effort to impress us makes the unceremonious good-bye on the last page a bit abrupt, but probably not surprising either for Elena Poniatowska, the interviewer and immediate target of reproach, or for the public eavesdroppers we readers become. From the scandalously unsentimental epigraph to the 1969 testimonial novel, *Hasta no verte Jesús mío* (*Till We Meet Again, Dear Jesus*), Jesusa has been rebuffing, rebuking, and otherwise putting us off: "Miss me?" she quips rhetorically on the epigraphic page; "the hell you will when I'm no use to you any longer."

Identifyng *Hasta no verte Jesús mío* as a testimonial novel is already to notice a tension between two genres and two narrative agents.[2] *Testimonio* is precisely not fiction. It is a first-person narrative in Latin America that, like

other oral histories, can be elicited by sympathetic intellectuals who interview illiterate or semi-literate working people. The intention, as the generic
term indicates, is judicial and broadly political, as the speaker "testifies"
against abuses suffered by a class or community. The genre, in fact, was given
official literary status as a politicized alternative to fiction when Cuba lost
the support of Latin American liberal novelists after Castro defended the
Soviet invasion of Czechoslovakia. Cuba's response was to say, in effect, that
there were more interesting stories being produced than the difficult experimental prose of late modernist "Boom" novels; there were real stories about
real people in struggle. In 1970, Cuba's official publishing house, Casa de Las
Américas, designated *testimonio* as a category in its annual international
awards for literature. Since then, it has been the object of sustained critical
attention, and some debate.[3]

Is *testimonio* "authentic" history? How much does the intellectual interlocutor interfere with the informant's narrative transmission? Can a first-
person singular voice presume to represent a group? In a strong case for the
genre's distinctiveness, John Beverley recently argued that *testimonio* is
poised against literature, that its collective denunciatory tone distinguishes
testimonio from the personal development narrative of standard autobiography, and that it tends to erase the tracks of an elitist author who is mediating
the narrative. This allows for a "fraternal or sororal" complicity between narrator and reader; that is, a tighter bond of intimacy than is possible in manipulative and evasive narrative fiction.[4] A testimonial novel, then, would be a
contradiction in terms, between immediacy and manipulation. But it is just
the kind of disturbance that Pontiatowska wisely leaves through Jesusa's controlling voice, and through her own confessional glosses. Poniatowska has
worried about the ethical conundrum unavoidable in socially unequal conversation that can take lives, to display them like so much evidence at a trial.

> An ethical problem arises around the writing of testimonial novels. Are those
> who create them writers or not? Are they simply opportunists who…plunge
> into the manufacture of easily consumed works that will fill the void between
> the elite and the illiterate in Latin American countries?… They confiscate a real-
> ity, present it as their own, steal their informants' words, plagiarize their collo-
> quialisms, tape their language and take possession of their very souls.[5]

Jesusa won't be easily consumed, thanks to Poniatowska's acknowledgment of her Jesusa's disturbances. Why should one imagine that only privileged intellectuals master the techniques of manipulation? The question most
professional readers have asked of this book is who is the writer; and the
answer has almost always been Poniatowska, even if she prefers to blur the
signature by including Jesusa in a 1985 essay about professional authors in
Mexico.[6] Does it flatter a narrator like Jesusa to be considered artless, transparent, available for easy intimacy? Poniatowska evidently, does not think
so, because she sends us on a cautionary and sobering sidetrack, beside the

denunciatory points of the story, towards a point about strategic telling. Beth Jörgensen dares to notice the obvious, in contrast to so many sentimental readers of Jesusa, "The speaking I...scolds, fusses, and shouts her way...into history."[7] If the editor had preferred to control the indifference, sometimes shrillness, if the story did interpellate her effortlessly and intimately, one would have to imagine little or no political and cultural differences between narrator and her sororal other. This unethical, and generally deluded, imagining is one injustice that Jesusa targets as she testifies and Poniatowska listens.

Until now, readers have been taking quite literally Jesusa's question about missing her when she's no use any more, shrugging off the rudeness as an untutored expression of a gendered reticence to share intimacy, or of a generally hermetic national character.[8] Poniatowska herself described the initially reluctant subject as "hermetic," as if that were a grudging signature of Mexican authenticity; Jesusa's early refusals to talk are precisely what make us insist on hearing her. But as we listen, the ring of Octavio Paz's classic meditation on Mexican solitude may deafen our ears to Jesusa's specific performance, explaining her away before she can explains herself.[9] We both expect her reticence and exact its removal, and thereby threaten to dissolve the object of scrutiny by our very effort to understand it. If refusal identifies her, then overcoming it may menace the very identity we demand to know. Almost half a century ago, Paz participated in this paradox by saying something literally unspeakable about Mexicaness, about its quiet defensiveness:

> The Mexican, whether young or old, criollo or mestizo, general or laborer or lawyer, seems to me to be a person who shuts himself away to protect himself: his face is a mask and so is his smile. In his harsh solitude, which is both barbed and courteous, everything serves him as a defense: silence and words, politeness and disdain, irony and resignation. He is jealous of his own privacy and that of others, and he is afraid even to glance at his neighbor, because a mere glance can trigger the rage of these electrically charged spirits.[10]

Why, then, are readers not wary about provoking Jesusa? Do we imagine ourselves to be immune to verbal barbs, or to be cozily inside the electrically charged borders that safeguard subjectivity from other, less trustworthy trespassers? If Jesusa is truly Mexican (an identity that Poniatowska banks on), and if Paz is right about the impenetrability of "Mexican masks" (which seems taken for granted in Poniatowska's choice of hermetic Jesusa as representative), why should readers anticipate anything like intimacy with the protagonist? But readers have managed to insulate themselves from the occasional barbs and shocks of reading Jesusa with the apparently harmless fluff of unprocessed sympathy. To the self-evidently (and reciprocally) dismissive "Miss me?" of her epilogue, readers have been responding, "Of course we will miss you, Jesusita," protesting almost defensively, as they continue to use her cult-like figure to celebrate feminism and the working class.

A specific example of her usefulness may be evident from the very evocation of Paz's Mexican myth-making that her telling style practically
demands. Jesusa's story can be read to counter or to adjust Paz's magisterial
voice. The glibness of his sustained, recursive style rings false alongside her
gruff interruptions; and his self-disavowing third-person report about
Mexicans should make any reader suspicious about Paz's own authenticity
as a representative speaker. Readers will do well to wonder about his positionality, even when the observer doubles as a participant within a plural first
person: "we believe that opening oneself up is a weakness or a betrayal" (30).
How can contemporary readers not hear a different kind of betrayal here?
Those who can hear the anger at exclusions in Jesusa's defensive dismissals
can hardly miss the message that Paz's slippery inclusion of himself in the
solidary "we" of serial and solitary Mexicans is won by the exclusion of
women. They are biologically open to penetration, and therefore literally and
physiologically incapable of integrity. It is perfectly possible that Paz, in this
passage, is being perversely critical of machismo as masquerade, when he
reports that women's "inferiority is constitutional and resides in their sex,
their submissiveness, which is a wound that never heals" (30). Nevertheless,
he associates Mexicanness with masculinity, whatever its value or liability,
as if a hardened woman like Jesusa were Mexican only to the extent that she
herself is perversely *macha*.

Solicitous readers come to the unsolicited rescue. Of course she is authentically Mexican, and her very identity, *pace Paz*, rips a compromising gash
on the masculine rigidity of his page. Whether Jesusa makes unfriendly gestures because she is an authentic Mexican recluse, or because gender specific
resistance to public intercourse awaits our sisterly support in "breaking the
silence," sympathetic readers have tried to smooth out jagged spots along the
barbed border of Jesusa's contour with the sustained ardor of unstinting
patronage.[11] What accounts for the degree and the duration of heat? Is it
Jesusa's intrinsic attractiveness? Or, is it her continuing usefulness (despite
the editor's protestation of disinterested love that we read out of Jesusa's initiating rebuff) for our own difficult projects of feminist and culturally specific self-fashioning?

The question is so obvious—and so obviously embarrassing—for Jesusa's
fans that it is just now being asked aloud. Not everyone finds her fascinating. In literature classes about Spanish America, where *Hasta no verte Jesús
mío* is regularly featured, students are incautiously candid. They don't like
it, more often than not; it is heavy, even sometimes offensive, reading. And
privately, some privileged professional readers will confess to feeling less
enthusiasm than politically incorrect boredom, indifference, even anger. "She
won't get me to donate to the orphanage or to the people's struggle," was one
telling response. An anecdote about a possible publication in English translation repeats the point. Almost ten years ago, a very able translation, judging
from the published passages, was prepared and scheduled to come out with
a trade publisher evidently eager to cash in on the book's popularity and its

promise to become required reading in the burgeoning industry of women's studies. But publication has been delayed, perhaps indefinitely. Could the book have seemed disappointing to uninvested readers?

The difference between public admiration and typically private disenchantment makes me wonder which is the more appropriate, that is more authorially calculated, reception. Does Jesusa want us to want her, or does she want us to keep at a safe distance? And if the answer is appropriately mixed, pulling at our intimacy and pushing at the bad faith of disinterested love, why might Jesusa have programmed her own partial failure to engage us? Is it possible that her ingenious specificity is to share information without sharing herself, and is it equally possible that she wants neither to be the stuff of mass sales nor the beneficiary of charitable contributions?

Critics have typically treated *Hasta no vert Jesús mío* as Poniatowska's production, a necessarily fictionalized and unauthentic life; they have cautiously measured its truth value and found it wanting, upbraiding Poniatowska for her self-authorized license to represent, for her artistic freedom, and for implying the writer's unavoidable and almost tragic irresponsibility, because writing necessarily reduces life to lies.[12] With loud beating of breasts and laments for the inescapable unreality we inflict on a life converted into text, critics take unlimited license to speculate about Poniatowska, to interview her and to elicit more writing from the professional writer. No one except for Jörgensen has yet attended to Jesusa's remarkable performance. It is her story after all. Otherwise, why would readers fret about the liberties taken in Poniatowska's version? But fretting hasn't yet renamed our focus onto Jesusa; readers have not yet stopped to notice her controlling voice in the conversion from experience to exemplum.

Poor Jesusa looks like so much raw material to guilt-ridden readers tormented by their own power of agency as collaborators with the writer. Jesusa may be active and proud, of course; she is even respectably masked in her hermetic Mexicanness, but the simple woman could hardly be calculating or strategic, could she? We should learn to stop at the possibility; not to stop and wonder is to overshoot the problem with a kind of misfired sympathy that does more character damage, than could any penchant for fiction in the editor. To her credit, Poniatowska hears Jesusa's haughty humility; and she leaves the unfriendly apostrophes on the page. This is one indication that Poniatowska continues to be Jesusa's best reader, allowing the other woman's voice to interrupt the flow of what passes for intimacy. Those interruptions may be symptoms of an entire unspeakable language that refuses scrutiny, making the audible text a pretext, perhaps, for noticing a resistant silence.[13]

Roland Barthes might have put his finger on those breaks as sites of textual bliss, spots where diagetical meaning shows gaps, like the spaces where skin shows tantalizingly between pieces of clothing and distracts the mind in a glimpse of ecstasy. Unlike the lulling pleasure of continuous and therefore predictable rhythms of telling, bliss marks an edge, a stop, a gasp of the text's language;[14] or it is the invitation to be the clandestine, perverse voyeur of other people's pleasure.[15] In either case, Barthes takes for granted that the text—eroticized and magical—exists to give him pleasure, that in fact he is its reason for being: "The text is a fetish object, and this *fetish desires me*."[16] The reader as object of desire, the solicited partner for an intimate entanglement, Barthes performs tirelessly in his extended essay to reciprocate. The result is a book composed of flirtatiously neurotic intermittence, deliciously anticipated but unpredictably timed interventions at unsuspected gaps in the body of conventional criticism.[17] This boldly self-celebratory role for the reader sounds almost scandalous against the drone of academic theories; and it rubs dangerously against the sensitive skin of sexually correct comportment in today's American academy. But how fundamentally different it is from other strains of reader-response theory that also flatter readers by locating them as objects of textual desire, elevating them from the perverse role of voyeur to the category of partner, collaborator, co-author?

In critics as different from one another as Georges Poulet is from Wolfgang Iser, the focus is on the agency of readers. Whether agency is understood as interiorizing (not to say cannibalizing) instead of talking back to a text (in Poulet's version),[18] or as setting the text into dialogic motion (as in Iser's classic and familiar studies),[19] readers are necessary and equal partners in the shared pleasures of esthetic production. Poulet's claims selflessly to "accede" to a text can prove the outlying example of an inclusive culture of criticism.[20] He protests modest passivity only after initiating his own surrender to helplessly dependent objects that crave his attention:

> Books are objects. On a table, on shelves, in store windows, they wait for someone to come and deliver them from their materiality, from their immobility. When I see them on display, I look at them as I would at animals for sale, kept in little cages, and so obviously hoping for a buyer. For—there is no doubting it—animals do know that their fate depends on a human intervention. Isn't the same true of books?... They wait. Are they aware that an act of man might suddenly transform their existence? They appear to be lit up with that hope. Read me, they seem to say. I find it hard to resist their appeal.[21]

Once the reader-prince succumbs to his own sensitivity and to the text's charming eagerness for a kiss, the rest of Poulet's essay follows the flirtatious rhythm of reciprocal possession. The analogy between book shops and pet stores is a provocatively flimsy cover for love for sale.[22] The first move is to purchase a partner, and to feel chosen by the book; the next is to appreciate its "offering, opening itself.... It asks nothing better than to exist outside itself, or to let you exist in it. In short, the extraordinary fact in the case of a book is the falling away of the barriers between you and it. You are inside it; it is inside you."[23] As the entanglement proceeds, Poulet manages some distance; he takes a breath of reflection on such breathless activity. ("On the other hand—and without contradiction—reading implies something resembling the apperception I have of myself.... Whatever sort of alienation I may endure, reading does not interrupt my activity as subject."[24]) But the repeatable rhythm of contact and consummation concludes by celebrating abandon to the writer who "reveals himself to us in us."[25] Perhaps celebration is in order because abandon, far from diminishing the reader as ventriloquist and vehicle, returns him to princely primacy. "The work lives its own life within me; in a certain sense, it thinks itself, and it even gives itself a meaning within me," a universal meaning that finally does not belong to a particular work.[26] It is a haunting "transcendence" that is perceptible when criticism can "annihilate, or at least momentarily forget, the objective elements of the work, and to elevate itself to the apprehension of a subjectivity without objectivity."[27]

If Poulet's finally immodest and mutually penetrating dance with the death of authorship can suggest one kind of border in reader-response criticism, the frontier between unabashedly self-centered unscientific ludicism, and the philosophically cautious grounding in the reality of reading as an activity, a different border is the site of equally serious trouble. It is the promising but underdeveloped place where reader-response meets political imperatives. The trouble brewing there, like a comforting mist, is a hangover from the self-celebratory assumptions common in reader-response criticism. Rarely has the reader been cast as a victim, a target, an incompetent voyeur in the varied critical practices that focus attention on the critic herself.

Tellingly, standard feminist reactions to response theory repeat its fundamental assumption about the collaborative role of the reader. For example, Patrocinio Schweickart's review of reader-response criticism draws an intimate parallel between Poulet's "Criticism and the Experience of Interiority" (as a strong case of eroticized appropriation) and Adrienne Rich's reading of Emily Dickinson: "The reader encounters not simply a text, but a 'subjectified object': the 'heart and mind' of another woman. She comes into close contact with an interiority—a power, a creativity, a suffering, a vision—that is *not* identical with her own. The feminist interest in construing reading as an intersubjective encounter suggests an affinity with Poulet's theory…."[28] The problem for feminists has been that the reader in canonical literature is assumed to be male, and collaboration for women turned into treachery against themselves. The threat is immasculation, as Judith Fetterly called this male-identified training in 1978, a term that Schweickart approvingly repeats in 1986 as she develops the feminist solution to reading (like) men: In addition to resisting male-centered works, we can "read ourselves" in women writers.[29] The solution, in other words, involves a dissolution of difference between reader and writer, a stronger chemistry even than Poulet's eroticism. "Mainstream reader-response theory" tracks a struggle for control between the text and its reader; but feminist readings are pleasantly confined between the poles of relationship and intimate merger. The male reading paradigm strains but ultimately reaffirms the frontiers of personal subjectivity, while the female paradigm (here Schweickart invokes Nancy Chodorow and Carol Gilligan) weakens exclusionary frontiers and exchanges struggle for conversation.[30]

The lines are rather neatly drawn between boys's books and girls's books in Schweickart's essay, even though dissonant readings of the *Autobiography of Malcolm X* serve as the initial wedge into universalizing male-centered responses: For Wayne Booth the book is a standard Western paideia, but the excised passage in his quote shows that Malcolm wrote it as a confirmation of Elijah Muhammad's rejection of racist Western thought. Then, by an alchemy worthy of Booth's transformation of Malcolm's rejection into an embrace, Schweickart proceeds to evaporate issues of class and color. Malcolm X becomes the wedge to free some contested space in for a woman's position. Women read differently from men, and the books they write are just as different. Boys' books either ignore women or abuse them in other ways, as Virginia Woolf's persona at the British Museum found out; and girls' books attend to the intelligence and heroism of women who dare to respect themselves in a surprising variety of ways, above all as writers.

The assumption about reading and writing being positive opportunities for uncensored connection among women had become so standard that by 1989 that Julia Swindells is compelled to offer a caution in her comments on *The Diaries of Hannah Cullwick*. "With the best of intentions," she complains, the 1984 Virago editor of these Victorian manuscripts reads liberation into a woefully constrained writing project that was one more service to a master who loved to watch Cullwick work, and loved to feel her perform all sorts of tasks. "The paradox that exists here," the Virago editor had claimed, "is that the drudgery that was everyday life for the maid-of-all-work also in a sense liberated her." Freedom here is from the limitations of corsetted Victorian womanhood, which prompts Swindells to wonder, "Would we, by the same token, say that the black person in South Africa, or, for that matter, in contemporary Britain, manifests the paradox of freedom in not having to 'suffer' the position of the white person?[31]

Another way to pose the ethical and political error is to notice that feminist enthusiasm can sometimes underestimate the differences among us, and the difficulties in establishing conversation, in the interest of a new and better universality to replace the male-centered version. This is Schweickart's aspiration at the end of her essay: "Feminist reading and writing alike are grounded in the interest of producing a community of feminist readers and writers, and in the hope that ultimately this community will expand to include everyone."[32] The wish seems benign enough, even friendly, but the will to overcome difference can result in simply overlooking it. If feminist reading begins with forcing an acknowledgement of different positionalities, why should it not develop a sensitivity to difference, rather than dream of improving on the homogeneity of a "male-centered" culture? That sensitivity would alert readers, women and men, to textual strategies that are besides the point of coaxing a reader's identification with an author's position, either by "immasculation" or gender affirmation.

The possibility that readers may be the sustained objects of aggression rarely occurs to critics, even when they assume a contestatory position and read books that manifestly cultivate a defiant or elusive attitude. Alongside a feminist politics of reading (that can boil down to resisting one identification and cultivating an alternative), and a sympathetic reading of testimonios that casts the reader as brother or sister, another notable case of missing the aggressive point is Ross Chambers's *Room for Maneuver: Reading Oppositional Narrative*.[33] Beginning with an admirably ethical inspiration, the study is plainly a program for politically productive reading; "Changing the World" is the first heading of the introductory chapter. Chambers is therefore at pains to open a space beyond the action/reaction dynamic that reads resistance in a Foucauldian spiral of power and dissent which reinforce one another. He pries the dead-ended dyad of opposition open to real resistance; and the fulcrum, the third term, is the reader as a neatly dialectical solution to unproductive tensions. "The communicational relationship between text and myself, as reader, is of a different kind, and positions me in such a way that I coincide fully neither with 'Paddy' [narrator] nor with 'Stephen' [narratee] but find myself in a triangulated relationship in which the third position (mine, *sic*) is, with respect to the textual relationships, both that of *tiers exclu*—the excluded third party—and that of *tertius gaudens*, the third who enjoys or profits."[34] The reader, as the indirect object of discourse, the redeemable viewer of discord, is available for the kind of sentimental re-education that could amount to the social condition for political changes of heart.

To do justice to Chambers's important move here, is to acknowledge the stages of reader-response that lead to the narrative's "influencing the desires and views of readers."[35] The first is an identification between powerful narratee and privileged reader. The reader "slips into the slot furnished—often as a vacancy—in the text as that of the narratee, and becomes the object of the narrator's seduction."[36] But because Chambers assumes that the reader is excluded from the oppositional act directed at the narratee (or that he should exclude himself thanks to the distance vouchsafed as voyeur), a triangulated reading becomes possible in which the opposition is given the visibility that amounts to the reader's collaborative operation with the text.[37] "For my role as reader of a text is not so much to receive a story (identifying with the narratee position) as to collaborate with the text in the production of meaning, a task that redistributes—perhaps equalizes—the power relationship, and certainly dissolves the simplistic distinctions of self and other, sender and receiver that are inherent in the concepts of narrator and narratee."[38]

The danger may be evident in this bloodless *Aufhebung* of narratee stand-in to the oppositional narrator's ally. By excluding ourselves from the struggle we get away unscathed, possibly with our retrograde desire still in place. Despite the best intentions of Chambers to describe desire in politically altered states, thanks to sensitive and self-critical readings, our self-appointed role as coauthor/collaborator remains unchallenged. And the possibility of sustained hostility towards the reader vanishes in the dialectical magic of helping hands. Not that Chambers ignores that initial tension, but that he decides too quickly perhaps that it is a dead end, that readers are capable of self-criticism without enduring redundant reminders of complicity.

We have almost lost the trail of a truly humbling exercise that Stanley Fish might have taught us in *Surprised by Sin*. This early (and outlying) book focuses on the reader's role in Milton's *Paradise Lost*, but certainly not to illustrate any possible coauthorship or complicity, no eroticized *pas de deux* or transcendental erasure of the text. Instead, Milton is shown to set up his reader at every point, to cajole him into thinking he has understood something of God's divine pattern only to dash the reader's presumptuous satisfactions. The true Christian should know that God is unknowable, and the text plays on our stubbornly earthly expectations of enlightenment in order to counter them abruptly, aggressively, repeatedly.

This is the track we might tread again when we learn to listen to a narrative like Jesusa's. Like Fish's Milton, she too may be playing on the expectations of enlightened modern readers for whom the amount of energy expended should predict the level of mastery gained. But labor theories of readerly value will miss the specific use value of the raw material. Milton's poem refuses workerly improvements as arrogant examples of the work's main point: the mortal reader's incorrigible incompetence. Without making transcendent claims for Jesusa's privacy, and arguing more modestly that her particularly positioned life defies easy universalizing and transcendent appropriations that would allow readers to assume some ultimate knowledge of her, she too discounts the unsolicited labor of self-defined collaborators. Like Milton, she will insist repeatedly that we miss the point by striving after it so actively. From the very beginning to the very end, she dodges our efforts to close in enough to extend ourselves.

But Jesusa's technique is so different from Milton's dynamic rush of meaning followed by the crash of confidence. There are no long passages of lyrical lulling of dangerous possibilities, no theological bombast, no cajoling or threatening. In fact, very little is addressed to the reader in Jesusa's telling, except for the diegetic interruptions that question the value of telling anything at all, interruptions that implicitly question the value of the listener. Instead there is prattle, interminable drone, that results, perhaps, in the boredom of many of us. Boredom is no simple matter, only an undertheorized one, maybe because it is an inauspicious site for active, collaborative reader responses. But Roland Barthes, at least, stopped to consider it, in moments after bliss when the exhaustion frees the spirit even from the work of contemplation. He would surely have read the paradoxical stasis in Jesusa's active life because, in fact, instead of producing bliss at the site of her interruptions, she is careful not to let the erotic edges of diegesis show. Instead, she smooths readers beyond taking their possible pleasures of her, just beyond bliss and straight into boredom. "Boredom," Barthes writes, "is not far from bliss; it is bliss seen from the shores of pleasure."[39]

From that far shore, distanced and exiled from the readerly pleasures of partnership that we have been trained to expect, reader response theory recovers its chastening potential. It is the potential to notice the reader as a paradoxical function of the text, not its coproducer. If we are not involved, not engaged, not challenged to put pieces together, where are we? Unlike a modernist literary puzzle this one is straightforward. We don't interpret because the text is so transparent, or empathize because it is written long after or purposefully beyond any experience of emotion. Where are we readers, the darlings of purposefully difficult texts, of an entire industry in literary criticism that assumes our responsibility and privilege to activate a text and to coauthor it? The stunning observation is that we are not needed at all, not interpellated as necessary coconspirators or problem solvers. The only times we do figure, by extension, are in rather dismissive asides to the interrogator/writer, as if to underline our exclusion. "Now fuck off. Go away and let me sleep."

The effect is ultimately chilling, although ardent readers cool off very slowly in a cumulative and delayed response. Not that Jesusa is coy or even subtle about refusing us access to exciting intimacy, but that we are so stubbornly sentimental when we take literary lives, so sloppy that we confuse lip-synching a life with experiencing it, and so generally given to facile friendships in fiction. "We read fiction, in part, to widen our social circle: to make new friends effortlessly, receive their confidences and enter their worlds," is the blithe confession that begins the front page of a recent *New York Times Book Review*.[40] The possibility that effortless friendship may be immoral because it overrides the radical alterity of the Other, or that the protagonist may be indifferent to or offended by her interlocutor's presumption of competence or desirability as confidante—that possibility dawns very slowly.[41] We are utterly unprepared to recognize demands for respect and denials of intimacy, even when aggressive apostrophes to the writer/reader are sandwiched in a rich text. One example can be read out of the typo in the final program for the October 1993 "Life Likenesses" conference on biography and autobiography at Harvard University. The telling mistake changed my title for this essay from "Hot Pursuit and Cold Rewards" to "Old Rewards," as if the rhythm of vital literary give-and-take were too familiar and predictable, too literally vital for our projects of self-fashioning to allow for syncopated interruptions. What else but our empathetic readerly reflex allows us to assume that rich necessarily means gooey? Empathy, after all, is a denial of differences, as Georges Poulet unabashedly announces. But for Mikhail Bakhtin it is a mushy reflex that "introjects" the observer's feelings onto the object's exterior. It thereby cancels any need to appreciate a different interiority, so that Bakhtin draws contrasts between empathy and intersubjective engagements; whether they are esthetic or ethical engagements. And engaging with the subject of art, either the hero or the book, needs to safeguard distance as a condition of possibility. Empathy is a conflation, while love leaves room for growth.

> Sympathetic co-experiencing, "akin to love," is no longer pure coexperiencing, or an empathizing of oneself into an object or into a hero…. And it is true that

the feeling of love penetrates, as it were, into an object and alters its whole aspect for us. Nevertheless, this penetrating is entirely different in character from "introjecting" or empathizing another experience into an object as *its own* inner state, as we do, for example, in the case of empathizing joy into a happily smiling man or inner serenity into a motionless and calm sea, etc. These empathized or "introjected" experiences vivify an external object from within by creating an inner life that gives meaning to its exterior, whereas love permeates, as it were, *both* its outer *and* its empathized inner life; that is, it colors and transforms for us the *full* object, the object as already alive, already consisting of a body and a soul.... Coexperiencing in this form does not in the least strive toward the ultimate point of totally coinciding, merging with the coexperienced life, because such merging would be equivalent to a falling away of the coefficient of sympathy, of love, and, consequently, of the form they produced as well."[42]

Jesusa has no taste for overbearing, annihilating sweetness, and no trust in disinterested affection. Real love demands and delivers; it has use-value, like the love Bakhtin requires of his readers who are charged with the responsibility to "consummate" heroes from an enabling distance, providing what we might call a flattering "Lacanian" mirror that will reflect a pleasingly coherent image from narrative fragments and limited internal perspectives. Real love is like the love Jesusa felt for the strict step-mother who taught her to read in order that she might have a productive future and taught her domestic skills to benefit them both. Or it might even be a feeling Jesusa can read out of Pedro Aguilar's insistence on marrying her. "The young officer might have loved me, or not, I don't know. I figure that if he didn't love me, since he was a soldier in the revolution, he could just have grabbed me and done what he wanted."[43] But Poniatowska's attention is different; without mutuality or any visible benefit to Jesusa, the interest is apparently self-serving. So you can save your crocodile tears when I'm no use to you, Jesusa responds. You have taken my life, for what it's worth, and I have nothing more to give.

What that life is worth is precisely the question to ask. What is it worth to us, and why does Jesusa provoke a doubt about its value with a text that manages to flatten an exciting life into a boring read? This is not to evaluate the real, lived life, which we could never even presume to know, and which is probably a composite of her "real" informant, Josefina Bórquez, and other colorful lives that served to embroider the text. But it is to examine the storied version that journalist Poniatowska transcribed and embellished. For all its transgressive excitement, its gender-crossing, border-crossing, double-crossing, and spiritually enhanced complexities, that life is replayed here with a tone of indifference; it is one of Jesusa's signatures, not Poniatowska's. Poniatowska had an absolute horror of boring her public, and she made real efforts to make the story more exciting by cutting out details here, adding others there (notably in the Zapata incidents), killing off unengaging characters and inventing replacements.[44] The sheer quantity of material about

Jesusa's temple of Spiritual Work bored the editor so that she "wouldn't give it much emphasis. A little French logic."[45] Then remorse set in, an instance of a general and class-based guilt complex, for pandering to popular tastes: "I do feel that I should have fleshed out her inner life. But I'm always afraid that people will get bored, so I think I should have a lot going on."[46]

But Jesusa doesn't care about boring the readers she hasn't sought out; she isn't marketing published copies of herself. Her only interest, she says, is ending it all, whether or not the story gets told. "She's going to die on me, just like she wants to,"[47] Poniatowska worried. That full stop would effectively have deadened the interrogator, too. So while she could, intrepid Poniatowska pursued Jesusa, practically forcing her questions on the old woman who raised one objection after another to the weekly Wednesday interrogations. What was the clunky tape recorder doing in her rented room, and who would pay for the electricity? If Jesusa wasted her time answering useless questions, who would walk the chickens around the neighborhood (everyone knows that chickens need sunlight to lay eggs)?[48] Poniatowska dutifully let go of the tape recorder and took hold of the chickens, so long as Jesusa would talk.

Why is there such insistence on the interrogator's part, so much effort and deference to an old woman who might have been one of Poniatowska's many maids? Jesusa would have known why, with the unsentimental clarity that irks some readers: "I'm not loveable; I don't like people."[49] Poniatowska wanted something from her, her life, an authentic but uniquely aggressive Mexican life that could confer an admirable national identity even on eavesdroppers and voyeurs.[50]

By the time Elena Poniatowska insisted on listening, she had schooled herself in the available techniques and learned caution about easy conclusions, first as a reporter specializing in long interviews with stars and statesmen, and then as a short-term assistant to ethnographer and sociologist Oscar Lewis. Lewis was then in Mexico, gathering oral histories of poor people in preparation for *The Children of Sánchez*, his controversial representations of their circular, culturally determined, patterns of failure.[51] Unrealistic when their expectations are high, self-defeatingly resigned when they are not, indigenous American populations are a palate of tragedies for some "scientific" observations, from racially colored positivism to the "culturally limiting" effects of poverty. From the sacrifices on Aztec pyramids to the unstoppable Incan empire, the masses of indigenous hearts supposedly learned resignation long before the Spaniards arrived. And centuries of repressive colonial stability (ending with independence for the minority of white creoles), helped to fix the posture of political indifference into an almost innate feature of the Indian character.

This racialized stereotype purposefully forgets the pre-Columbian wars that Aztecs had to fight against their unmanageably rebellious colonies, the almost relentless battle they waged against Spain, and the long years of indigenous vanguard activity during the Independence struggle. Indians and mestizos are hardly resigned in Mexican history. To think of men like Guerrero, Juárez, and Zapata is also to think of their mass military and political support among indigenous people. And if observers had any lingering doubt about the potentially explosive quality of what passes for resignation during the pauses, if they could imagine that it translated as mere passivity rather than political quiescence, the recent rebellion in Chiapas is rather sobering. A local and overwhelmingly indigenous population in Mexico has literally disarmed a government that hardly expected such consistent and intelligent resistance. And a generation before the rebels roundly refused to be spoken for, Jesusa Palancares was resisting the universalizing embrace that threatened to squeeze her out of history. An active participant in Mexico's passionate and promising history, she kept reminding her cultivated interlocutor, like the rebels reminded the authorities, that despite poverty and years of apparent "conforming" to her fate, inviolable positions were being drawn.[52]

Poniatowska evidently learned to respect Jesusa's positions, despite the master Lewis's expectations of indigenous resignation and his socially scientific understanding. Poniatowska's ear was tuned to a range of active, even aggressive, compatriots after Lewis left, compatriots who were, after all, making history and being broadcast internationally through the generally popular student uprisings of the late 1960s. After the government's 1968 massacre of 400 students, she listened intently to a variety of voices that demanded historical agency, voices of outraged and militant Mexicans who testified in disbelief. She recorded the collective commemoration in *La noche de Tlatelolco* (1970), for which she was awarded (although she refused it) Mexico's most prestigious literary prize, the Xavier Villarrutia Prize.[53]She thereby also refused either to exonerate President Gustavo Díaz Ordaz or to accept the neat closure the prize would signify.[54] Both while she was working on *Hasta no verte* and afterwards, Poniatowska has been tracking testimonial nuances and becoming their vehicle, or—less generously—their ventriloquist. Among the books that followed are: *Fuerte es el silencio* (1980), a series of news stories about grass roots resistance including a hunger strike by mothers of the "disappeared" and about the student insurgence; *Gabby Brimmer* (1979), coauthored with the parapalegic subject of the book which became the basis for the movie *Gaby; Nada nadie: Las voces del temblor* (1988), which collects responses to the 1985 earthquake; and *Compañeras de México: Women Photograph Women* (1990, with Amy Conger).[55]

The novels take a different tack, with their autobiographical impulse and their quest for self-realization in creativity. *Lilus Kikus* (1954), about growing up Catholic and growing out of its constraints; *Querido Diego, te abraza Quiela* (1978) is a factually based but imaginary series of love letters to Diego Rivera by the historical persona of Russian born and Parisian resident painter, Angelina Beloff; and *Tinísima* (1992) follows the photographic peregrinations of Tina Modotti, a foreigner who rediscovered Mexico image by image. In these, Poniatowska recreates (herself in) Mexico through the transformative efforts of artists and outsiders who learn something about her unknowable homeland. Through Jesusa's testimonial novel, however, there was a qualitatively different promise, the haunting promise of reconciling factual with fictional writing, and beyond that, achieving an extraliterary, nationally grounded, self-realization.

In one interview after another, Poniatowska explains how estranged she had always felt from Mexico ever since her birth in Paris to a Polish aristocrat and his beautiful Mexican bride, ever since her school days in Philadelphia and her Mexico City home where only the servants spoke Spanish.[56] She grieves over her longing to be authentically Mexican and tells how be-long-ing led her to Jesusa's door. No doubt the same sad story was repeated there, along with some predictable flattery about Jesusa's being the real thing, a model and inspiration for national pride as well as for unfettered woman-hood; she is a corrective for machista masquerading and a local grounding for the Europeanized intelligentsia. We don't exactly hear Poniatowska's patriotic (and poignant) appeal in the book, though we will hear it later on:

> While she talked all sorts of images came to mind, and they all made me very happy. I felt strengthened by all those things that I never experienced myself. What grew in me, or what perhaps had been there for years, was my Mexican being, becoming Mexican, feeling that Mexico was inside me and that it was the same that was in Jesusa and that it would come out by simply opening the gate.... One night, just before sleep came, after identifying myself with Jesusa for a long time and reviewing the images she showed me, one by one, I could whisper to myself: Yes, I belong."[57]

We don't hear the desire and the demand until later, but we can surmise them from the sarcastic retort that Jesusa fires back in the book. She says, in effect, this is your problem not mine. First of all, I'm no hearth to warm yourself by, and second, none of this matters to me at all. The only Mexican here is you, she blurts out, since you're rich enough to afford a title, and privileged enough to fill up your time with worry instead of work: "I have no coun-try," says Jesusa directly, "I'm like the gypsies, from nowhere. I don't feel Mexican and Mexicans are nothing to me. The only thing that matters here is...self-interest. If I had money I'd be Mexican, but since I'm not even as good as garbage, well, I'm nothing" (218).

Casting herself as an outsider to everything, country and kin and kind-ness,[58] Jesusa therefore has nothing to lose, and her information flows freely, as if nothing were being held back. She doesn't protest the occasional indis-cretions of her interrogator; she doesn't block the narrative with stop signs at secret passages, the way Rigoberta Menchú would do in her 1983 testimo-nial. Reading the story of the young Guatemalan woman who won the 1992 Nobel Peace Prize provides a real contrast in strategy; Menchú conspicu-ously announces that secrets are being kept from us, lest our enlightened and universalizing drives presume to offer a better understanding than her own, and lest we therefore proceed to make moral and strategic decisions in her stead. By performing a series of flamboyant suppressions, Menchú says, in effect, that her document is a screen, in the double sense of showing and covering up,[59] allegedly hiding the largely "public" secrets, known to the Quichés and kept from us in a gesture of self-preservation.[60] "They say that the Spaniards raped and destroyed the best of our ancestors' children...to honor them we must guard our secrets. And those secrets no one will discover except for us, the indigenous people."[61] By some editorial or joint decision, Menchú ends her book with a reminder of what remains beyond it. "I continue to hide what I think no one else knows. Not even an anthropologist, nor any intellectual, no matter how many books he may have read, can know all our secrets."[62] But this text is full of information about Rigoberta herself, her community, traditional practices, the armed struggle. A reader may wonder, then, what secrets we cannot know, and why so much attention is being called to our insufficiency as readers. Does it mean that the knowledge is impossible or that it is forbidden? Is she saying that we are incapable of knowing, or that we ought not to know? Her withholding seems to be an investment in diversification, knowledge, and the power it portends. It is socially constructed and therefore not interchangeable, not substitutable.

How else are we to take Menchú's protestations of silence as she continues to talk? Are there really many secrets that Rigoberta is not divulging, in which case her restraint would be "true" and real? Or is she consciously performing a kind of rhetorical seduction in which she lets the fringe of a hidden text show in order to tease us into thinking that the fabric must be extraordinarily complicated and beautiful, even though there may not be much more than fringe to show? If we happen not to be anthropologists or historians, how passionately interested in secrets does she imagine the reader to be? Yet the narrative makes this very assumption, and therefore piques a curiosity that may not have preexisted the resistance. The refusal is performative; it constructs metaleptically the apparent cause of the refusal. Before Menchú denies us satisfaction, we are not aware of any desire to know her secrets. And that desire denied, that intellectual and intimate demotion of readers used to better treatment may humble us enough to let an unfamiliar kind of respect complicate desire. No one tags Menchú in her game of hide and seek, because she refuses to change places and to risk losing her place to the reader; instead she taunts us by escaping before we get a full view. And playing at chastity, covering up discursive spaces to produce inviolable private parts, makes modesty a reader's requirement for engagement.

Menchú, in fact, teaches us to read modest-making moves in politically particularist literatures, to expect those moves and remain respectful before them. Taking Menchú's lesson in reading, we can begin to locate some of these overlooked strategies in a more general project that reads resistance to "comprehension" not as difficulty, but as a defense of one's positionality, a defense against presumptuous "competent" readers.[63]

By contrast to Rigoberta, cynical and apolitical Jesusa hides nothing, it seems. "I don't feel anything, from feeling too much."[64] What difference would hiding make anyway, since any strategic seduction would be beside the point for a woman just waiting to die in peace. Unlike Menchú's coquettish omissions, Jesusa delivers an unpunctuated and practically seamless text. Consider how differently they discuss the *nahaul*, for example, from their particular corners of Mayaland throughout which the concept is current. For Menchú this spiritual *doppelgänger* from the natural world is the subject of sacred and social secrecy; small children are not told if their *nahaul* is a sheep, or a lion, or a tree, because that knowledge could bias their development, and outsiders are even less reliable repositories for that knowledge.

> We Indians have always hidden our identity and kept our secrets to ourselves. This is why we are discriminated against. We often find it hard to talk about ourselves because we know we must hide so much in order to preserve our Indian culture and prevent it being taken away from us. So I can only tell you very general things about the nahaul. I can't tell you what my *nahaul* is because that is one of our secrets.[65]

But Jesusa cares nothing for these pretenses of propriety in the devalued cult she knows; secrecy only allows for basely human deceit:

> The *nahaul* is a Christian in disguise so that he can rob like an animal. He's a Christian in a dog's skin and walks around on all fours, on his hands and knees, but when he comes to a house to rob it, he has to get up to get what he wants. But at the moment he's discovered, he runs away howling and everybody in the house crosses himself in horror. He goes out at night when there's a full moon, to see better. Nothing more than a plain crook dressed like an animal, a dog or a coyote or a wolf. People short on spirit are very afraid of them, but not me because I have really seen them. I saw him. I was alone one morning and...[66]

Instead of frustrating titillation, which is what we get from Menchú, Jesusa puts out a full story, as smooth and infuriatingly independent as the boundless Pampa that maddened some of Latin America's founding fathers.[67] But to compare Jesusa's story with the virginal land seems patently wrong. Her text is hardly barren, but full of detail, even compromising detail about her own drunkenness and rage (like the time she got so angry with a cop, she pulled down his pants and sunk her teeth into his b...berries), about her successes and failures with work and with people.[68] Nevertheless, the life is seemingly impenetrable, because, paradoxically, penetration makes no sense when there are no holes to fill in. There is no engagement in this ready-made, disturbingly smooth product. It keeps us idle, never running the risk of confusing observer with participant. And idleness can infuriate us more surely than the effort a difficult book demands. Like the endless and unmarked desert that turns out to be a labyrinth more deadly than the complicated maze in Jorge Luis Borges's story about rival kings, Jesusa's book confounds the sophisticated reader by refusing to supply conquerable challenges; it loses the reader in an arid monotone of indifferent telling.

None of Menchú's tantalizing intimacy is withheld, nor is there any mention of the corollary lesson about the ethical hazards of unsolicited sympathy, hazards of informant removal through ethnographic renewal. Instead, Jesusa seems to give it all away with a verbal shrug: What does anything matter? Why bother telling you; what good does it do me?[69] Somewhere between indifferent and resigned, she repeats these rhetorical questions and so puts the value—or the purpose—of her performance into serious question.

Perhaps we are not getting something we had bargained for, some intimacy or borrowed authenticity that autobiography is supposed to deliver. But if we stopped to calculate the deal, we might ask how we could possibly get what we want vicariously through Poniatowska. The very Mexicanness that she craves is characterized by intellectuals like herself, following Octavio Paz, as unavailably "hermetic." Her pursuit of intimacy already predicts her failure; it marks her as an unauthentic Mexican. Paradoxically, desire gets in the way of satisfaction. If Mexicans keep silent even as they speak, in Paz's apt articulation, if they reserve themselves even as they expend words, then to exact intimate withdrawals for the purpose of revealing a personal account is literally counterproductive; it is to render that account empty, to leave nothing to bank on. This means that the bargain Poniatowska wants to strike with Jesusa—the informant's private authenticity for the writer's public hand in breaking silences—leaves Poniatowska necessarily empty-handed. If her informant is really Mexican and hermetic, little real meaning can change hands; and if she offers intimacy, it hardly has any authentic(ating) value.

Perhaps purposefully tone deaf to the paradox of silent speech or meaningful muteness, Poniatowska persevered with Palancares. Breaking silence is, after all, the slogan for intellectual feminists of the period. Even if Jesusa did not want to be saved from solitude, Poniatowska would force the rescue. And her force proved irresistible to the working woman. Maybe it was the flattery of Poniatowska's persistent interest, or the poignancy of a privileged woman's pursuit after Mexican meaning for herself. In either case, or in both, Jesusa responded with a torrent of words whose worth is drowned by the very flow itself. What intimate purchase can they have?

Perhaps the uncensored revelations of this adventurous woman are something so eviscerated by practiced indifference that they are meant to leave us cold. Even the promisingly mysterious opening sequence about the spiritist sessions and visions, a sequence that Poniatowska must have chosen for its dramatic effect, is immediately demystified, sanitized, interpreted away. "They told me that all that white clothing was the habit in which I was supposed to appear at the hour of Judgement and that God had allowed me to contemplate myself like that and how I behaved during the three times I came to earth" (11). Jesusa has no patience for mystery. The life of the spirit, yes, but how dare we imagine this is anything mysterious, to be interpreted, possibly by us.

If Jesusa needn't bother telling us her life, and if she gains nothing by our taking it from her, why indeed does she keep holding forth as if nothing were being held back? Could she be deploying an almost comical strategy of refusal that defies an insistent authority by apparently pandering to it, like the strategy that everyone in Eastern Europe associated with "The Good Soldier Schweig" who would infuriate his interrogators by answering with so much detail it was impossible to tell what piece of it mattered? Might we notice that the game of hide-and-seek, so obvious in Menchú's maneuvers, is announced in voluble Schweig's very name, which means "Silence?"[70] And is it possible that Jesusa too is staging a performance that makes the information irrelevant, so available and public that it offers no political or personal pathos for readers? Then self-aggrandizing empathy would be impossible, as impossible as our imperious tendency to substitute the autobiographical subject in a game that Paul de Man called reciprocal replacements.[71] Some readers actually manage to ignore Menchú's demand for distance and to embrace her in an autobiographical reflex that invites identification with the writer. And Poniatowska went on record about her identifications with Jesusa. The projections of presence and truth are hardly generous here. Instead, they allow for an unproblematized appropriation which disregards the text's insistence on the political value of keeping us at a distance. Used to a metaphoric persona in autobiography that shuttles between writer and reader, we may miss Menchú's metonymic alternative of contiguity based on irreplaceable difference.

Poniatowska sometimes worried about her own morality as a player in the game of "de-facement"; but she need not have worried about Jesusa's mortality, that is her enduring serviceability, because Jesusa offered everything required of her during two years of what must have looked like amateur therapy sessions, as one woman probed and the other disclosed one intimate story after another. "Jesusa has been freed to speak by the timely intervention of Elena Poniatowska," writes one approving reader.[72] But the speaker seems less grateful than we expect her to be. Her integrity does not flinch before the interest she kindles or the kindness her interrogator proffers. And as for the therapeutic value of middle-class sympathy, it is less than nothing, she objects, because the language of paralyzing pain entirely misses who she is; it obliterates her. "I don't know what sadness is. You're talking to me in Chinese, because I don't understand sadness. Crying is one thing, but sadness is another. It's bad, doesn't work, means nothing to anyone but yourself."[73]

The dismissal of Poniatowska's sentimental language, towards the end of this hybrid between oral history and novelized hagiography, makes the off-putting epigraph resonate with more than just skepticism about the possibility of friendship *hors de texte*.[74] That uninviting initiation also predicts a series of disencounters with curious and impertinently sentimental writers and readers.[75] The message is not only to save your crocodile tears after you have taken my life, but also that the life you have managed to eke out over years of diligent plunder (or hours of voracious reading) is undigestible for you because it needs no digesting; it is too simple to be processed or to leave nourishing traces; so it is simply expelled and forgotten. As if Jesusa were taunting us with lavish adventures, serving them up one after another, she purposefully reserves any flavor or meaning for disappointed and possibly chastened readers. You can take away the frantic activity of my life, she may be saying, but you leave this purloined person hiding in full view, safely untranslated and unassimilable. Empty-handed readers are then caught red-handed, singed by a frustrated desire to have our way with Jesusa. When she refuses, refusing to be our matrix for narcissistic self-duplication, we confront our limited contours before trying to take another literary life.

NOTES

1. Later on, Poniatowska will admit that the scenes with Zapata are of her own invention, inspired by Jesusa's admiration for Zapata alone among the important figures of the Mexican Revolution. See María Inés Lagos-Pope, "El testimonio creativo de *Hasta no verte Jesús mío,*" *Revista Iberoamericana* núm 150 (January–March 1990): 243–53.

2. Beth E. Jörgensen's discussion is particularly useful on this "Creative Confusion," as she calls her essay about *Hasta no verte Jesús mío,* Chapter Two in *The Writing of Elena Poniatowska* (Austin: Texas University Press, 1994), 28–66, esp. 53. Her reading coincides with several of the points I developed here independently.

3. For collections of essays, see the special issue of *Latin American Perspectives, Voices of the Voiceless in Testimonial Literature,* ed. Georg Guggelburger, 70 (Summer, 1991) and 71 (Fall, 1991); René Jara and Hernán Vidal, eds., *Testimonio y literatura* (Minneapolis: Institute for the Study of Ideologies and Literature, 1986); John Beverley and Hugo Achúgar, eds., *La voz del otro: Testimonio. subalternidad y verdad narrativa* (Lima and Pittsburgh: Latinoamérica Editores, 1992); Sherna Gluck and Daphne Patai, *Women's Words: The Feminist Practice of Oral History* (New York: Routledge, 1991).

4. John Beverley, *Against Literature* (Minneapolis: University of Minnesota Press, 1993), 77, and in general Chapters 4 and 5.

5. Poniatowska, "Literatura testimonial" (1984). Quoted in Jörgensen, 60–61. See also Judith Stacy, "Can There be a Feminist Ethnography?" in Gluck and Patai, 111–20; and Daphne Patai, "U.S. Academics and Third World Women: Is Ethical Research Possible?" in Gluck and Patai, 137–53.

6. 1985 Essay on La Onda, reference from Jörgensen, 52.

7. Jörgensen, 36.

8. The expectation is prepared by standard feminist assumptions about women being trained to control expressions of desire. Poniatowska herself is one example: "The effort to hide personal preoccupations, her own intimacy is a constant feature of her creative work." Lagos-Pope, 249 (my translation).

9. Julia A. Kushigian, "Transgresión de 1a autobiografía y el Bildungsroman en *Hasta no verte Jesús mío,*" *Revista Iberoamericana* núm 140 (Julio–Sept.

1987): 667–77. She quotes Paz, as if Jesusa had posed for his Mexican portraits. He wrote, as she quotes on p. 668: "Como todos los idolos, es dueña de fuerzas magnéticas, cuya eficacia y poder crecen a medida que el foco emisor es más pasivo y secreto. Analogía cósmica: 1a mujer no busca, atrae." *(Laberinto de la soledad* (Mexico: FCE, 1979), 33.

10. Octavio Paz, *The Labyrinth of Solitude: Life and Thought in Mexico*, translated by Lysander Kemp (New York: Grove Press, 1961), 29. *Laberinto de 1a soledad* (Mexico: FCE, 1979, first published by Cuadernos americanos, 1950). "Viejo o adolescente, criollo o mestizo, general, obrero o licenciado, el mexicano se me aparece como un ser que se encierra y se preserva: máscara el rostro y máscara la sonrisa. Plantado en su arisca soledad, espinoso y cortés a un tiempo, todo le sirve para defenderse: el silencio y la palabra, la cortesía y el desprecio, la ironia y la resignacíon. Tan celoso de su intimidad como de la ajena, ni siquiera se atreve a rozar con los ojos al vecino: una mirada pinede desencadenar la cólera de esas almas cargadas de electricidad," 26.

11. See Lisa Davis, "An Invitation to Understanding among Poor Women of the Americas: *The Color Purple* and *Hasta no verte Jesús mío*" in Gari Laguardia and Bell Gale Chevigny, eds., *Reinventing the Americas: Comparative Studies of Literature of the United States and Spanish America* (Cambridge, NY: Cambridge University Press, 1986) 224–41; and Bell Gale Chevigny, "The Transformation of Privilege in the Work of Elena Poniatowska," *Latin American Literarv Review* XIII/26 July–Dec. 1985, 49–62, where a parallel is made between Jesinsa and her antithesis Angelina Beloff (From *Ouerido Diego*), "sharing with her only a will to survive and a need to break silence, to assert herself," 53. Also Scott, in Poniatowska's "desire to identify with Mexico's *intrahistoria* as well as to affirm her own self...there is also a perceptibly feminist desire to give voice and visibility to women marginalized and silenced" (412).

12. See, for example, Lucille Kerr, "Gestures of Authorship: Lying to Tell the Truth in Elena Poniatowska's *Hasta no verte Jesús mío*" in *Reclaiming the Author: Figures and Fictions from Spanish America* (Durham: Duke University Press, 1992), 46–64. The hybrid genre, novela testimonial, "seems to testify to the truth of what it tells through the language of literature, a good many questions may be raised about how such a text may become accepted (or not) as truthful, and about how the figure of the author associated with it may come to exercise any authority at all," 47. Also see Nina M. Scott, "The Fragmented Narrative Voice of Elena Poniatowska," *Discurso* vii/2 (1990): 411–20. "As fine a text as Poniatowska has produced, the ambiguity between fact and fiction still undermines the effectiveness of Jesus's testimonial" 414.

13. See *Languages of the Unsayable: The Play of Negativity in Literature and Literary Theory*, Sanford Budick and Wolfgang Iser, eds., (New York: Columbia University Press, 1989).

14. Roland Barthes, *Pleasure of the Text* (New York: Hill and Wang, 1975), 40.

15. Ibid., 17.

16. Ibid., 27.

17. Ibid., 6.

18. Georges Poulet, "Criticism and the Experience of Interiority," in *The Structuralist Controversy: The Language of Criticism and the Science of Man*, Richard A. Macksey and Eugenio Donato, eds. (Baltimore: The Johns Hopkins University Press, 1972) 56–72. [Reprinted in *Reader-Response Criticism: From Formalism to Post-Structuralism*, edited by Jane Tompkins (Baltimore: The Johns Hopkins University Press, 1980), 41–49.

19. See, as a representative piece, Wolfgang Iser, "The Reading Process: A Phenomenological Approach," in Tompkins, 50–69. Also, for a study of the operations readers perform and the "spurs" that texts provide for interaction with the reader, *The Act of Reading: A Theory of Aesthetic Response* (Baltimore: The Johns Hopkins University Press, 1978). In *The Implied Reader: Patterns of Communication in Prose Fiction from Bunyan to Beckett* (Baltimore: The Johns Hopkins University Press, 1974) Iser offers readings of representative novels based on their requirement of active readerly participation. Among his many essays, one that is most promising for the readings I attempt here is "Narrative Strategies as Means of Communication" in *Interpretation of Narrative*, Mario J. Valdés and Owen J. Miller, eds., 100–117. It focuses on the particular shape of readings as imposed by the author's regulation of the process.

20. In the "Discussion" (Macksey and Donato, 73–88) that follows Poulet's paper, he responds that unlike reading, conversation "becomes instead, quite the contrary, a sort of battle, a radical opposition, an insistence on *differentiation*. The act of reading, as I conceive it, is…above all an acceding, even an adherence, provisionally at least, and without reserve" (73).

21. Poulet, 56.

22. That unreflective, universalizing love can produce perverse confusions between pets and partners is provocatively argued in Marc Shell's "The Family Pet, or the Human and the Animal," in *Children of the Earth: Literature, Politics, and Nationhood* (New York, Oxford: Oxford University Press, 1993), 148–75.

23. Poulet, 57.

24. Ibid., 60.

25. Ibid., 61.

26. Ibid., 62.

27. Ibid., 72.

28. Patrocinio P. Schweickart, "Reading Ourselves: Toward a Feminist Theory of Reading," in *Gender and Reading: Essays on Readers. Texts. and Contexts*, Elizabeth A. Flynn and Patrocinio P. Schweickart, eds., (Baltimore: The Johns Hopkins University Press, 1986), 52.

29. Judith Fetterly, *The Resisting Reader: A Feminist Approach to American Fiction* (Bloomington: Indiana University Press, 1978), xx, and Schweickart, 41.

30. Schweickart, 52–54.

31. Julia Swindells, "Liberating the Subject?; Autobiography and Women's History, A Reading of *The Diaries of Hannah Cullwick*" in *Interrogating Women's*

Lives: Feminist Theory and Personal Narratives, the Personal Narratives Group, eds. (Bloomington: Indiana University Press, 1989), 24–38.

32. Schweickart, 56.

33. Ross Chambers, *Room for Maneuver: Reading Oppositional Narrative* (Chicago: University of Chicago Press, 1991).

34. Ibid., 24.

35. Ibid., 12.

36. Ibid., 32.

37. Ibid., 33.

38. Ibid., 26.

39. Barthes, *Pleasure of the Text.*

40. Alison Lurie, "Love Has Its Consequences: Three novellas about women who haven't come such a long way." *The New York Time Book Review*, August 8, 1993, 1.

41. Emmanuel Levinas, *Totality and Infinity* (Pittsburgh: Duquesne University Press, 1969).

42. Mikhail Bakhtin, *Art and Answerability* (Austin: University of Texas Press, 1990), 81–82.

43. "Me quedría el muchacho oficial o no me quedría, no sé. Entiendo yo que si él no me hubiera querido, como era militar y andaba en la revolución, pues me arrebata y me lleva y ya." At the nadir of sentimentality, she describes their "intimacy": "Yo nunca me quité los pantalones, nomás me los bajaba cuando él me ocupaba, pero que dijera yo, me yoy a acostar como en mi casa. eso no, Mi marido no era hombre que lo estuviera apapachando a uno, nada de eso. Era hombre muy serio. El tenía con qué y lo hacía y ya." (85)

44. García Pinto, 175. "But now it seems to me that there are some things that could have been deleted and others that could have been worked on more, things about her inner life, not so many anecdotes or adventures.... There are people who think it's like a picaresque novel."

45. Pinto, 175.

46. Pinto, 176,

47. Kerr, 185. n. 13. quotes from "Jesusa Palancares" (p. 9) about the informant terrorizing interrogator by threatening to die before she tells the whole story: "Y se me va a morir, como ella lo desea; por eso, cada miércoles se me cierra el corazón de pensar que no podría estar."

48. Chevigny, "Jesusa did not want to be interviewed, however, and Poniatowska for some time visited Jesusa once a week in what appears a tacit understanding of an equalizing ritual. Jesusa would set her to the task of taking her thirteen hens, a little leash tied to a leg of each, out into the sun.... Although Poniatowska has said she made up details, her deference to Jesusa is patent in everything she says about her." 54.

49. *Hasta no verte*, 273. "Yo no soy querendona, no me gusta la gente."

50. Jesusa's uniqueness is clear from her interview with Lorraine Roses, "Entrevista con Elena Poniatowska," *Plaza* 5–6 (1981–82), 51–64. "I see her as unique. In the first place, she's not at all like other Mexican women because she's no self-

denying little Mexican mother; she's not mild, but fundamentally rebellious. Her pride is enormous" (60–61). But Julia A. Kushigian reads her as typical, in fact as a model for Paz.

51. Oscar Lewis, *The Children of Sánchez: Autobiography of a Mexican Family* (New York: Random House, 1961).

52. Ibid., 135. "Bendito sea Dios porque he sufrido tanto. Seguro que yo nací para eso.... Pero me conformaba."

53. Translated as *Massacre in Mexico*, by Helen R. Lane. (Lincoln, MO: University of Missouri Press, 1992).

54. Bell Gale Chevigny, "The Transformation of Privilege in the Work of Elena Poniatowska," *Latin American Literary Review* XIII/26, July–December, 1985, 49–62, 50.

55. University of Washington Press, 1990.

56. "Elena Poniatowska," *Women Writers of Latin America: Intimate Histories,* interviews with Magdalena Garcia Pinto, trans. Trudy Balch and Magdalena Garcia Pinto (Austin: University of Texas Press, 1991), 163–81, 163. "All the Pontiatowskis were French-Polish. One, for example was one of Napoleon's marshals. They had been expelled from Poland precisely because the last one was Stanislaus Augustus, the last king of Poland" (164). "I was born in Paris. [in convent school in Phila.] We got special treatment because we were considered princesses, because of my father's family name" (165). "We came on a refugee boat...in 1942 or at the very beginning of 1943" (166). Spoke only French, was sent to British school in Mexico; "But I learned Spanish from the servants very quickly. From that time on I have always had very sympathetic feelings for housemaids, or whatever you want to call them. That explains why I like Jesusa Palancares...so much."

57. Elena Poniatowska, "*Hasta no verte Jesús mío*: Jesusa Palancares," *Vuelta* 24 (noviembre 1978), 7–9. "Mientras ella hablaba surgían en mi mente las imagenes, y todas me producían una gran alegria. Me sentía fuerte de todo lo que no he vivido.... Lo que crecía o a lo mejor estaba allí desde hace años era el ser mexicana; el hacerme mexicana; sentir que México estaba adentro de mí y que era el mismo que el de la Jesusa y que con sólo abrir la rendija saldría.... Una noche, antes de que viniera el sueno, después de identificarme largamente con la Jesusa y repasar una a una todas sus imágenes, pude decirme en voz baja: 'Yo sí pertenezco'" (8).

58. See Kerr: "Jesusa's opinions and actions situate her as ever at odds with, and sometimes openly critical of, the major institutions and political or popular myths of Mexican culture (the family, the military, the church, the Mexican revolution and its heroes)" (57).

59. Henri Lefebvre, "Toward a Leftist Cultural Politics: Remarks Occasioned by the Centenary of Marx's Death" trans. David Reifman. *Marxism and the Interpretation of Cultures,* eds. Cary Nelson and Lawrence Grossberg, 75–88. See esp. 78.

60. "Se dice que los españoles violaron a los mejores hijos de los antepasados, ...y en honor a esas gentes más humildes nosotros tenemos que seguir guardando

nuestros secretos. Y esos secretos nadie podrá descubrir más que nosotros los indígenas."

61. Sigo ocultando lo que yo considero que nadie lo sabe, ni siquiera inn antropólogo, ni un intelectual, por más que tenga muchos libros, no saben distinguir todos nuestros secretos."

62. See my "Resistant Texts and Incompetent Readers," *Poetics Today* 15: 2/3 1994.

63. *Hasta no verte*, 256. "De tanto que siento ya no siento."

64. Menchú, 20.

65. *Hasta no verte*, 120. "El nagual es un cristiano que se disfraza para robar en figura de animal. Es un cristiano con una piel de perro y camina así con las cuatro patas, con las manos y los pies, pero cuando llega a robar a una casa, a fuerza se tiene que levantar para alcanzar lo que va a echar en su morral. Pero a la hora en que lo descubren se echa a correr aullando y todos los de la casa se persignan del horror. Sale en las noches de luna para ver mejor. Nada más es ratero de conveniencias que se transforma en animal, perro o coyote o lobo. La gente corta de espíritu les tiene mucho miedo pero yo no porque los he visto de a deveras. Yo lo vi. Estaba yo sola y...."

66. Domingo Faustino Sarmiento is my main reference; it is his rhetoric that recurs in later writers. See my *Foundational Fictions: The National Romances of Latin America* (Berkeley: University of California Press, 1991), chapters 2 and 9.

67. *Hasta no verte*, 209. "Le bajé los pantalones, que me agacho y que me le cinelgo del racimo. ¡Daba unos gritos! Al final lo aventé después de darle una buena retorcida."

68. Palancares complains of the idle questions women asked her after her husband died in battle (97). "¿Que me gano con decirles? No me gano nada. No con que les cuente yo mi vida, se me van a quitar las dolencias. Yo no cuento nada."

69. "Elena Poniatowska," *Women Writers of Latin America: Intimate Histories,* interviews with Magdalena Garcia Pinto, trans. Trudy Balch and Magdalena García Pinto (Austin: University of Texas Press, 1991), 163–81, 169.

70. I thank Kim Sheppele for this association. The variable spellings Schweig and Schweik are part of the Point of Czechoslovakian mongrelization of several languages.

71. Paul de Man, "Autobiography as De-Facement" *MLN* 94 (1979), 919–30. "Autobiography, then, is not a genre or a mode, but a figure of reading or of understanding that occurs, to some degree, in all texts. The autobiographical moment happens as an alignment between the two subjects involved in the process of reading in which they determine each other by *mutual reflexive substitution* ... in a text in which the author declares himself the subject of his own understanding, but this merely makes explicit the wider claim to authorship" (my emphasis, 921). Julia A. Kushigian finds the movement a source of unproblematic affirmation, as if she missed de Man's point about loss. See "Transgresión de la autobiografía y el Bildungsroman en *Hasta no verte Jesús mío*," *Revista Iberoamericana* núm' 140 (Julio–Septiembre, 1987), 667–77. She quotes de Man on "Autobiography as Defacement," 921–22, about "substitutive exchange that constitutes the subject," but concludes: "En determinado

momento el intercambio entre ambas mujeres domina; así se transforma en sujeto independiente, libre de cualquier oposición que pudiera impedir la sustitución y la inevitable fusión de los dos mismos sujetos" (668).

72. Lisa Davis, "An Invitation to Understanding among Poor Women of the Americas: *The Color Purple* and *Hasta no verte. Jesús mío"* in Gari Laguardia and Bell Gale Chevigny, eds., *Reinventing the Americas: Comparative Studies of Literature of the United States and Spanish America* (Cambridge, New York: Cambridge University Press, 1986), 224–41, 225. Davis continues, "much as Alice Walker has served Celie and the other characters of *The Color Purple* as 'author and medium.'"

73. 89. She claims that even her father's death at the hands of Zapatistas didn't make her sad: "A mí no me dió tristeza porque no lo vi. Como ya me había casado y no andaba con la gente de mi papá, la cosa hasta ahí quedó. No supe más de él, hasta que pasaron los años y en el Defe encontré a un joven espirita que le dio poderes a la facultad para que fuera a levantar su espíritu entre los abrojos."

74. García Pinto, 166. After Poniatowska offered her a copy, Jesusa complained that the book was not a testimonial; she told me, "You don't understand anything..." (167). She wanted more episodes about the Obra Espiritual, and was angry that Poniatowska didn't detail the meetings and people; that I made people up and killed others off.

75. Susana Beatriz Cella keeps the asymmetry of the relationship in focus, but for some reason concludes that the struggle between narrator and editor has had a happy outcome, the book itself. Is the end felicitous for us or for the narrator? The asymmetrical relationship would seem to impose the question. See "Autobiografía e historia de vida en *Hasta no verte. Jesús mío* de Elena Poniatowska." *Literatura Mexicana* II/i (1991), 149–56.

POSTMODERNISM AND THE POSSIBILITY OF BIOGRAPHY

○ Introduction

Marjorie Garber

IF THERE IS no "self," how can there be biography or autobiography? This is the question poststructuralism poses to postmodernism.

In a way it is a specious question, like the question recently posed to a group of avant-garde literary critics: if the self has been deconstructed, can there be any meaningful concept of human rights?[1] To accept the concept of a "split subject" is not to deny the existence of persons, or of history, or of oppression (or indeed of pleasure). For the biographer and the autobiographer, postmodernity means understanding that there is no secure external vantage point from which one can see clearly and objectively, can "realize" the subject. As if biographers ever thought they were doing that. That biography—and, even more, autobiography—is a species of fiction-making is a truth so old that only a willed cultural amnesia can make it new.

Still, there are issues.

Freud's sentence, "*Wo Es war, soll Ich werden,*"has been variously translated. "Where id is, ego shall be." "Where it (id) was, there I (ego) must come about." Does this mean "the ego should replace the id"—the answer of ego-psychology, which urges the subject to take charge of, indeed to master, his/her own desires? ("Psycho-analysis is an instrument to enable the ego to achieve a progressive conquest of the id."[2]) Or does it mean "the id forms the ego"—in effect the reverse sentiment, suggesting that it is desire and its displacements that produces the construction that we call the self?

Jacques Lacan paraphrases Freud this way: "Là où fut ça, il me faut advenir."[3] There where it was, I must come to be. What does this mean, and what are its implications for biography?

More than a hundred years ago the issue was framed and dismissed by the testy egghead rhetorician Humpty Dumpty: "The question is, which is to be master, that's all." Dumpty was speaking of language, and it is language, according to Lacan—and poststructuralism—that instates subjectivity. Instates it as a "split subject," already self-divided. In Freud's terms, *Ichspaltung*, the splitting of the ego.

Lacan asks his own question: "Is what thinks in my place, then, another I?" The concept of the split subject depends upon the idea that the subject is constituted in and through language. Something is missing, something is desired; language fills the gap. Words name the thing that is wanting, and wanted. "Identity" and "wholeness," as Jacqueline Rose points out, "remain precisely at the level of the fantasy."[4] Meantime who "I" am shifts, depending on who is speaking, depending on who is listening. As Shakespeare's Cassius long ago remarked to Brutus,

> since you know you cannot see yourself
> So well as by reflection, I, your glass,
> Will modestly discover to yourself
> That of yourself which you yet know not of.[5]

Is what looks in my place another eye?

Like Lacan's "mirror stage," Cassius's "glass" reflects not an objective record but a fantasy image, offering Brutus an ameliorative *misrecognition* of self—one that imputes unity, purposefulness, admiration, and control: "that of yourself which you yet know not of." Shakespeare is always already our contemporary, since every age invents its own Shakespeare to authorize its idiosyncrasies as "human nature."

If poststructuralism bequeaths to biography the question of the split subject, postmodernism acts out that ambivalent bequest, testing and transgressing the borderline between "fiction" and "reality," or "fiction" and "nonfiction" in novels, films, and popular culture. Through technological wizardry Woody Allen's Zelig and Tom Hanks' Forrest Gump appear on screen with heroes of the past brought to "life" again. Forrest Gump shakes hands with President John Kennedy—as did a young Bill Clinton in his campaign ads. Oliver Stone invents grainy "documentary" footage that rewrites the Kennedy assassination. Ronald Reagan, as President, "remembers" life experiences that were actually parts of his movie scripts. A breathless nation watches O. J. Simpson circumnavigate the L.A. freeways in a white Bronco van followed by a phalanx of police cars, impatient for the denouement: the arrest, the car crash, the suicide. In the movie *Speed*, which played to huge audiences all that first Simpson summer, viewers could see the same car chase—the white van, the police cars—uncannily filmed months before Simpson's flight. Is history a tape loop? Does all documentary evidence partake of this same quality of fantasy? Phone sex, Court TV, and the "dramatized reenactment" of current events in tabloid television and insta-films mark the apparently inescapable postmodernization of modern life: simulation, "morphing," lip-synching, animation.

Is what performs in my place another I?

The essays in this section not only describe and name postmodernism as a mode of what Marilyn Brownstein calls "life writing"—they also exemplify it. Sherley Anne Williams describes a novel in progress that takes a biographer as its narrator, and shows the inevitability of a crossover between the biographer's life and that of her subject. Biography begets autobiography. Marilyn Brownstein takes Walter Benjamin and Virginia Woolf as examples of what she calls "autograph." Clark Blaise puts "postmodern" in the very title of his essay, reflecting upon the temporality and imaginative geography of a life, where the nearest exit may be behind you.

"As for living," wrote Villiers de l'Isle-Adam in a phrase that both perturbed and fascinated the modernists, "our servants will do that for us." Thus spoke an exemplary fin de siecle decadent of the last century. In this fin de siecle, in this differently decaying decade, is it the *biographers* and not the servants who do the living?

NOTES

1. *Freedom and Interpretation: The Oxford Amnesty Lectures 1992*, ed. Barbara Johnson (New York: HarperCollins, 1993). Contributors include Hélène Cixous, Frank Kermode, Wayne Booth, Paul Ricoeur, Terry Eagleton, Julia Kristeva, and Edward Said.
2. Freud, *The Ego and the Id*, SE 19: 56.
3. "L'Instance de La Lettre Dans L'Inconscient." *Ecrits*. (Paris: Editions du Seuil, 1966), 524.
4. Jacqueline Rose, in Jacques, Lacan, *Feminine Sexuality: Lacan and the école freudienne*, ed. Juliet Mitchell and Jacqueline Rose, trans. Jacqueline Rose (New York: W.W. Norton, 1983), 32.
5. Shakespeare, *Julius Caesar* 1.2.67–70.

14

TELLING THE TELLER
Memoir and Story

Sherley Anne Williams

AUTOBIOGRAPHY AND BIOGRAPHY are the provenance of history, the factual, and the real; fiction is the provenance of imagination, and what happens there is only make-believe. There is some affinity between the two, however. Every fiction is about someone or something's life story, whether in whole or in part. And writers in each discipline are challenged to select and arrange the events they tell in some purposeful sequence that is revelatory of meaning and insightful of nature, human or otherwise. Because characters and events in fiction exist only in the mind, fiction writers seldom confront questions of privacy, accuracy, or access that may confound real life biographers—unless, of course, we do so through a character.

Amah Dean Graham, the central character in my current fiction, *Meanwhile in Another Part of the City*, is a historian, a tenured professor. Why history? I am writing a novel, not an autobiography. Why academia? I am familiar with its professional culture, and I wanted a character grounded in one—for reasons which may become clear later. Amah's first book, was published while she was still in graduate school. It was the "biography," in the sense of life story, of an all-black township in California, told through the memoirs and in the voice of Lady Jewel Ivory, the elderly daughter of one of the township's founders.

But whatever professional seductions biography might have held for Amah are long in the past by the time my fiction opens. Amah's book was thought quirky in what little press it got when it first appeared in the 1970s; Miss Ivory was neither famous nor dead, nor had she hinted at sizzling love affairs or had children; the town itself had been short-lived. Amah's departure from conventional third-person biography had not impressed her advisor. He turned down the material as a dissertation project: the transcribed ramblings of some old woman did not constitute biography. The book had no footnotes, had not been referred by a scholarly press and, published while Amah was still a student, had been little help in the job market. Amah is still an Afro-Americanist, but now works in broader and more academically accessible areas of inquiry, her scholarship and professional style no longer an issue.

The major structural convention of the written story is Amah's telling of events in the life of another character, Celeste, a pivotal figure in Amah's intellectual life. Years before and, perhaps, unwittingly, Celeste had given Amah the first inkling that her aspirations toward an intellectual life and an academic career were not beyond the reach of a bright, industrious, black girl such as Amah had been in the sixties. Almost thirty years later, Celeste remains for Amah a symbolic figure distinct from the militant integrationists who led the Civil Rights movement and the militant separatists of her own generation who called for Black Power. Amah uses Celeste's life as proof of a point in discussions about black men and black women with new friends. The group meets yearly at an academic convention and Amah, convinced of the symbolic value of events in Celeste's life, reveals more and more details about Celeste, the telling blossoming from anecdote to vignette to full-blown story.

Rather than naming Celeste in her stories, Amah identifies her by elegant attire and eccentric behavior, which she considers part of the public domain. Theirs is a small community of intellectuals where everyone mostly knows everyone else, by reputation and name if not by sight. It is one thing, Amah tells herself, to gossip about people one will never meet, as the group regularly does, and quite another to talk about someone whom one is likely to see professionally at any time. Amah is aware that the biography, the cumulative story she tells, is both a chronicle of an individual black women in the sixties and a critical commentary on that era; she worries that in telling it she may have crossed the line between public domain and Celeste's privacy. But the life study presented in *Meanwhile in Another Part of the City* is not Celeste's.

Amah's tales of Celeste are first-person narratives told in a framing story. The framing story is set in the present and narrated from a third-person perspective generally limited to Amah's point of view. In the story's present, Amah is confronted with another chance to try sex at an age—forty-something—and in an era—the present—when black people seldom talk about love or relationships, when they seem in fact to have stopped speaking to each other and with each other. And true to her "diasporic identity," she tells these tales to a white person, the would-be lover, who is the only one of their mostly black crowd who wants to hear them. She is fully aware of the irony. What she had not expected, however, is that her act of biography would also call forth her own autobiography. She discovers that she cannot tell Celeste without also telling herself. Her own subjectivity fills the space her "biography" should have made for Celeste's voice; her assumption of biographical voice, the third-person point of view masks her own place as a character in the tale. Nor can Amah tell herself as an intellectual without also telling herself as a woman. The oral autobiography that results, like the oral biography to which it responds, is at once open and veiled, the personal subsumed under the analysis of the political historian—barbed and frank, perhaps to a fault, about issues of nationalism and gender relations, reticent about personal affairs and family relationships.

Amah's deliberate disembodiment of her own voice echoes the rhetorical strategy of classic autobiography where the subject disembodies herself in order to abstract the higher and therefore "real" meaning of the life. Amah, however, grows uncomfortable with her self-edited narrative and, in the present of the story, begins to tell herself the things she cannot tell the white man, Horace. She constructs a counter-autobiography, one forced into existence by the meta-text she creates through her biography of Celeste. The full-blown story, then, is both biography and autobiography and perhaps manages to suggest, as Amah hopes it does, what a generation of black women scholars looked for and found to sustain them. Her telling of this story, however, is truncated; she suppresses one ending and substitutes another, deciding she will only speak so much of her generation to the white man.

Fiction always carries with it some element or dimension of the autobiographical; a writer, as James Baldwin once observed, writes out of one thing and one thing only: her (or him) self. That there is something of the writer's experience and perception in each of her or his characters is a truism of writing workshops and numerous handbooks that tell how to "turn your life" into fiction. But no matter how true to life one's fiction is, there comes a point in the writing when the fiction's likeness to life no longer matters, when the story or character is no longer being driven simply by the writer's will. Rather, the story unfolds out of its own logic and momentum and is then honed or otherwise manipulated by the writer in subsequent revision. And no matter how dominant the autobiographical content that goes into a characterization or plot development, in fiction the factuality of the autobiographical element or its likeness to the real life is seldom at issue or even the most significant level of meaning.

Amah, the character, is close to Sherley Anne, the writer, but I have no trouble distinguishing myself from my characters. This is why I turned away from poetry where the disembodied voice is always taken as the poet. Even students hear the disembodied voice of modern fiction not as the writer but as the character—think of Richard Wright's *Native Son*, in which Wright's presentation of Bigger's thoughts is sometimes taken as a measure of Bigger's ability to articulate them and even sophisticated readers sometimes take the very real vitriol of Wright's work for his character's expression of his inchoate longings. I do not mind talking about myself but there are not that many things I want to say, or can say in a voice constrained to the one-to-one correspondence of writer and subject. The challenge in writing Amah's imaginary autobiography and constructing the fiction of her life is to displace the issue of "real" life and make autobiography the issue, as a type of fictional—rather than an historical—project.

The final elements of the autobiographical form in the Amah Dean fiction are found texts, letters, pseudo papers, recipes, and song lyrics. The title is taken from Jesse Fuller's "San Francisco Bay Blues," and its verse, "Meanwhile in another part of the city, I'm about to go insane; I thought I heard my baby call the way he used to call my name," serves as the epigraph to the whole story. These texts are used as internalized documentation, as Robert B. Stepto calls the use of such incidental material in the autobiographical narratives of escaped and former slaves. They serve as implicit authentication of Amah's cultural, generational, and professional status. But Amah does not control these texts as did the antebellum narrators; nor are all of them integrated within framing episodes or nested tales. At times they may even seem to comment on Amah's actions. The found texts thus emphasize the story's ties to the traditions of black autobiography even as they also point up the fiction of Amah's story.

Amah's life is so other than that of Frederick Douglass and Harriet Jacobs (to name only the two most famous escaped slave narrators), that a narrative form that fit the two of them could not be expected to contain hers; or that Amah's narrative is forced beyond the conventions of these liberation narratives by the actual presence of a sympathetic white man in her story. In truth the texts are a way for me to short-circuit that constraining correspondence between writer and subject and remain quite firmly Amah's "biographer." The texts, by their very existence, often outside the unfolding of the plot and thus beyond Amah's consciousness, call attention to the artifice of the story. Their placement and content evoke the role of editor, organizer, writer, author. I am Amah's biographer, the tellee in the phrase "as told to," presenting someone else's tale, the subject's "auto" subsumed under my own. And this idea of exterior, authorial control is at the heart of a fiction writer's imagining of *auto*biography. The trueness of the first-person voice is a function of artifice, technique. The reader is meant to recognize, however unconsciously, that the voice is assumed; it is the subject that has been possessed by the author and not vice-versa.

Such possession is not the kind of control I want over representations of a real person's life, so I am less interested in autobiography or even biography as a form than I am in fiction. Biography and autobiography as the provenance of history are part of the official, "factual" story of the past. Yet the facts of the American past are such that black people have only been able to confront—imaginatively—the official story that is history, through wordless sounds, the wild cries and hollers of our music, and, sporadically, our words and stories. Thus our greatest literature (until black women began to write it) was rigorously present tense. The living experience, fiction, since World War II, has carried more authority of experience in Afro-American letters than either biography or autobiography, i.e. history. We have tended to distrust biography and even "as-told-to" autobiographies because, until the last decade or so, the most thoroughly researched ones were often done by whites.

The chasm between black and white life in this country is such that we have been unable to legitimately disabuse ourselves of the idea that no white person can truly see through the eyes of a black person. And too many white people are unable to disabuse themselves of the notion that a black person in this country cannot have true self-agency, that enablement must always come under the auspices of some white person. So biography and autobiography, the (more or less) factual story is less credible, less real, less of a life-likeness than the imagined fiction. Additionally, biography and autobiography are about what made a person, whereas fiction is about the making of someone; one is product, the other is process, one is forever past, the other is always present. With Amah's fiction, I want to move into the present with both feet.

The balance between representations of past and present Afro-American experience as the subject of fiction shifted in the eighties. The past, near as well as distant, has come under intense scrutiny from imaginative as well as scholarly writers to such an extent that the country, to judge by popular talk-shows, does not want, really, to hear all that old-ass shit no more. Black history is seen as securing "special" rights—as though, for example, the laws securing rights for black people did not also secure those rights for all people. And truly, it makes very little difference that one slave escaped to freedom if one more child gets hooked on crack, or if another baby perishes in a shooting. The times call for nothing less than a fiction as true to the totalities of our contemporary lives as contemporary black fiction has been in portraying the essential-isms of our past. Fiction now has the burden of doing something of what self-authored, black autobiography used to do for us; I speak now of Frederick Douglass and Maya Angelou, even Booker T. Washington and Richard Wright. All had some vision of a higher, finer meaning for our lives, saw some possibility of improvement in ourselves and our immediate circumstances, and so imbued us with a sense of change and progress as real possibilities in our lives.

Amah lives right now; she confronts AIDS, drugs, economic stagnation, and interracial sex with the same bewilderment as the rest of us. Nonetheless, she tries, and even if she does pick up her marbles and goes home; she always comes back. And if she speaks to anything, it is to the present and our dreams for the future. She is the star of the vignette she substitutes for the end of Celeste's story. She offers the white man something other, perhaps, than what he had sought, but it is something she is finally willing to give. Amah—scholar, female, black dissenter—is seduced, as our young people must be if we are to survive as a people, not by biography, someone else's story, but by the vitality and possibility of her own life.

"CATASTROPHIC ENCOUNTERS"
Postmodern Biography as Witness to History

Marilyn L. Brownstein

RECENTLY I FOUND among my notes this sentence of uncertain origin: *fragments of lives create a social fabric in which the laws for social life are not made but found.* I would like to think it my own, but, in fact, I suspect Walter Benjamin (a writer who deemed plagiarism a rhetorical trope and dreamed of an essay constituted from the sentences of others). No matter the attribution, the uncited sentence bears, in a preliminary way, the weight of some things I would like to consider, namely, questions about the role of the personal in life writing and the inevitably twinned matters of autograph and authority. Best of all, this sentence serves as an axiom for life writing and specific procedures responsive to poststructuralist and postmodern critiques of the possibility for biography.

As such, the sentence deserves scrutiny. The independent clause, *fragments of lives create a social fabric*, is not controversial; what is problematic awaits the unpacking of the dependent clause, *in which the laws for social life are not made but found.* The ordinary challenge of the passive voice, the question of the subject, is compounded in this case by seemingly antihistoriographic intimations of the personal as the source of authority. That is, it could be the case that the finders of social laws are the same as the keepers of the creative fragments of the sentence's subject. Thus, I want to take up a special case of a postmodern theory of representation, a version of life writing in which authority is located, at least initially, in autograph. The term *autograph* refers to a subjective space opened within discourse by a dialectical process, the effects of which facilitate the finding of the law.

The recovery of a facilitating process that has its origins in the personal need not imply, moreover, an aesthetic of individualism (at least in any conventional sense) or a search for authentic identity, but rather the potential for the life writer to reproduce a discursive occasion that is open-ended and therefore an occasion on which subjectivity may be restored to history. Thus I am able to restate my topic as a reconsideration of the relation between autograph and authority, initially suggested here in the paraphrase of Virginia Woolf in my title, fragments of her rallying cry in *Three Guineas*: "let biography be witness to history."[1] While considering the problem of life writing, Woolf, in her late-in-life, autobiographical "Sketch of the Past" (1939), demonstrates the historicizing function of a catastrophic encounter: Gerald Duckworth's sexual exploration of her juvenile body.

> I remember resenting, disliking it—what is the word for so dumb and mixed a feeling? It must have been strong, since I can still recall it. This seems to show that a feeling about certain parts of the body; how they must not be touched; how it is wrong to allow them to be touched; must be instinctive. It proves that Virginia Stephen was not born on the 25th of January 1882, but was born many thousands of years ago; and had from the very first to encounter instincts already acquired by thousands of ancestresses in the past. And this throws light not only on my own case, but upon the problem that I touched on the first page; why [in writing memoirs] it is so difficult to give any account of the person to whom things happen."[2]

Similarly, for Walter Benjamin, an archeology of personal experience managed by the diction of involuntary memory provides for the redemption of the historical subject and the historiographic project as well.[3] The dialectical methodology that I wish to propose for life writing, a recycling of Woolf's and Benjamin's memory themes, discretely names the penetrating interdependencies of the historical subject and the subjects of history. For both writers, the analysis begins in a specialized, sensational language, in acknowledgment of the radical representability of sensory memory and the historical implications of such reference.

> I find in my memory rigidly fixed words, expressions, verses that, like a malleable mass that has later cooled and hardened, preserve in me *the imprint of the collision between a larger collective and myself*. Just as a certain kind of significant dream survives an awakening in the form of words when all the rest of the dream content has vanished, *here isolated words have remained in place as marks of catastrophic encounters*.[4] (my italics)

The evocation of a scene of writing which insists upon the human body as subject of history and the specific suffering of the body in relation to historical conditions is a commonplace of dialectical methodologies of early twentieth-century feminist and Marxist writers and social critics. I take my examples from Woolf and Benjamin, not altogether an odd couple if one considers the historical and biographical contours of the lives of these two critics of literature and modern culture. The narratives overlap almost too perfectly, and all too poignantly. Both were, by their own reports, of upper middle-class origin. Born in the last decades of the nineteenth century—Woolf in 1882 and Benjamin in 1891, both died by suicide—Benjamin in flight from the Gestapo in 1940 and Woolf during the bombing of England in 1941. The autobiographical accounts figure powerfully, moreover, because both practiced a narrative mode dependent upon a dialectical resistance—the posing of difference, of strain, between the domain of private life and the public sphere as the initiation of an analysis.

The complementarities develop in reading a group of theoretical and autobiographical works: from Woolf, *Three Guineas*, an epistolary pacifist polemic published in 1938, in which she equates patriarchy with fascism, and "A Sketch of the Past," her analyses of the "merits and faults" of momentous events in her life[5]; from Benjamin, "The Author as Producer," a talk given at the Paris Institute for the Study of Fascism in 1934 and "A Berlin Chronicle," autobiographical sketches written in 1932, in which fragments of childhood memory illuminate aspects of Weimar culture.[6] Of course, Woolf and Benjamin both wrote biography as well. And the discursive principles I propose here are all-purpose, equally useful in both forms.

The uses of the personal are similarly and specifically defined in both of these writers. In "A Berlin Chronicle" Benjamin alludes to the cognitive principal that organizes subjectivity. The same principal delineates autograph in life writing: "[I]t is likely that no one ever masters anything in which he has not known impotence; and if you agree, you will also see that this impotence comes not at the beginning of or before the struggle with the subject, but in the heart of it."[7] "In the heart" is a term doubled by the sentence that follows in which Benjamin identifies the source of his "impotence before the city" in the generalized helplessness he remembers within the compass of his mother's scrutinizing gaze. Vulnerability, inextricably joined, developmentally, to mastery, is a congenital and lifelong condition for cognition and foundational to his dialectical practice. Thus, for Benjamin as well as for Woolf, a radical literary style has its origins in the intentional reproduction of an ambivalent cognitive mode. This formulation, is key to dialectical tendencies which produce and reproduce the margins of difference. A mode of discourse based in difference, moreover, is a mode that resists not only the ideology it examines but the ideological aspects of its own production, the orders of ordinary language and their mediating effects as well.

In "A Sketch of the Past" Woolf reflects upon cognitive ambivalence, an elemental and precocious linkage of powerlessness and mastery she discovered at age thirteen.

> [I]t was partly that my mother's death unveiled and intensified; made me suddenly develop perceptions.... Of course this quickening was spasmodic. But it was surprising—as if something were becoming visible without any effort.... I...began to read some poem. And instantly and for the first time I understood the poem; it was as if it became altogether intelligible; I had a feeling of transparency in words when they cease to be words and become so intensified that one seems to experience them; to foretell them as if they developed what one was already feeling.[8]

Such unintegrated states, according to cognitive psychology and studies in the neurobiology of memory, represent the activity of sensory memory, a recall of the personal record of vulnerability that is the key survival lesson in these works by Woolf and Benjamin. Neurological studies of memory confirm the possibility of thought without words, of memory stored as sensory detail and ordered according to the principles of the spatial mind, a mind without categorical, linear, or serial imperatives—a mind that resists abstraction in the concrete particularity and radical urgency of its plight.[9]

In irrational or preverbal or unintegrated states, survival is neither a matter of abstraction nor rationalization but a pursuit of the body's most practical objectives—a pursuit not dependent upon a myth of the wholeness of identity or subjectivity or even the practical exigency of time in which to make up one's mind. Instead at moments of stress or extreme challenge one operates out of fragments of the self, out of memory's echoes of strategies designed to cope with environmental particularities. Powerlessness and a concomitant unintegration, natural to all key phases or challenging occasions throughout human life, are the sources of one pole of Woolf and Benjamin's dialectical praxes.[10]

Under such circumstances the writing subject, unequivocally open to the particular processes of her own developmental history—inevitably, a narrative of incalculable gain at the site of unmollified loss—reproduces the vulnerability and the receptivity of the infantile body at key developmental moments. In discursive formations such experiences contain, as the passage from a "A Sketch of the Past" indicates, a space in which language means beyond the confines of lexicon or linguistic orders, a moment, to paraphrase the poet Marianne Moore, when images are so clearly represented they are taken for thought.[11] In these instances the familiar registers of rationality that contain and mediate the chaos of experience give way to "moments of being," to a world ordered by the recall of significantly matching moments, and by discursive strategies that recall, idiosyncratically, the particular sensory makeup of the vulnerability of the speaking or writing subject.[12] In this context, autograph may be defined as the reproduction of vulnerability and authority, located at the intersections of vulnerability and mastery that both

Woolf and Benjamin situate in subjectivity, in memory. In life writing the intentional production and reproduction of the specific nature of idiosyncratically embodied discourse prepares the occasions on which, according to Woolf and Benjamin, the law may be found.[13]

Both writers specifically theorize the general terms of such occasions and thus begin to provide answers to the problem of authority, the question of who it is that finds the law. For both, the scene of writing in this context is closely related to the scene of reading, equally significant occasions for finding the law. In "The Author as Producer" Benjamin cites Bertolt Brecht's theory of the alienation effect in epic theater and a concomitant refunctioning of art (234–35). Revolutionary art's new function, like the radical function of Woolf's experimental college imagined in *Three Guineas*, begins in the disruption of expectation that releases the audience from a focus on the conventions of plot and performance, thereby granting its members the individualized discomfort that precedes original thought. According to Benjamin, the psychology of the alienation effect constitutes a theory of reception involving producer, director, playwright, actors, and audience in a moment of being, an embrace of crisis in the terror of not belonging and not understanding that precedes a willed reintegration, a making up of what one doesn't know, a reconstitution of meaning from difference and by difference.

Woolf's matching occasion for finding the law in *Three Guineas* has mythic roots and contemporaneous potential. In studying the *Antigone*, she marks the distinction between written and unwritten law; the latter must be "discovered afresh by successive generations, largely by their own efforts of reason and imagination."[14] In this category she names practical knowledge, "the unpaid for education of daughters of educated men," and regards the achievement of its principal lesson, "freedom from unreal loyalties," as a model for the nature of life experience in which laws are found not made.[15] In this way Woolf links the paradigmatic dilemma—can vs. ought—of classical tragedy with heroic conflict in everyday life, employing narratives of middle-class women who brave poverty and patriarchal censure in order to find themselves in work and in pursuit of their own histories.

The fragments of lives that Woolf gathers in *Three Guineas* function cumulatively to demonstrate potentially rich relations between social and epistemological laws. The cumulative biographies of "daughters of educated men" deconstruct patriarchal economic oppression, revealing how an ideology of feminine dependence mediates paternal vulnerability and preserves patriarchal power. The economic oppression of the daughter is revealed to be the overdetermined symptom of patriarchy's "infantile fixation." This naming of the projection or displacement of patriarchal vulnerability marks the radical conversion of historiographic agency in *Three Guineas*. For in the histories of formerly dependent daughters of the middle class who strike out on their own, Woolf revives the practical connection of vulnerability and mastery as a developmental chore guaranteeing membership in the "Outsiders' Society." Such ambivalence, the basis for social change and revolutionary practice, breaks the binaristic, ideological, and practically false principles of masculine power and feminine vulnerability.[16] The recovery of originary ambivalence—by definition a resistance to the ideology of power—authorizes historical subjectivity.

Consequently, one could say that the achievement of a dialectic in which no synthesis can occur becomes a criteria for a particular kind of postmodern life writing. Its distinctive feature and distinctive advantage as a methodology rests in the preservation of the specific ambivalence of an individual life as one term of the dialectic. This term in its complexity is preserved even in the momentum toward the larger second term, an historical concept. In this analysis of Woolf's and Benjamin's similar methodologies, resides the originary ambivalence of the personal. The incommensurabilities of the doubled term of biography and the abstracted singularity of an historical context effectively stall the momentum toward synthesis.[17] The ambivalence of the personal in this work is not to be confused, moreover, with the doubleness of a Lacanian split subject. Instead, the theorizing of biographical ambivalence marks the return of subjectivity to history. That is, the speculative moment consists of a weighing of personal need against a social demand or prohibition already internalized; ambivalence is the essence of the speculative moment, originary to the flight toward consonance, the predictably human impetus to achieve an equilibrium of need and demand. It is the embrace of difference, however, the preservation of the personal or bottom-up analysis within the dialectic of need and demand or need and prohibition, that provides resistance to, and deconstruction of, ideology. Resistance in the formal ambivalence of the speculative moment is the historicizing feature distinctive to a radical dialectical practice.[18]

Ideology—or the second term of the dialectic—is measured by its reproduction in the life of individuals, quantified in the degree to which the social role mediates our relation to the real. This is not to define ideology as "a conspiracy against authenticity," nor as an oppressive "cloud of ideas," but simply to press Woolf's recognition, similar to that running throughout Marxist thought that ideology, as the source of social identity, manages not the real relations of the individual to the relations of the means of production but the imaginary relation of the individual to the relations of production.[19] For example, unconscious support for war or the imaginary relation is disclosed in Woolf's discussion of women's benign or humanitarian service to the war effort: nursing the war-wounded or taking over the peace-time jobs of soldiers. Here she indicates that the rewards of patriotism (an ideology) mediate the individual's belief that she opposes war; thus, an ideological construct abets the transformation of the desire to be against war into activity in support of war.[20]

Two passages demonstrate the operation of an unsynthesizable dialectic and situation of the relation within dialectic of the personal to the social law—of autograph to authority—one from *Three Guineas* and the other from "A Berlin Chronicle." If Benjamin's ambivalence was born in relation to the figure of the maternal, Woolf's would seem to be a reaction to her father Leslie Stephen, whose raging temper, according to her report, was a symptom of his inability to cope with the death of his wife Julia and his mourning children.[21] In "A Sketch of the Past," Woolf recalls Leslie's "savage" treatment of his daughters on Wednesdays during the weekly review of household accounts. Her diction in this context ("vicious, animal, brutal" is the string that characterizes her father's verbal attacks) preserves her rage at the gendering of economic abuse in the father-daughter relation that is her topic throughout *Three Guineas*. In the following passage on nepotism and women's exclusion from the professions, Woolf exploits male terror by means of projection: that is, by reproducing specifically gendered sexual terror as economic advantage. Here Woolf's art attempts to refunction the arrangements of capital.

> ...we shall agree at the outset that the professions are very queer things. It by no means follows that a clever man gets to the top or that a stupid man stays at the bottom. This rising and falling is by no means a cut-and-dried clear-cut rational process.... But the giving of...perquisites, the exercise of such influence, queers the professions. Success is easier for some, harder for others, however equal the brain power may be, so that some rise unexpectedly; some fall unexpectedly; some remain strangely stationary; with the result that the professions are queered. Often indeed it is the public advantage that they should be queered.[22]

Woolf's usually light hand is heavy here; it is not a matter of narrative but of risks she takes with respect to lexical disruptions of her narrative (another sort of "catastrophic encounter"). In this case, the repetitions of "queers" significantly distracts and displaces our attention. We move through a brash litany that begins at the seat of masculine vulnerability with unexpected rising and falling; or the "strangely stationary" option; from "hard success"—and our doubts about the bad puns and uncharacteristically heavy-handed prose—to subsequent play on "infallibility" of examiners; and the "cut-and-dried clear-cut" "fallibility" of the impersonal, culminating in a recognizable "queerness in the ties of blood and friendship." Inevitably, this litany of "queers" takes on sexualized resonances in which homosociality is wed to nepotism—all matches consummated between the sons of educated men and their nearest male kin.[23]

The sensory level of the text, achieved here in repetition, rises to the grand occasions, all in the family of man, before degen(d)erating to a synaesthetic (which is to say, sensory and irrational) evocation of the possibilities for nepotism in the work-lives of "the daughters of educated men." In the passage that follows, the sensory effect is achieved in a distasteful recital of a patriarchal ideology of female otherness: the queer "flavors" of sex in public office yield the "savours" of a feminine applicant who is single. Should she be married, however, the "scents of sex" become "odours," growing "rank and penetrating" until the plot sickens in a narrative clogged with the impediments confronting married women who could only wish for positions in public office.[24] Thus a refunctioning of language attempts to produce a change by pungently reproducing the unspeakable in resistance to the unspoken laws of patriarchy.

The nature of autograph in Woolf is anger that turns on the domestic economy as sexual economy—a telling public response to a household in which paternal diffidence with regard to the incestuous abuse of Leslie Stephen's daughters was joined to paternal rage over finances (at least in the long-term memory of one of his daughters).[25] These then are the souvenirs of loss, foundational to Virginia Woolf's ambivalence. Woolf's autograph (a memento of loss in language) functions to create the dislocations of a writerly text, enabling her reader to find the law, not of Woolf's making, but in a discursive field of Woolf's distinctive preparation. Autograph here (and according to the Brechtian model which Benjamin cites) releases authority to the reader, who, in a hermeneutic turn, becomes, herself, a producer.

The aim, in all cases, is to exploit radically demediating techniques (catastrophic linguistic encounters). Besides repetitions of the nature discussed above, the leaping conflagrations of Woolf's war-like, antipatriarchal polemic style are joined to content, for example, in neologisms that generate shocking conclusions: After listing many "bloodthirsty" battles among male professionals (including the battle of Harley Street, the battle of the Royal Academy, the battle of Westminster), Woolf coins "timeshed" and "spiritshed," intended, no doubt, for the more familiar category that harbors *bloodshed*. Thus she is able, quite matter-of-factly, to observe, "you will agree that a battle that wastes time is as deadly as a battle that wastes blood."[26] From Virginia Woolf who had experienced such loss first-hand in the death of her nephew Julian in the Spanish Civil War, a loss that caused her enormous anguish, we can only take the preceding statement unhyperbolically. Linguistically, hyperbole is a trope of mediation; here, the literal equation— the waste of time and the waste of life (the latter in its most physicalized manifestation, the waste of blood)—is the immediate, historicizing turn of a catastrophic encounter. We learn through this and similarly designed discursive refigurations throughout not, in fact, to take anything hyperbolically in *Three Guineas* despite the autographic anger that traffics in oppositions turned full circle, in sensory insult and public rage marking the fierce autograph of a feminist pacifist.

Benjamin's refunctioning effects in "A Berlin Chronicle," a sixty-page autobiographical essay cum historical document, are derived from rearrangements of "impotence" and ideology in a materialist analysis of patriarchal power and the domination of women and children in the farce of bourgeois family life. The dynamic is distinctively different from Woolf's, as are its tropes. Nonetheless, with both authors, the agent of refunctioning is the ambivalence of sensory experience, recovered in subversions of the rational orders of discourse and in public disclosures of conventionally personal and private responses.

In Benjamin's essay dialectic is established by narrative: a re-membering of occasions of "impotence," moments of Benjamin's terror which he attributes to his mother's power over him. Her power is purchasing power, a mirror of patriarchal authority, except that it includes her "humiliation," her "impotence." The technique is retrospective narration in which details evoke simultaneously the muted sleepwalking of secure childhood alongside the tyrannies and terrors of middle-class privilege. The passage to follow, occurring at the midpoint of the essay, documents the family's wealth which was accumulated in association with Lepke's auction house and the commerce of art and artifacts. Bourgeois excess is inventoried in the epistemological excess of a four-page paragraph in which an empire of objects obscures the human figures at the scene.

> Even if I never heard the rap of this gavel, there is another sound that became indissoluble from the image of my father's power and grandeur—or, rather, from those of a man in his profession. It is, implausible as it may seem, the noise made by the knife that my mother used to spread the rolls that my father took to his work in the morning, when it was scraped for the last time, to remove the butter still adhering to it, against the crisp surface of the cut roll. This signal preluding the labor of my father's day was no less exciting to me than, in later years, the sound of the bell that announced the start of a performance at the theater. Apart from this, the real token of my father's profession in our apartment was a Moor, almost life-size, who stood on a gondola reduced to one-thirtieth of its size, holding with one hand an oar that could be taken out, and lifting on the other a golden bowl.[27]

The father's silent gavel and his unseen engagement with work are matched by the mother's "noise" and the industry of her knife. In the theatre of familiar sensations the mother is reproduced as a knife, a bit of butter, and a cut roll. Her presence, however, is recorded in the canine peculiarity of her son's Pavlovian excitement. What follows in the logic of the memory theatre is the nearly life-size Moor "urgently oriented toward its companion piece that I cannot tell today whether a second Moor...really stood there originally or is a creature of my imagination."[28] The list of strangely disparate objects ends with recollections of family outings, first to the Ice Palace, recorded in the boy's vision of a prostitute in a tight white sailor suit. The narrator sentimentally links this remembered gaze from the threshold of puberty with the "initiation" of his erotic life at the first artificial ice rink in Berlin, an enterprise in which his father had "a sizable stake."[29]

The section concludes with representations of the links between sexual vulnerability and economic power, and, as with Woolf, a revelatory matching of sexual abuse and economic abuse. "...I got to know the town...as the theater of purchases...my father's money could cut a path for us between shop counters and assistants and mirrors, and the appraising eyes of our mother, whose muff lay on the counter. In the ignominy of a new suit we stood, our hands peeping from the sleeves like dirty price tags...."[30] Thus, the domestic inventory as record of a domestic economy includes specifically coded intersections of race, class, gender, and sex that are affecting not because they are intersections of raceclassgendersex but because they are rooted in the body's responses: in records of feeling dirty, abandoned, for sale, on display, chilled to the bone, inappropriately dressed, shamed, ubiquitously watched and judged, in states of arousal and impotence.

The autograph in Benjamin is vulnerability made public, comparable to Woolf's rage in *Three Guineas*—all presentations of the historiographically productive "catastrophic encounter." In this example, racial shame and terror of oppression organize the attempts at assimilation of a middle-class German Jewish family. The extent of the family's vulnerability can be weighed and measured in the images and effects of material excess—a commodity fetish of monstrous proportions. The material expression of these assimilative tedencies would seem to reify a wish to disappear into or to be indistinguishable from a mountain of objects. The list of possessions does accomplish the obliteration of individuals in their objectification as dismembered part objects of a familial body of goods. The list also functions in opposition to the desire for anonymity which is part of the assimilative impulse; it foregrounds, highlights, brings into sharp focus the household economy in its overdetermined signatures of racial terror, sexualized domination of women, and rigid economic management of family roles.

Benjamin's narrative list, read as a proleptic deconstruction of the ideology of assimilation, could be labelled postmodern. According to Lyotard the postmodern is the "nascent" form, coming both after (*post*) and anterior to (*modo*) its constitutive patterns.[31] In "A Berlin Chronicle" commodified desire deconstructed by Benjamin's domestic inventory betrays the failed displacement of racial terror. For example, the family's possession of the lacquered Moor reproduces itself as a mindless and carefully preserved and contained embrace of racism, imperialism, colonization—literally at dead center in everyday domestic life.[32] The multiple tolls of slavery are enshrined moreover in Benjamin's bizarrely animated phantasy of the Moor's "urgent" orientation toward a lost "companion piece." This fragment of Benjamin's imagination, a "chip of Messianic time" reflects upon the loss of companionship, destruction of families, and objectification of the exotic other—all exigencies of racism and economies based on trade in human lives.

Gaps in the narrative form confirm displacement (with its psychoanalytic as well as diasporic valences), moreover, as the trope of choice. "A Berlin Chronicle" begins with a meditation on impotence and an account of Benjamin's perverse sense of direction and ends with the deferred solution to the mystery of a lost term. That is, early in the piece, a forgotten word forestalls closure of the memory of a bedtime story told to the young Benjamin. The missing word, ultimately recalled, becomes the text's last word: "syphilis." As such, "syphilis" summarizes and reifies the brute fatality of inescapable identity, the legacy of the Benjaminian autograph in which his tragic death would seem to be (post *modo*)—racial, ethnic, filial, gendered—fulfillment.[33] Thus, memory's repetitions historicize a life; life writing produces and reproduces the logic of the historical subject.

Moreover, from the perspective of the present the domestic inventory in the content of Benjamin's list is as chillingly postmodern as the narrative of Benjamin's death at the Spanish border. The list reproduces both pre- and post- Holocaust images of lost connections; booty in inventoried heaps; trunks and suitcases stuffed and abandoned; death lists and mountains of paperwork. These are artifactual evidence of the Nazi attempt to end diaspora—which had come to include a Jewish colonization of German culture—in the annihilation the Jewish people. Thus Benjamin's list prefigures and recalls the meticulous Nazi bureaucracy in its obsession with record-keeping, bookkeeping, files, films, and photographs—the detritus of an unassuaged feeding frenzy as historical record of what is *only apparently* the same paradigm that dictated the commodification of German Jewish assimilative tendencies. That is, while the irony of the list persists, perhaps, in the anticipatory effect of this representation of the assimilative tendencies among middle-class German Jews, the proleptic list as rhetorical trope underscores a politically motivated rearrangement of the relations of power and vulnerability. Perhaps it is Benjamin's fantasy of the Moor lacking a companion, the bringing to life of a *memento mori* in the reproduction of a tender conceit of memory rather than of a remembered object, that makes the difference.[34] Thus, if German Jewish commodity fetish is a mirror of German bourgeois life, it is also a neurotic symptom, a demonstration of ambivalence, of vulnerability and mastery in its obsessive repetitions of loss—its oft-cited unrequited love affair with German culture. Nazi accumulative tendencies, on the other hand, represent the impossible fantasy of control, a psychotic (schizoid) embrace of power. The neurotic tendencies, in both Benjamin's and Woolf's anticipatory paradigms, are dialectic; incongruities are preserved, side by side, autonomous but linked. The schizoid (fascist) response, on the other hand, produces the aftershocks of the rejection of dialectic (impotence and mastery) by conflating the realms of the real and symbolic (to use the terms in their Lacanian emphases) in the self-aggrandizing and thus self-annihilating pursuit of omnipotence.

Autograph is the intentional reproduction of originary ambivalence, recorded in the dimensions of difference, a sensory representation that recapitulates the particular shape and dynamic of originary vulnerability and originary mastery and productivity. Authority is the moveable commodity, occurring initially as a function of autograph but with potential for shifting under the agency of the dialectical arrangement of biography and history to authorize the writerly reader as producer. Both author and reader deserve, you might say, the cognitive dissonance from which mastery (Benjamin's term)—or more simply put, an unencumbered embrace of the real—becomes a matter of learning to open our minds simply by trusting our guts.

NOTES

1. The idea of biography as witness to history is an organizing theme of Virginia Woolf's *Three Guineas* (New York: Harcourt Brace and Company, 1966) and pervasive throughout.

2. Virginia Woolf, "A Sketch of the Past" in *Moments of Being* (New York: Harcourt Brace and Company, 1976), 69.

3. In factoring in Anson Rabinbach's discussion of Benjamin's theological Messianism, I am employing a description of language and memory in Benjamin convergent with my own and an approach quite distinct from my own. I do so because Rabinbach's work lends explicit support to a central theme in mine: the politics of connections among personal traumata, radical language usage, and the projects of historical materialism. Also Rabinbach cogently specifies the relation between "im-mediate" and mediated expression as a Messianic—and thus, philosophical—project, which is to say, an immanently historicizable project. I thank my editors for pointing me toward Rabinbach's essay "Between Enlightenment and Apocalypse: Benjamin, Bloch and Modern German-Jewish Messianism." (*New German Critique*, no. 34, Winter 1985, 79–124.)

4. "Catastrophic encounters" is Walter Benjamin's phrase for the language of involuntary memory and the potential for a renewed referential relation that definitively includes the historicity of the speaking subject (c.f. "A Berlin Chronicle" in *Reflections*, ed. Peter Demetz. [New York: Harcourt Brace Jovanovich, 1978], 14).

5. Interestingly enough, Woolf claims to have started "A Sketch" as relief from the labor of writing a biography, the life of Roger Fry ("A Sketch of the Past," 64).

6. Walter Benjamin, "A Berlin Chronicle" and "The Author as Producer" in *Reflections*, ed. Peter Demetz (New York: Harcourt Brace and Company, 1978), 3–60, 220–38. To fill out my discussion of Benjamin's anti-Enlightenment historiography, I have also drawn upon "On Some Motifs in Baudelaire" and "Theses on the Philosophy of History," both in *Illuminations*, ed. Hannah Arendt (New York: Harcourt Brace Jovanovich, 1968), 155–200, 253–64.

7. Benjamin, A Berlin Chronicle," 4.

8. Woolf, "A Sketch of the Past," 93.

9. Sensory or spatial memory is a key neuroscientific topic. A recent collection of symposium papers across several disciplines in the neurosciences, *Thought Without Language*, ed. L. Weiskrantz (Oxford: Clarendon Press, 1991) is a good introductory source.

10. In all likelihood Benjamin would not have put it quite this way, yet his own version is close. In his discussion of memory in "On Some Motifs in Baudelaire," he moves between Bergson and Proust to describe memory's function in the *Fleurs du mal*. In this essay he captures the role of culture, of time and place, of "*memoire involontaire*," distinct from the conscious, intellectual associations of "*memoire volontaire*," in shaping the nature of present experience: "[t]his concept [*memoire involontaire*] bears the marks of the situation which

gave rise to it; it is part of the inventory of the individual who is isolated in many ways. Where there is experience in the strict sense of the word, certain contents of the individual past combine with material of the collective past...producing the amalgamation of these two elements of memory over and over again.... In this way voluntary and involuntary recollection lose their mutual exclusivity" (159, 160).

11. See Bonnie Costello, *Marianne Moore: Imaginary Possessions.* (Cambridge: Harvard University Press, 1981), 69–70.

12. Woolf elaborately glosses this phrase in "A Sketch of the Past" (70–73).

13. Within Messianism Rabinbach notes (1) the potential for an "anti-Enlightenment return of thought to the realm of experience denied by rationalism" ("Between Enlightenment and Apocalypse," 102); and (2) that the function of language is related to the function of culture: "[t]hought focuses upon the restoration of lost meanings, suppressed connections, and is often linked to a sense of redemption through language and through reading of texts which reveal the hidden presence or traces of a Messianic epoch" (84, 85). In this realm the nature of the law would be recovered in the "restoration of lost truth" rather than the "embrace of power"(85).

14. Woolf, *Three Guineas*, 138.

15. Woolf, *Three Guineas*, 78.

16. Although Benjamin's version is not based in a gender distinction, he makes exactly this point in "The Author as Producer" in a tautological hoop tossed around "tendencies" that are "literarily correct" because they are "politically correct" (221).

17. It is possible to say then that Benjamin and Woolf revise the notion of the proletariat as ideal historical subject in recognition of involuntary memory, the privileging of ambivalence teleologically driven to find the law. The experience of marginality within any class creates potential for dialectic in owning rather than dismissing-repressing-projecting the effects of one's powerlessness. Both authors acknowledge the revolutionary function of the writer as betrayer of her (any) social class—a betrayal implicitly double since class identity is simultaneously lived out and resisted.

18. The closing sections of "Theses on the Philosophy of History" (xv–xvii) prescribe for the materialist historian who must reject "telling the sequence of events like the beads of a rosary. Instead he grasps the constellation which his own era has formed with a definite earlier one. Thus he establishes a conception of the present as the 'time of now' which is shot through with chips of Messianic time" (261). "...he recognizes...a revolutionary chance in the fight for the oppressed past...in order to blast a specific era out of the homogeneous course of history—blasting a specific life out of the era or a specific work out of the lifework" (263).

19. Rosalind Coward and John Ellis, *Language and Materialism* (Boston: Routledge and Kegan Paul, 1977), 71.

20. Woolf, *Three Guineas*, 39.

21. Leslie Stephen brought one daughter, Laura, to the marriage and Julia

Duckworth, brought two sons, George and Gerald, and a daughter, Stella; four
children, Virginia, Vanessa, Adrian, and Thoby, were born to them.

22. Woolf, *Three Guineas*, 49, 50.

23. Although I have been unable to uncover evidence that "queer" was used specifically in the context of homosexuality before World War II in British or
American English, there is an unaccountable density of the term in this essay,
even given a preference for its widespread uses in British English.

24. Woolf, *Three Guineas*, 50–52.

25. In "A Sketch of the Past" (69) and in "22 Hyde Park Gate" in *Moments of
Being* (New York: Harcourt Brace and Company, 1976), 155, Woolf recalls sexual abuse perpetrated against her by Gerald Duckworth and, after the death of
Julia Stephen, by George Duckworth: "not only the father and mother, brother
and sister to those poor Stephen girls" but "their lover also."

26. Woolf, *Three Guineas*, 63.

27. Benjamin, "A Berlin Chronicle," 37.

28. Ibid., 37–38.

29. Ibid., 39.

30. Ibid., 40.

31. Jean Francois Lyotard, appendix to *The Postmodern Condition: A Report on
Knowledge*, trans. Geoff Bennington and Brian Massumi (Minneapolis: The
University of Minnesota Press, 1984), 79, 81. Rabinbach's analyses of the
Messianic function of language interestingly coincides with Lyotard's description of postmodern representation both in the sense of time (Messianic time
has to do with a recovery of the past in the future—in Lyotard, "what will have
been done"); and representational potential (Messianic utopian perfection cannot be imagined but can be hoped for in exile but not reached—in Lyotard, the
postmodern acknowledges the unpresentability of reality but attempts the presentation nonetheless).

32. See Jean Baudrillard for a discussion of lacquered surfaces of household objects
as devices of containment: a whole ethic of "protection, care, and cleanliness
which converges with the disciplinary ritual of framing." *For a Critique of the
Political Economy of the Sign*, trans. Charles Levin (St. Louis: Telos Press,
1981), 44, 45.

33. As my editors helpfully pointed out to me, "syphilis" here can be read as a critique of middle-class assimilation. In this context the disease of the blood, cru-
cially, inextricably connected to prostitution, is an overdetermined mark of the
brute fatality of racial, economic, and familial identity. Here the word in memory produces historically particular and unmediated relations: a one-to-one
connection of "syphilis" and "fatal identity," also, "prostitution" and "assimilation." Thus we read back and forth between assimilation and prostitution and
include the notion of inherited practice in, for example, the maternal role and
maternal vulnerability, summarized in the overdetermined and vulgar images
of vaginal exposure (the cut roll, the muff on the counter); the initiation of
Benjamin's sexuality; and, additionally, in his father's predictable fidelities to
provincial merchants (his regular business trips) coupled to equally regular mar-

ital infidelities (39). These associations of fatal identity would also hold for Benjamin's uses for the narrative of his own encounters with prostitutes (11). Here fatal identity is historicized in his frequenting of prostitutes and politicized as this passage demonstrates a requisite betrayal of the writer's social class in his simultaneous resistance to and adherence to the habits of his class. The experience of marginality he recounts in inhabiting his own precincts (of the city and the mind-body) while, like Baudelaire's *flaneur*, perusing the borders of others, inaugurates the methodology of the materialist historian's analysis, according to its codification in "Theses on the Philosophy of History."

34. "Language shows clearly that memory is not an instrument for exploring the past but its theatre" ("A Berlin Chronicle," 25).

YOUR NEAREST EXIT
MAY BE BEHIND YOU
Autobiography and
the Post-Modernist Moment

Clark Blaise

THE ADVANTAGE OF SPEAKING in the last session of a conference is the opportunity it gives to integrate scattered notes made during earlier sessions. But when the margins begin to squeeze the central ideas, and commentary clogs the text, some of the unwelcome side-effects of postmodernism become all too manifest. As one of the few autobiographers invited to this biography conference, I do wish to emphasize that autobiography is the opposite of biography—as opposite as subject is from object. Biography is an act of literary reconstruction, a celebration of, and identification with, achievement.

True autobiography (deleting the "autobiographies" of film stars, generals, and politicians, which are really ghost-written self-biographies), is a denial of celebrity. Paradoxically, autobiography is an act of self-destruction. We have repeatedly seen in this conference that biography's identification with achievement causes the biographer to struggle with questions of tact, delicacy, and ethics. These are questions which the autobiographer cannot for even a moment consider. Tactlessness and indelicacy, humiliation and embarrassment, are precious deconstructive tools. Autobiography celebrates only consciousness, and it can arrive at that goal only by deconstructive acts, a series of self-erasures.

My invitation to speak to this conference derives from the publication of *I Had a Father: A Post-Modern Autobiography*,[1] an attempt to align my placid, academic life with that of my violent, immigrant father. I felt that there were parallels in our lives, particularly as I entered my fifties which placed me in intimate relation to the decade of my father's deepest influence on me. I also felt that the parallels were so deeply buried that his "story" became historical as well as familial or psychological. Not knowing him well, I gave myself sanction to contextualize him through his distinct French-Canadian culture, history, language, and geography. The almost accidental result of that reconstruction became my autobiography. This means I am speaking about the Seductions of Biography both as a seducer and as one of the seduced, and that like any lover, my insights into the presentation of self, its process and theoretical underpinnings, may be clouded by infatuation or outright prejudice.

If we are here collectively in thrall of selfhood, we owe ourselves some answers to a few fundamental questions—again, I feel definitions are useful, and even possible. Is any "life story" an autobiography? How is memoir different from autobiography? Is it just a browser's perception, or have we entered a silver age of autobiography? If so, could it have something to do with the postmodernist ambience we inhabit? And most bedeviling—what is postmodernism, and does *it* even exist, or is it the name we give to a collection of symptoms that elude a single diagnosis?

I take a very limited view of true autobiography. I think of it as clearly distinct from memoir, however distinguished the best work in that genre can be. Memoir is applied memory, a memorialization from a serene distance of the times, people and places in one's semi-famous life. We would not read the memoir unless we were previously interested in the person or the times. In other words, the life somehow certifies the enterprise.

Autobiography is more democratic. It assumes—or manufactures—a kind of anonymity. Anonymity, in fact, may be its supreme artifice and achievement. Autobiographers are, or pose themselves as being, gifted amateurs. If you pick up my autobiography it is not because you have heard of me, or my father, or the places I have lived, or the times I have lived through. I must capture your interest only as a voice, a consciousness, an energy and an urgency. That urgency begins in crisis, in a memory, or a moment of shame or grief or simple dysfunction that translates into the revelation: *I cannot go forward*. The past has suddenly arisen within me. I must go back, pick up pieces, dig up truths, bring them back, and integrate them.

If this appears to place autobiography in thrall to psychoanalysis, I can only suggest that autobiography—the quest for self-knowledge and psychic integration, for cultural and social demystification—is by far the older impulse. Autobiography is a mediation between time-lines, linked through a single consciousness. The autobiographer is present at his/her birth, is father or mother to an emerging self. But the account does not start, conveniently or biographically, with "I was born one cold bleak morning," and its parts are not linked arbitrarily by a series of "I remember." Linkage of events follows a freshly-wakened consciousness rejoining and rejecting freshly-upturned fragments, not the meditative mind ordering its well-preserved memories.

Autobiography differs from another stepchild: fiction. The techniques and conventions of fiction—the artifices that are intended to lead to climax and catharsis, such as plot, character revelation, withheld information—are too manipulative for autobiography. What is attractive in autobiography is the reader's access to the author's naked agony of choice, the author's continual presence. The pleasure of most fiction, with the exception of meta-fiction or the work of certain Italians or central Europeans, is the seamless disappearance of an apparent author.

Autobiography is the drama of consciousness gaining sovereignty over its own experience. An autobiographical novel might be the inverse: experience out-muscling consciousness. The paradoxes of autobiography lie in the realization that each life is both unique and commonplace, that our fifty-year pocket of interactive time and space is both infinite and infinitesimal, that our achievements are both singular and accidental. Our sex, race, orientation, native language, religion, ethnicity, and country of birth are utterly determining and totally irrelevant. To convince you to read my book, I must convince you of my uniqueness, but to resolve the book, I must conclude with a vision of my lowest common humanity. Otherwise, I will be a grotesque, I will have failed. In a novel, I would try to create a unique character, someone memorable and unrepeatable. In autobiography, I begin with someone unique and reduce him to an emblem: son. It is for that reason that I term anonymity an achievement—anyone is, and can be, exceptional.

In a novel, we mark the climax of the work with the protagonist's "change of heart." In a biography, we plot the growth of the biographee's awareness and power. In an autobiography, we celebrate the opposite: the consistency of character through disparate experience, the birth and permanence of consciousness; in a word, selfhood. Earlier this year, for example, during a reading from my autobiography at a Florida bookfair, a hostile woman arose from the front row and demanded, "What have you ever done? Why am I listening to this? I've done more than you and no one will publish me!" If I had had more presence of mind and less irritation, I would have answered, "Everyone's *done* more than I have. You are confusing self-narration with autobiography. You don't want to write your autobiography—you want someone else to write your biography." I would say that the resolution of all the paradoxes of autobiography lies in the management of time. The autobiographer must find a technique for removing selfhood from the flattening anvil of time; he or she must restore all the wrinkles of self from the mangle of narrative.

The autobiographical subject is distinct from the biographic object, or the fictional character, by reason of its adversarial relationship to time. Autobiography succeeds when it masters a kind of time-travel. When autobiography fails, it surrenders to the artifice of creaky recollection, dutiful recitation, chronologically-correct toe-dabbings into the flow of past events. In other words, autobiography fails when it loses the drama of consciousness-retrieval, when a passive surrender to time seduces it into becoming its own authorized biography.

An important contemporary autobiography is *Stop-Time* by Frank Conroy, the title of which could serve as a banner for the entire genre. Published in 1967 when the author was thirty-one, it gave the illusion of staying still in time, the equivalent of Michael Jordan's hang-time, or perhaps of certain jazz riffs. Conroy captured the sinister pull of pure consciousness in the following manner:

> The nature of time had changed. Sitting at the bar I slipped effortlessly from one moment to the next, each perception dying gradually like a slow movie fade-out while the next built up underneath it. I got up from the stool and crossed the empty room, surprised to find myself in motion. Outside, on the deck in the darkness, a cool wind made my jacket billow around my body. I went to the rail and stared down at the water. I imagined jumping. The ship would keep going, eventually disappear, and there would be only the sea, me, and the sky—nothing else. For a moment the purity of it overwhelmed me. I felt I had to jump, not just to die, but to experience the moments of total solitude as I waited. From another deck I could hear the music of a small orchestra. Someone passed behind me. I turned and walked along the deck, my fingers trailing along the surface of the rail.[2]

The true subject of any autobiography is this struggle of consciousness ("for a moment, the purity of it overwhelmed me") over flux ("from another deck I could hear the music of a small orchestra. Someone passed behind me"), the emergence of fixed points of character, like boulders, from the whitewater of downstream spillage. To extract these moments of pure fixity (the certainty, that for just a moment the world is speaking to me) requires enormous concentration, and luck. Think of this, slightly more-celebrated paragraph from *Stop-Time*:

> One afternoon at the Select, John handed me a small drawing. "You know what that is?"
>
> I smoothed the paper on the small table and looked closely. It appeared to be a machine of some sort, various cogs, levers, and bars against a flat surface. "You mean something in reality?"
>
> "Yes."
>
> After a while I shook my head. "I don't know."
>
> "It's the lock on the Metro door."
>
> I looked again and recognized it instantly. In a single moment I understood distortion in art. The drawing was highly complex, much more elaborate than the simple bar and catch I had watched interacting countless times on the Metro doors. What he had drawn was the *process*, the way the bar approaches the catch,

slides up the angled metal, and drops into the locked position. He had captured movement in a static drawing. For a moment I was speechless. When I looked up he was smiling at me. "You see?"[3]

Autobiography is the dialogue of the individual and all that makes him/her unique, with the vastness of time and space, all that makes him/her indistinguishable from anyone, indeed anything that has ever existed, including brass doorlocks. It is the ancient argument with anonymity without being a bid for celebrity. It is the release of consciousness, or selfhood, from the sequence of events which we might term plot. From Augustine contemplating the paradox of the ever-new, ever-permanent river to Conroy discovering process in a static drawing, autobiographers have realized that the true enemy of selfhood is the enemy of life itself: time. How to stop time, to stun it long enough to enter its flow, when to divert it, and to step outside it, how to contemplate its passage from some eternal moment—that is the impulse behind autobiography.

The application of the techniques of postmodernism—what I will call the postmodernist moment—provide many of the tools for intense self-scrutiny. At the same time, the more amorphous postmodernist condition that surrounds us virtually elevates autobiography and the personal memoir to privileged status among contemporary literary genres.

A quarter-century ago, Conroy might have struggled to see process—the self-conscious slowing of time—in a Metro doorlock. Now we have learned, almost automatically, to employ ubiquitous, inescapable time-stopping and truth-bending processes. James Merrill, in a flippant aside from his "memoir" (the genre-description is his) *A Different Person*, describes the present moment in pure postmodernist terms, dipping into the commercial culture that surrounds us, even in describing intergenerational gay politics:

> Jerl (a politically-correct young friend) and I represent the difference between classic psychotherapy—that constricting and expensive underwear once made-to-order in Vienna—and its postmodern evolution toward letting our lives hang out in vivid, one-size-fits-all attitudes cheaply available at Benetton or The Gap.[4]

How easily the commercial allusion flows, even from such a Late Modernist as Merrill.

Postmodernism, for my purpose, is the acceptance of discontinuity and simultaneous multicentrality—that is, of shifting contexts creating instant, equivalent realities which justify "violations" of tone, or style, and the whole gamut of Jamesian unities. In fact, the traditional Jamesian unities, along with other buttresses of the canon, have themselves become identified as primary violators of reality. Along with this perception comes the breakdown of other convenient notions of high and low art, of commercial and hermeneutic influence, of technological and pop inspiration. High Modernism had banished commercial, media, and technological imputs from any discussion of serious art; postmodernism has offered those sources more than just an olive-branch. It has integrated and elevated them into the literary culture, while leveling the high peaks of canonical expression.

Take the rich, almost inexhaustible ironies and implications for art—especially for autobiography—surrounding the Rodney King beating—and the subsequent attempt to agree upon precisely what was seen. In the first trial, defense lawyers announced that the videotape, far from condemning the police officers, would guarantee their acquittal. How could this be? The world had seen the tape, seen it repeatedly, and shared the same response. By slowing down the tape and commenting on each frame, aided by a change of venue and a susceptible if not complicit jury, the team of lawyers repetively attacked familiar notions of contingency, cause-and-effect, agency, responsibility, and victimization, until they had finally destroyed the inherent link between deed and retribution (or should I say between plot and catharsis). They turned a cinema-verité tape into a "Road Runner" cartoon. A foot-on-the-neck pinning of the victim to the ground became exculpatory evidence of compassion. "Evidence," even in the form of a fortuitous visual record, can no longer be trusted. Postmodernism accepts the ambiguity of "Rashomon" without the Modernist courtesy of separate takes. The separate takes are implicit in the single image. Postmodernism, with its suspended moments of nonstop nonsequiturs, delivers juicy significance without coherence ("Look at that!" replaces "What does that mean?"). The implicit belief that truth resides in "external reality," the faith in Mimesis, as has been pointed out, has broken down.

Justice, or catharsis, can be readmitted in Los Angeles only after billion-dollar riots and fifty deaths have grossly distorted the context, and only by the political expedient of a second trial on a different charge. (It is tedious to list the various "Sons of Rodney King" trials in the past two years, where "evidence" finds itself defeated by pervasive, multicontextual, extranarrative subjectivity.)

For all of those reasons, and for their future implications, American writers at the close of the 20th century might be said to be living in the Rodney King Era—an era that discounts physical evidence and relies on commentary, and accepts massive physical destruction as a consequence of rejecting causality and accountability—no less than Emile Zola lived in the time of Dreyfus.

I was writing *I Had a Father* while the Rodney King trial, verdict, and riots went on. My method of presenting my life, and that of my father, could have been taken from the defense team's handbook. I too slowed down the narrative of my life, commented incessantly, introduced documents and ephemera, leaped through time and space by a hundred years and four continents, revisited scenes and moments, and by the end I literally doubted my own existence. I stopped time so effectively and so often, commented upon it so analytically, and introduced so many alternative contexts for interpreting my character—literary, geographical, historical, linguistic—that I erased my self entirely from the operations of my life.

The King trial proved that without a theoretical apparatus, no evidence of the eye will be trusted. Thomas Lacqueur's book *Making Sex* showed that prior to about 1800, women did not exist as a medically recognized distinct sex (that is, medical school illustrations posed organs and cadavers in such a way as to minimize, if not eliminate sexual differences).[5] We know that modern society has created the categories of childhood and adolescence, which did not exist when children had economically useful roles to perform. We know, or can be reminded by ironists like E. L. Doctorow in *Ragtime*, that immigrants and African-Americans did not "exist" at the turn of the century, even as they lined the streets and filled the tenements to bursting. Most of us can remember a similar "birth" of gays and Chicanos, to cite only some obvious examples, as groups with history, culture, dignity, and a distinct social, psychological, and literary identity. Women were defective men, immigrants were imperfect Americans, gays were perverse straights. They were all funny and harmless. They were always there; they were never there. While we can all applaud the humanist impulse that widens the realm of the known to the familiar, and the accepted, we might also predict that the role of autobiography will become increasingly important in reserving individuals's rights to self-exclusion. *Tout comprendre, c'est tout pardonner*—but who wants to be forgiven all the time? New understanding has robbed the newly inducted of the rights to individuality, eccentricity, and rebellion.

Once a postmodernist consciousness takes hold, its examples proliferate. I even chose as the title of this paper the sinister words of flight attendants: *in the event of an emergency, your nearest exit may be behind you.* In other words, your immediate future, your possible survival, is in your past, courtesy of a corporate disclaimer. I was much attracted to the familiar pink rabbit of the early Energizer battery commercials, and the way in which this pink rabbit, by crashing through the frame of a bogus commercial, made all commercials, all bespectacled men in white lab coats pushing pain medicine, potential targets for parody. Knowing the possibility of the past, you discounted the present and waited for the rabbit, which often didn't come. Sometimes, ads for headache medicine were just ads for headache medicine, and they looked utterly foolish. Ads had to be created that seemed bunny-proof. On the national political stage, policies had to be devised, or presented, to be Jay Leno–proof.

Those of us who compose on word processors are accustomed to shifting vast blocks of type, effectively obliterating traditional notions of narrative in the name of a consistent voice. Narrative therefore surrenders to juxtaposition, plot to non sequitur. After component passages become equivalent, sequences take on open-ended—perhaps even accidental—depth or humor. We begin behaving without the constraints of context. The past, like a compliant corpse, can be "accessed" or autopsied for accusatory or exculpatory evidence—the remains are eternally contemporary.

At the University of Massachusetts, some students want to drop their "Minuteman" mascot because its white, male, militarist appearance is at odds with present-day campus reality. (The movement to change offensive American Indian mascot-names, which have only a commercial/athletic institutional significance, and which never pretended to understand or "honor" native American culture, has merit. To see the Minuteman as equatable, just another offensive mascot-name to be corrected by expunging, is a mark of deep and, I'd argue, postmodernist, confusion.) It is another form of postmodernist time travel, imposing contemporary sensibility on the past by reading history backwards, eliminating context, reediting *Huck Finn* or Flannery O'Connor. This not reading the past, but trying actually to reformat it by deleting offending words (as though history were a giant text to be scanned by a word search program), moving blocks, ignoring and perhaps not even recognizing comic anachronism.

Groups of African-American students at Berkeley demanded that Eudora Welty, Flannery O'Connor, and William Faulkner drop the "N-word" and use the term "African-American" in their writing, and the professor who included those authors on her reading list was reprimanded for her insensitivity in assigning the offending texts. A word which unleashes contemporary anger is erased, at the cost of eliminating an historic referent of monstrous proportion.

These are postmodernist absurdities; the Los Angeles riots are postmodernist tragedies. What postmodernism can teach us, positively, is that there is, literally, no limit to the dimension of an individual human life. It is not only great lives that intersect the 20th century, as Modernism taught, but that every life is a complete cultural history of its time. Every life is a Great Life. This is the motivation behind the boom in contemporary autobiography. I had the feeling when my mother succumbed to Alzheimer's Disease that a shelf of history, a branch of knowledge, had disappeared with her, the only Canadian in the Bauhaus. I had the feeling when my father, a French-Canadian gunman turned Pittsburgh Rotarian, died that immigrant history had lost a resource that not even a Nathan Glazer could replace. In a postmodernist world, their lives are as esssential as those of Truman, Churchill, and Roosevelt to an understanding of the twentieth century.

Postmodernism helps us see that every life is larger than the circumstances that inhibit it, or the events that shaped it. The trouble with postmodernist narrative is its denial of catharsis, its reliance on shock, and the multiple contingencies, re-beginnings, and evasions built into its fabric. The denial of consequence feeds a hunger for retribution. Catharsis must be sought outside the frame, from the cuddly pink rabbit assuring you that it is all a parody to the Molotov cocktail, telling you it was not.

The postmodernist age is upon us, time travel is a fact, narrative has shattered, and the postmodernist self, capable of infinite inflation, infinite expansion, is fast becoming the most adaptable human analogue (dare I say character?) for a fiber-optic, 500-channel, cellular age.

NOTES

1. Clark Blaise, *I Had a Father: A Post-Modern Autobiography* (New York: Addison-Wesley, 1993).
2. Frank Conroy, *Stop-Time* (New York: Penguin, 1967), 240.
3. Ibid., 276.
4. James Merrill, *A Different Person: A Memoir* (New York: Alfred A. Knopf, 1933), 90.
5. See Thomas Laqueur, *Making Sex: Body and Gender from the Greeks to Freud* (Cambridge, Mass.: Harvard University Press, 1990).

◯ Contributors

K. ANTHONY APPIAH is Professor of Afro-American Studies at Harvard University.

CLARK BLAISE is a novelist and Director of the International Writing Program at the University of Iowa.

MARILYN L. BROWNSTEIN is Visiting Assistant Professor of English at the Ohio State University.

BLANCHE WIESEN COOK is Professor of History and Women's Studies at the John Jay College and the Graduate Center of the City University of New York.

JOHN D'EMILIO is Professor of History at the University of North Carolina.

JEFFREY LOUIS DECKER teaches in the English Department at UCLA.

MICHAEL ERIC DYSON is Professor of Communications Studies at the University of North Carolina at Chapel Hill.

MARJORIE GARBER is William R. Kenan, Jr., Professor of English at Harvard University, and Director of the Center for Literary and Cultural Studies.

HAYDEN HERRERA is a biographer.

MAURICE ISSERMAN is Professor of History at Hamilton College, Clinton, New York.

BARBARA JOHNSON is Professor of English at Harvard University.

WILLIAM S. McFEELY is the Abraham Baldwin Professor of Humanities at the University of Georgia.

DIANE WOOD MIDDLEBROOK is Professor of English at Stanford University.

RICHARD J. POWELL is Associate Professor of Art History at Duke University.

MARY RHIEL is Associate Professor of German at the University of New Hampshire.

PHYLLIS ROSE is Professor of English at Wesleyan University.

BETTY SASAKI is Assistant Professor of Spanish at Colby College.

DORIS SOMMER is Professor of Spanish at Harvard University.

MARITA STURKEN is Assistant Professor in the Annenberg School for Communication at the University of Southern California.

DAVID SUCHOFF is Associate Professor of English at Colby College.

SHERLEY ANNE WILLIAMS is a novelist, poet, and Professor of English in the Department of Language and Literature at the University of California, San Diego.

JEAN FAGAN YELLIN is Distinguished Professor of English at Pace University.

○ Index